ALIVE IN THE WILD

FOR

Doria Jim, & Jimmy
with Love,
Ruth & Charlie

Editor: Victor H. Cahalane

Graphics Editor: Charles C. Johnson

Drawings by Robert Candy

PRENTICE-HALL, INC.,

ALIVE
IN
THE
WILD

ENGLEWOOD CLIFFS, N.J.

Alive in the Wild, Editor: Victor H. Cahalane
Graphics Editor: Charles C. Johnson
© 1970 by Prentice-Hall, Inc.
Copyright under International and Pan American
Copyright Conventions
ISBN 0 - 13-022160-0
Library of Congress Catalog Card Number: 77-81581
Printed in the United States of America · *T*
Prentice-Hall International, Inc., London
Prentice-Hall of Australia, Pty. Ltd., Sydney
Prentice-Hall of Canada, Ltd., Toronto
Prentice-Hall of India Private Ltd., New Delhi
Prentice-Hall of Japan, Inc., Tokyo

CONTENTS

INTRODUCTION
VICTOR H. CAHALANE

One June afternoon several years ago, Charles Johnson walked into my office. He was chuckling about the baby raccoons that he had left in the kitchen of his farm home back in New Hampshire that morning. After a week's bout with "colic," they were still putting their hands over their bellies and complaining shrilly as if they were in pain. They had learned that these gestures and cries brought whiskey and warm milk, and although they had made a rapid recovery and no longer needed this medication, they still wanted it. (Raccoons learn fast!)

A former advertising man, Charlie had been making superb photographs from coast to coast for numerous publications. That spring he had built a stockade and was hosting numerous animals for several months of observation and photographing. It would be with great regret in September that he must open the gates and let his guests and their new families return to wilderness homes.

Out of these experiences developed the idea for this book, *Alive in the Wild*. Robert Candy, a talented artist and writer who has illustrated many wildlife books and periodicals and authored two successful books and numerous articles, was the logical person to make it unique. A pilot for four years during World War II with combat duty in the Aleutians and Burma, Bob is now Information and Education Chief for the Vermont Fish and Game Department.

Obviously one book could not contain all the animals and all the distinguished scientists who had studied them. Which animals would we choose? Which authorities would we ask? Could their research be ready and would they be available?

We were fortunate to persuade thirty-five outstanding biologists in the United States and Canada to each contribute a chapter about an animal that he has known through years of study. Most of these authors are friends whom I have made during my twenty years as chief biologist of the National Park Service and twelve years as assistant director of the New York State Museum.

In the past I have carried on research in many of the states, been boat-wrecked in Alaska, had armed escorts among hungry lions in Africa, and barely escaped avalanches in Switzerland. I feared that my days of excitement were over, but reading the manuscripts for this book was a new and vivid experience. The chapters are bursting with exciting life-history facts, some of which have never been published before. Many years of research by air, by land, and by sea are capsuled in the accounts.

A pair of golden eagles cartwheel down the skies in their nuptial dance. A deer pursues a coyote, and a prairie dog "buries" black-footed ferrets alive. Alligators make incubators for their eggs, and wolves answer taped voice recordings miles away. Walruses try to rescue their dead and dying; bellowing sea lions and fur seals defend their harems. Muskoxen grow long-skirted coats in the Arctic where there is no daylight for as much as four months of the year and the temperature reaches sixty below zero.

Among the authors in this book is Fran Hamerstrom, who has given the freedom of her home to great horned owls and shared an eyrie with an eagle. The impressively bearded Richard Van Gelder, with a twinkle in his eye, declares that "to know a skunk is to love him!" Karen Pryor trains rough-toothed porpoises to carry tiny transmitters and track wild schools of their relatives. Alan Sargeant has used as much radio tracking and telemetry to discover land-mammal secrets as anyone. Clifford Pope and Carl Kauffeld have hobnobbed with thousands of snakes. How does the male rattlesnake court the female? This and other snake problems are explained. For years Carl Hubbs has censused, pursued, and nearly bumped into gray whales. No one pretends to know more about the turbulent mating and mass nesting of the giant sea turtles than Archie Carr.

Many of the authors in this book have led expeditions and carried out research in different parts of the world, received honors and awards, and published both technical and popular books. All are distinguished in their fields, and most have devoted much time and energy to promoting conservation. Some of them have provocatively opposing opinions. For instance, do predators control the size of a prey population—or do they not? In spite of what some zoologists say, why is it not safe to hoist a skunk by its tail?

In addition to reflecting different points of view and research procedures, the thirty-five chapters provide a contrast in format and style. These unforgettable accounts by scientists—and about them—are in the following pages.

ALIVE IN THE WILD

PART ONE
BIRDS

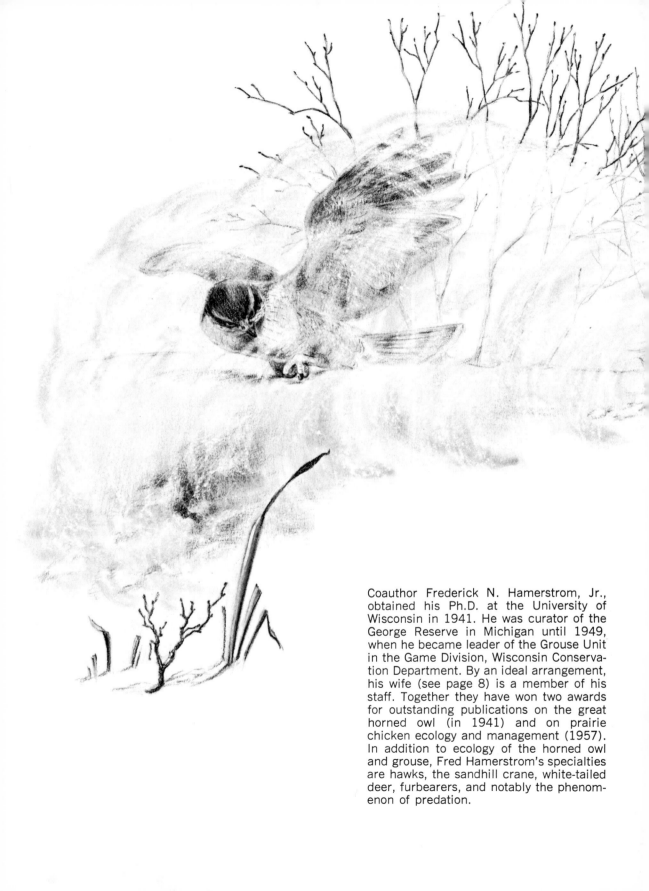

Coauthor Frederick N. Hamerstrom, Jr., obtained his Ph.D. at the University of Wisconsin in 1941. He was curator of the George Reserve in Michigan until 1949, when he became leader of the Grouse Unit in the Game Division, Wisconsin Conservation Department. By an ideal arrangement, his wife (see page 8) is a member of his staff. Together they have won two awards for outstanding publications on the great horned owl (in 1941) and on prairie chicken ecology and management (1957). In addition to ecology of the horned owl and grouse, Fred Hamerstrom's specialties are hawks, the sandhill crane, white-tailed deer, furbearers, and notably the phenomenon of predation.

SCAR SAC
FRANCES AND FREDERICK HAMERSTROM

It was after daybreak in mid-February when Scar Sac, a greater-prairie chicken, left his roost, a tunnel in the sedges where the snow had drifted deep. The frost lay thick and silvery on the feathers of his back and tail. As he walked, the "snowshoes" he had grown last autumn on both sides of each toe helped support his weight and made small fringe-like tracks.

Soon the sun struck the distant birches white under the dark winter clouds. The prairie cock started running in a curious, purposeful way, as though he had an important engagement, which he did. He was on his way to the ancestral booming ground. The sun rose higher, the temperature warmed up to 30°, and the air was still. The cock felt the spring urge to mate, although it was long before the swans would fly low over the marsh toward their breeding grounds in the north.

As he ran, rather awkwardly wobbling from side to side, he looked like a plain, sparrow-colored chicken. But when he arrived at his goal, which looked to us like any other place on the great marsh, an astonishing transformation began. Head down, with short steps, he stamped excitedly. His prints

3

in the snow were no longer neat and well spaced but "booming tracks" resembling feathery fronds of ferns.

His tail feathers spread and rose. Long, three-inch neck tufts erected until they looked like horns. Orange skin patches over his eyes projected. The great orange sacs on either side of his neck swelled and filled with air. He started to boom.

The sound was eerie—like blowing into a bottle and also a little like organ music. Rolling over the vast marsh, it called other prairie chickens to the area which had been used spring after spring, longer than the memory of living man. He boomed again and again; then flutter-jumped, awkwardly leaping three to five feet into the air. With each jump he looked like a cripple, but when he boomed again, every motion was precise.

With each boom his air sacs inflated. They were orange but still rimmed with cherry color, for he was not yet in full breeding condition. There was a small mark on the left air sac. It was definitely purplish. Brown or black spots on the sacs of prairie chickens are undependable as distinguishing features, for they may be ticks and simply walk away. This tiny scar remained, and so we had named him Scar Sac. Later the mark would be obliterated, but not until Dark Tail arrived.

The temperature dropped during the next few days, and the prairie chickens gathered into great flocks, gleaning corn where they could find it. As we trapped and banded for our survey, we found that the wild hungry birds were much less difficult to catch at the end of a hard winter.

"What is the wildest animal in the whole world?" a neighbor's son once asked us. We didn't know the answer then and don't know it now, but of all animals we have ever handled, the prairie chickens make the most desperate attempts to get away. One must be firm, gentle, and quick, or they will hurt themselves, perhaps spraining or dislocating a wing or a leg.

Our traps were six feet long, four feet wide, about two feet high, and covered with soft fishnet so that the birds could not harm themselves. Each had a broad funnel at both ends for the birds to enter and was baited with ears of corn as well as loose kernels. The whole set looked like a banquet.

Seven traps were set in a field of shocked corn about a mile from where Scar Sac had boomed, and three times a day we snowshoed into the field to brush the drifted snow off the bait. One day we saw tracks of about sixteen prairie chickens near the traps; one wary bird had walked around and around a trap, bypassing the funnel entrances.

The next day we flushed the entire flock at noon, and a goshawk tail-chased them. Singling out one prairie hen, the raptor followed her, almost closing the gap between them. We have clocked prairie chickens in flight at fifty-five miles an hour even when they weren't hurrying! It was hard to say how fast this bird was flying—to save her life.

When the goshawk was only ten feet behind his quarry, the hen flew lower over the snow. He was about to strike when the chicken plunged downward. Soft, powdery snow puffed high in a sparkling cloud where she disappeared. Baffled, and blinded by snow, the gos missed his strike as he smashed to the ground. Seconds later, the hen, quicker than any hawk on the takeoff, was head-

4

ing for the safety of open spaces. Had she been sick or injured, death would have been swift, for predators usually catch the weak and miserable.

On February 23, with the wind out of the northwest and the temperature at 5° below, we made a big catch. The traps were bouncing with prairie chickens. Barehanded, to avoid pulling feathers accidentally, we caught each bird by both legs, weighed it in a sock, determined its age, banded it, and let it go. We caught Dark Tail that day.

Some of the cocks showed only a tinge of orange on their air sacs, with no thickening of the skin; others had a narrow cherry-colored rim around the orange center. (The cherry color is simply the birds' concentrated blood supply showing through the still-thin skin on the bare patches on either side of the neck.)

Dark Tail's air sacs were fully thickened and orange except for the very tops, which always remain red. Ready for mating and a big bird, he weighed over two pounds. He was an exceptionally handsome and powerful cock.

On five separate days we made catches. One hen was recaptured each time—the food was irresistible! The last time we released her, she cut back behind us, smashed into a fence wire, and tumbled into the snow. She tried to take a step, but one leg was broken. We ran, hoping to catch her and set it, but she flew away with one useless leg dangling beneath her. We never expected to see her again.

In late March we put up a blind where we had seen Scar Sac performing weeks before. Perhaps he would come running and booming again. Dawn that day was a pale lemon streak when we were surrounded by the sound of booming. There were sixteen cocks! They looked like gnomes, and as the sun came up, their breath rose in the still air like puffs from tiny steam engines. When Scar Sac raised his pinnae and boomed, we saw the small purple mark on his left sac, and knew for sure that it was he. He was booming just where he had boomed before, but part of the territory he had fought for and defended was now usurped by our blind.

Needing more room, Scar Sac trespassed on Dark Tail's claim. Dark Tail rushed for the intruder, grabbed him by the wing, and pulled him around in circles, breaking two primary tips. Suddenly Dark Tail let go and Scar Sac slipped on the ice. In a moment he flew up and jumped on Dark Tail's back, where he clung, holding on by a mouthful of feathers, and repeatedly beat his assailant with his wings. More and more feathers marked the battleground. The fight raged without pause for sixteen minutes.

At last each cock retreated to the heart of his own territory to boom. Scar Sac raised his pinnae and tail, stamped his feet, and lowered his head, but no sound came forth, for his air sacs hung baggy and useless on each side of his neck. (Actually the so-called air sacs are one sac which bulges on both sides of the neck.) He tried again to boom, and blood oozed from a triangular gash which covered the small purple scar that had once identified him. He had been so beautiful.

A three-way fight began on the far side of the booming ground. A female harrier hunting mice swooped low and then, swerving, crossed the booming ground, flushing all but one of the cocks. The flock flew about a hundred yards and lighted. They stood alert with necks outstretched in mild alarm. There was no booming, no fighting. Soon reassured,

5

they walked, ran, and flew back to the booming ground.

Dark Tail landed in his territory first —with noisy wing beats. A moment later Scar Sac reached his domain, stamped his feet, and raised his pinnae. The thick fluid beneath the skin of his air sacs had already closed the great gaping hole. Scar Sac blew up his giant sacs. He could boom again!

In spite of being wounded in battle, he had succeeded in increasing the southern boundary of his territory by about two feet. Each morning when the flock returned to the booming ground, Scar Sac and Dark Tail would take time out from booming to spar over the boundary. Each knew exactly where the line was, and regardless of bickering, it was respected by both.

Toward the end of the morning their urge to boom and fight was exhausted, but the two birds still crouched facing each other—sleepily—until it was time to fly to the feeding grounds and then to doze and to dust on a sand island where they showed no hostility.

Day after day the cocks returned. On April 3 the melodious roar in the early morning mist suddenly increased. With it this time was a new call of the male— rather like the honk of a Canada goose but higher and clearer. *A hen was approaching!* The cocks flutter-jumped excitedly trying to attract her—Scar Sac as high as any of them. A few cocks, near a patch of marsh grass, boomed in full display.

The first hen of the season raised her slender neck and walked, uneasy and shy, out of the marsh grass onto the booming ground. She picked at bits of

grass and preened her midback feathers, behaving as though the magnificent display of the cocks were nonexistent. One might have thought her to be feeding on the meadow by herself. Because her feathers had an unusually reddish tinge, we called her Rusty.

She came again the following morning, but now she walked the ground making quick little runs, visiting each cock. As she moved through the booming ground, the cocks forgot their territorial boundaries when she came near. Each one boomed in a frenzy as though to keep her close.

Other hens came from day to day, staying together. Most of them lingered in Dark Tail's domain, but Rusty singled out Scar Sac. Flirtatiously she spread her wings and repeatedly ran and stopped as he boomed to her in the dawn.

The rising sun glowed on his orange air sacs. He stopped booming to bow to her. Spreading his wings wide, he bowed slowly till his beak and body touched the ground. Then, as in a minuet, Rusty also paused and spread her wings. Head high, neck arched and with pinnae towering in a single peak above his head, Scar Sac turned and mounted her.

A moment later, as though spurred by success, Scar Sac rushed over to pick a fight with Dark Tail. Rusty shook her feathers until they seemed to stand straight out from her body. Then she flew across the wide meadow to where she would make her nest. Her mission had been accomplished; she would not return to the booming ground again that spring, for soon she would have eggs and chicks.

It was a year later. Four hens flew to the booming ground at sunrise on April 19. The cocks stamped, boomed, flutter-jumped, and gave the high, whooping *"females present!"* call. Three hens were exquisite, sleek and in perfect plumage. The fourth limped. Falling at each step, she kept spreading her wings wide to steady herself. The plumage on her breast and belly was caked with mud. It was the hen that had hit the wire in the winter and flown far over the popples with dangling, broken leg.

What hope for her to woo a cock?

She landed in the territory of a weak young male. Pitifully, she spread her wings to keep from falling. The young cock acted as if he could not believe his good fortune. A hen was spreading her wings before him, as though in invitation. He boomed once triumphantly and, wasting no time, mounted her.

Scar Sac rushed over, knocking him off, and sent him flying with the impact of the blow. The crippled hen hesitantly took a step. Then Scar Sac mounted her. The other cocks, frenzied and competitive, circled her like Indians in a war dance. The sleek, pretty hens, almost ignored, preened in the marsh grass.

Scar Sac lived five years—far longer than most prairie chickens. Each spring he boomed in the same area. The fifth spring he no longer occupied the strong position near the center of the booming ground, but stayed on a small knoll to the side, where he had neither occasion nor necessity to fight. Day after day the hens passed him by. The next spring he was gone.

The Hamerstroms, who coauthored the preceding chapter, work so closely in biological research that they are always mentioned simultaneously. In this case, however, owls are a distaff specialty. Since 1940, Frances Hamerstrom has been a biologist in the Wisconsin Game Department, where her work on the ecology and population dynamics of grouse earned her an honorary doctorate from Carroll College. Her interests include raptorial birds and falconry; during her research she has shared an eyrie with a golden eagle. The Wildlife Society's award for the outstanding publication of 1941 went to "Fran" and Fred for their *The Great Horned Owl and Its Prey in North-Central United States*.

AMBROSE

FRANCES HAMERSTROM

Ambrose, a great-horned owl, was hatched on March 20 in an abandoned hawk's nest. He was only a few hours old, a heavy-headed ball of white fluff, when I found him. I carefully put him inside my shirt next to my skin, where he lay quietly.

Although people nearby complained that horned owls were making heavy inroads on the pheasants stocked by the game farm, the only prey at the nest were seventeen deer mice. I slipped a few into my pocket, climbed down the tree, and got into my car.

It was good to be driving homeward with my owlet.

He was quiet until I stopped at a restaurant and ordered supper. Then he started calling "Cheep, cheep." The waitress looked me over with interest. I was alone, wearing flannel shirt, blue jeans, and field boots, but I had put on an overcoat to look dressy enough to go into a nice restaurant.

"Do you have a radio in your purse, ma'am?" she asked.

"No," I answered. I tried pretending the sound came from the next table, but Ambrose was hungry, and when the waitress brought my meal he became insistent. "Cheep, cheep, cheep."

9

"Are you *sure* you don't have a radio, ma'am?"

"No," I said, "I'm wearing an owl."

She eased away from me and over to the manager. Just then an extraordinary old man, with grayish-brown hair down to his shoulders, came in and started explaining his visions and how he had been sent to this earth. No one paid the slightest attention, however. The manager continued to look at me warily. The waitresses clustered and whispered. Patrons turned around and stared.

"Cheep, cheep, cheep." My shirt moved slightly. It was high time to feed Ambrose. I bolted my supper, paid my bill, and ran to the car.

First I started the heater going so that he would not get chilled. Then I warmed up some pieces of raw meat by holding them in my mouth and took him out of my shirt for feeding. "Ready now," I said softly. To imitate the arrival of a parent owl at the nest, I bumped the hand holding him and hoped that it felt like the bump of an adult landing. Although he was blind, I thought perhaps he could distinguish between light and dark, so I cast a shadow between him and the bright lights of the restaurant. Then I gave him the first warm, wet morsel and followed with another and another. Each time the food went down his throat I whistled softly. He must first learn to associate my whistle with food so that later on he would come out of the woods and across the fields to me.

As soon as he was satisfied, I tucked him back under my shirt and started the car. During the next two hours of driving, Ambrose slept. All he could feel was skin, nylon, warmth, and a little motion. Unexpectedly, he would seem to remember that nylon years later.

As soon as we reached home, I started warming meat again. Already, each time I whistled, Ambrose fed eagerly. When he was sleepy again, I put him on a wool sock in a strawberry basket, covered him with another wool sock, and set him high behind the tall wood-burning stove.

I dared not wear him at night, lest I roll on him. For the next ten days Ambrose was to spend his nights in the strawberry basket and his days on me, just above my belt. This was the nearest thing to a brood patch that I had to offer.

When he was three days old, he could raise his head and open one eye a little. He weighed 86 grams—three ounces. The next day he preened. Four days later he weighed 123 grams—a nice gain. If I left him on the table, he would come to my voice, but not to other people's. All young birds become "imprinted" to certain sounds soon after hatching. Normally this helps them to recognize their parents and later to choose a mate. Ambrose, when his eyes were not yet three-fourths open, not only knew my voice but was imprinted on *me*.

Every five hours I fed him on morsels of rump of freshly killed house mouse or breast fragments of English sparrows. His white downy coat was being replaced by tawny juvenal plumage. At twelve days he weighed 316 grams and had more than tripled his weight. (That gain would have scared our doctor if our babies had done the same.) Now I gradually cut down the number of meals per day and began to add fur and feathers to his diet.

He still had his egg tooth at seventeen days of age. This was the whitish tip on his beak which had helped him break his eggshell when he hatched. Two days later he lost his egg tooth, and the bluish, milky film was almost gone from his eyes. Another important event took place that day.

Ambrose had started eating bones, which he could not digest. That day he coughed up his first pellet; stretching his neck, gaping and shaking his head, he finally worked it up. It fell on the living-room table. We both looked at it with interest. It was smaller than an adult would cough up but beautifully formed —oblong with the bones for the most part covered by partly digested fur and feathers. It gleamed with the iridescent sheen of mucus which denotes a freshly cast pellet. Later in the day, astonishingly, he coughed up another. Even as an adult, he rarely produces more than one a day. I can sometimes whistle the pellets up, for he knows full well that my whistle means food, and he is in no mood to eat with a pellet still in his stomach.

Ambrose was growing up. By the time he was twenty-eight days old, his ear tufts ("horns") stood downy and soft. The beautiful white patch on his lower throat showed up well. He jumped with both feet for the first time, and in the evening we heard the patter of little feet running through the house as he played.

His days were spent outdoors, untethered and free. He needed sunlight to prevent rickets and spent the mornings sitting on the grape arbor or sleeping by the woodpile. He still slept like a baby —on his belly. When the sun got too hot, he moved into the shade.

By May 14 he was stalking bumblebees and earnestly pouncing on corncobs. He made short flights to sit in an elm or on one of the windowsills. His daily cruising radius had increased to about 130 yards—still mostly on foot. He had just learned to sleep standing up like an adult!

He celebrated the Fourth of July by hooting—softly and weakly.

Brigitte, a charming German girl, had been visiting us, and it was time to take her East. We packed the station wagon and took off. Ambrose and Baldur, the young red-tailed hawk whose hearing ability I was studying, sat perched on top of the back seat. Both enjoy riding and Brigitte was thrilled with our big car and the American countryside. She took the birds for granted by now.

Traffic was heavy. Car after car slowed up to look at our feathered passengers. One old lady was pointing out the birds to her husband. With a straight face I asked Brigitte, "Isn't it strange that everybody can tell you are a foreigner?"

Our car jerked to a stop at the next intersection. Both birds raised their big wings for balance. All eyes, enchanted and excited, were on our passengers. "How can they know I am a foreigner? I look just like everybody!" Blushing, she gave her hair little pushes patting it into place, "How can they know?"

We stopped for lunch, and by the time we got back to the car the birds had drawn a crowd. "Look at those eyes . . . See their big feet: I wouldn't want to mess with them! . . . Will they bite you?" A plump, well-dressed woman was standing on tiptoe on the sidewalk so that she could lean deep into the car through the open window. With her face a few inches from Ambrose's breast, she kept reiterating, "Polly want a cracker? Polly want a cracker?"

When we returned, I decided to get down to business with Baldur. He had not been responsive to hearing tests. In fact, for one whole afternoon he sat on a telephone pole ignoring my whistle. At sunset I went out in the last effort to call him down. Half-heartedly I whistled. Finally he deigned to leave the pole to lumber toward me. My owl, soft-winged, shot in from the woods to the north and intercepted him a few feet from the glove. In the last rays of the dying sun they fought, battling in the air over my head, turning and twisting for advantage, with bodies not quite interlocked.

Ambrose struck the glove first, and Baldur took to a tree. I homed Ambrose to the big screened porch which now belonged to the owls, gave him a rabbit's head, and went out on the lawn to try for Baldur. Baldur had learned a lesson, ordinarily learned from nest mates at an earlier stage: there is competition and he who comes first is winner. Almost before I could whistle, Baldur was on my glove. Forevermore thereafter his response to my whistle had style and speed.

When Ambrose was three we brought him Zulieka, an owl companion. She was a big, downy ten-day-old horned owl, and we hoped that someday, perhaps in three years, she would make him a mate. Like most female horned owls, she was to become far larger and more powerful than the male. As an adult Zulieka would sit almost two feet tall, have a wingspread of forty-two inches and weigh four pounds three ounces. Ambrose, smaller and gentler, would weigh three pounds four ounces.

Like most female horned owls I have known, Zulieka ranged farther, even on foot before she could fly well, than males of the same age do. The males are the homebodies.

They were playful when we brought them into the house together. Ambrose swooped from the top of the bookcase to snatch a pillow and fly across the room with it. Young Zulieka, in imitation, swooped too, but grabbed the sofa arm and struggled in vain to carry off the whole sofa. Both were exercising hunting muscles.

In late August rats invaded the corn-crib. Rats! The family murmured about poison, but not I. Full of joy, I planned a hunt. At dusk I took Ambrose from the porch. First I gave him a short flight to be sure he remembered his obedience lessons. Then I let him fly to a favorite perch.

Crickets called in the grass around me, and bats came out of the barn. A woodcock swung by, and soon a glowworm cast its delicate light near my foot. By now I could barely distinguish Ambrose's silhouette on a high branch. Then his head moved from side to side; he had spotted quarry! Ten minutes passed . . . fifteen. The crickets shrilled. Suddenly Ambrose swooped silently—one long sure glide—and made his kill. I ran to the sound of the short scuffle, picked Ambrose up, and let him take his pleasure on the fresh, dead rat.

Even though my owls knew me well, I had to keep conditioning them with my whistle, plus food, or someday I might lose an owl. Each evening I whistled to them, even when they were on the porch, and offered meat on my glove. Often it was a dead mouse. If Ambrose was hungry, he swallowed it whole. But if not hungry, he often flew to my glove just to be "polite" and held the mouse in one foot like holding an ice-cream cone. His big eyelashes swept downward as he closed his eyes with each bite. If he and Zulieka were still hungry after the first offering, they were treated to a chicken leg or road-killed squirrel. The next morning the broken bones of the drumstick would be pulled bare by the beaks of the owls. What was left of a squirrel —the skin—would be lying inside out, like a discarded sweater. Often we fed them in the house, or invited them in for the pleasure of their company.

With the onset of cold weather Zulieka became more quarrelsome. Whenever Zulieka saw anything, anywhere, that she wanted, she took it. She was easily strong enough to kill Ambrose if she had a mind to, and Ambrose knew better than to argue.

Breeding season approached. We nailed a wooden nesting box, lined with nylon stockings as it happened, to the wall of the porch. Ambrose took to it right away. Head down, with soft clucking noises, he turned and nestled into the stockings. Zulieka had no interest in this effete luxury. It was not until we built a stick nest for her that she would abandon her stand-up perch. Then she took possession, sat on it, and defended it from all intruders, even me. We never saw her let Ambrose even perch on it. She had been hatched in a stick nest: Could it be that this influenced her now? Ambrose's early memories were of being worn inside my shirt: Did nylon stockings remind him of his earliest days? Who knows how owls select their nests?

That autumn we decided to have our best sofa reupholstered, and it was gone for weeks. When the old man who had done the work and his son proudly carried it into the house, they put it in position under the gold-framed mirror which set it off so well.

"I hope you got no birds?" he asked.

"Birds?!" we exclaimed.

"Yes," he nodded. "Them parakeets makes an awful mess." We tried to reassure him and hurried him and his son out of the house. We could have told him

a thing or two: the dark mutes of an owl must be scrubbed off promptly with soap and water! The white ones if allowed to dry become chalky and can be removed by hard work with a stiff brush.

It was late in January, mating time three years later. Zulieka sat low in her nest. If she felt like it, she perched on Ambrose's nest box but never settled down. Once or twice we saw the two owls sitting side by side and hoped that they would stop behaving like brother and sister. But no. Far more often there was a flurry of wings and an angry chittering—Zulieka had bumped Ambrose off a perch.

Ambrose, in courtship display, raised his tail, lowered his head, and hooted. Like a great powder-puff, his throat patch loomed white in the twilight. "Hoo-hoohoohoo-hoo," the deep sound carried far over the snow-covered fields. And close upon his call came Zulieka's, higher and with more notes. Night after night they hooted, but Ambrose was not displaying to Zulieka, nor to faraway wild females; he was displaying to *me!*

Somehow a new element must be introduced to break down his early imprinting, but what?

Moon shadows mark the sparkling snow tonight. Frost fringes Ambrose's beak. The owls are calling. There is an owl high in the elm and another sits on a pine stub. *The wild owls have come.* Ambrose, Zulieka, and the wild owls, all four hoot, and hoot again. Perhaps . . . perhaps tonight, with the music of his own kind ringing all around him . . . two great females and a rival male . . . perhaps he will at last forget about me, and mate with Zulieka.

13

Although a neuroanatomist by profession, Walter R. Spofford has been a bird enthusiast since boyhood when he became acquainted with the great Massachusetts state orinthologist Edward H. Forbush. Along with medical school teaching, Dr. Spofford has found time to study golden eagles and peregrine falcons in the Appalachians, and to investigate the effect of the eagle on the sheep industry in western Texas. In 1967 he devoted three months to research on raptorial birds on Alaska's Arctic Slope. He maintains several African eagles for studies of behavior, plumages and molt.

The following chapter is based on Dr. Spofford's many experiences with golden eagles, but he is indebted to Mrs. Emilie Curtis for information, and especially for the doubly verified observation of the egg-bulge as the eagle flew (page 16).

THE GOLDEN EAGLE
WALTER R. SPOFFORD

Cresting the low pass, first one eagle and then the second sailed on partly flexed wings—two dark shapes as silent as their shadows that raced along the slope below . . . Now they wheeled in an updraft of air, spiraled, and topped the ridge. Their circles of flight tightened, crossed, and recrossed. At times the long-feathered legs and feet of the male seemed to touch the back of his larger mate.

Suddenly the eagles interlocked talons, and with wings outspread, they cartwheeled down the sky in a breathtaking spectacle.

Separating from his mate, the male shot upward and dropped. With wings folded close to his body, his speed quickened. A dark wedge, he hurtled earthward at nearly 200 miles an hour. Just as he seemed about to crash into the treetops below, his wings opened, spread hard, and he banked steeply upward. With powerful thrusts he bounded high until, closing his wings again into a flying wedge, he made an arc against the sky . . . Slowing, like a spent rocket, he folded backward into a second headlong plunge.

The nuptial flight was reaching its climax. The female followed her mate in each figure of the sky dance. At times the pair tumbled backward over and over, slid sideways down the sky, and then rose again in great continuing arcs.

No longer silent, the eagles chittered excitedly down long spans of air. After a half hour of ecstatic display, one eagle shallowed out of a steep descent and landed gently on a grassy knoll of the ridge. Immediately the other followed, and the great birds with their golden hackles rested. Then for a few seconds, the cock mounted the hen and spread his wings slightly. Afterward, side by side, they stood, looking off into the distance for nearly half an hour.

Eagles are thought to mate for life. Their breeding season lasts for about six months, including courtship, mating, and raising the young. Together the cock and hen build their nest and add to it over the years. On a cliff the largest accumulation may on rare occasions become as much as six feet wide and eight feet high. When there is no longer headroom because of an overhanging edge, the nest is abandoned until it settles or, more usually, falls to the ground.

Most eagle pairs have several nests in their home range—using one or another as fancy dictates. Although some naturalists suggest that the birds change their nests because of ectoparasites, I doubt that eagles are motivated by any desire or need for sanitation. An eagle pair with several nests may use the same one for five years in succession. Some eagles have as many as ten or twelve homes; others have only two or three, depending on the number of cliffs that are available. Although typically built on ledges or cliffs, nest platforms are also lodged in trees.

While the hen takes her turn at brooding, the cock may sky-dive repeatedly within sight of the eyrie. The hen gets very excited, stands up on the nest, and "K'YELPS!" loudly throughout his performance.

When the female herself is in flight, the bulge of a nearly-ready-to-be-laid egg may be seen. Two eggs are usual—the first is often spotted with reddish and the second more plain or completely whitish. Although both eggs usually hatch, only one eaglet—the first—is likely to survive. The smaller, later one often dies of neglect or from being smothered, or sometimes from being persistently attacked by the three-or-four-days-older nest-mate. A single chick may be better fitted to survive than two, particularly when the food supply is limited. The laying of two eggs serves as a buffer against the loss of one. In good rabbit country, three eagle chicks may be found in a single nest—but this is rare.

Eagles carry green branches to their eyrie—pine, spruce, or juniper early in the season, and deciduous growth later on. They may be placed there long before the eggs are laid and are replenished at various times until fairly close to the fledgling period. Sometimes a fresh sprig is found there late in autumn. Perhaps the sprays, often brought in quick succession by both cock and hen, perform some kind of ceremonial function. To human observers, they are only decorative, but to the eagles they may also be useful. They may help maintain the nest bowl, regulate the temperature of the eggs, partly protect an eaglet from the sun, and possibly act in some obscure way as does "anting" (sensuous pleasure) for many birds. However, none of these factors may be the cause of the ceremony.

A few weeks ago I watched a hen eagle coming in over a western mountain ridge, carrying a bushy green juniper in her talons. Suddenly she dropped. Her seven-and-a-half-foot wingspread was horizontal, her tail was up and her head and feet down, trailing the juniper. Straight down she parachuted for some 300 feet into the eyrie, and there she sat, almost hidden in the greenery.

Both parents bring food to the young, and the hen tears it up in small pieces as long as this is necessary. The eaglet may remain in the nest eleven or twelve weeks and after that be fed by the parents for some time. The fledgling often leaves the nest before it can fly properly. Al-

though it hides away among the rocks and brush, its presence is broadcast by noisy demands both for its parents and for food.

The eaglet begins yelping even before it is hatched, and by the time it is six weeks old, the loud and piercing "Kee-Yelp! KeeYelp! KeeYelp!" can be heard for a surprising distance across the clear air of a western canyon.

Once I heard an eagle concert. Late in the afternoon a hen eagle in her eyrie turned toward the lake, looked at the sky, and then began to call very loudly: "KLEAP! KLEAP! KLEAP!" Almost imme-

diately the cock plummeted from the higher air, swung in a half circle, plunged to below the ledge, and then soared up into the nest in a graceful arc. "KLEAP! KLEAP! KLEAP!" the hen continued to exclaim. "KeeYelp! KeeYelp! KeeYelp!" the little eaglet joined in. The male flew across to the front perch (a dead pine) and contributed an obbligato with his softer "Kulp! Kulp! Kulp!" For some reason the excitement persisted. Eventually the eaglet lay down and went to sleep, but the adults kept up their alternate "solos" until after dark.

Both of our eagles in North America —the bald and the golden—are normally quiet birds. Contrary to much poetry and prose, neither of them gives voice to anything that can be technically called a "scream." Certainly it does not resemble the scream of a human, a cougar, or a bobcat. The bald eagle has an almost inarticulate rasping cackle and a sort of escaping-steam hiss with bits of voiced "caks." When a nest is approached by man, the golden eagle usually slips away quietly, often unseen, while the bald eagle will circle nearby giving harsh but nearly voiceless creakings and rattlings.

During the brighter part of the day, the golden eagle may preen and bathe at a remote water hole, or, circling above the plains, become lost to view. Sometimes, perched inconspicuously on a crag, it is revealed only because of harassment by ravens or crows. When flying in a light plane over hills in western Texas, I have seen an eagle here and there perched on the open ground and on the Valentine plain standing quietly in grass that was knee high.

Once, when flying over foothills of the Capitan Mountains of New Mexico, I came near an eagle carrying a large stick which it dropped at my approach. As I followed the bird and came close for photographs, it suddenly began a series of dives a few yards from the wing tip of the airplane. It plunged earthward out of sight, and then almost at once shot up again so close that I could see its bright yellow feet and cere, and its dark, deep-set eyes.

Another time a dark streak of an eagle hurtled out of the blue from a thousand feet above—straight at an eagle slowly coursing ahead of me. With a move almost too quick to grasp, the coursing bird rolled over in a complete loop with its feathered feet extended at the aggressor, and then in a second was flying level again. The would-be attacker banked and with both momentum and powered flight shot back up above the coursing eagle. Once more he made a stoop at his victim and then a roll-over, followed by a third dive. As my plane approached the pair, the birds separated and flew a few rods apart, but after I had passed, they were circling again and swinging up their feet at each other. I have sometimes seen fighting eagles come to grips briefly, but as long as we could see them, these adversaries were only sparring— following the usual course of making threatening maneuvers instead of actual contact.

A hunting eagle is a very different bird. Abroad at the first hint of dawn, it laboriously flaps low over slopes and desert, searching for a rabbit or other nocturnal animal that has not yet retired for the day. Failing a catch in the first light, the raptor hunts methodically, almost harrier fashion, coursing back and forth from low to somewhat higher elevations, contouring into and out of ravines and "draws," working an area for many minutes before sliding over a low ridge to the next draw.

The eagle is an opportunistic feeder. In much of the West, the chief prey is usually one of the "key industry" herbivores, such as ground squirrels, rabbits, or marmots. The prey varies considerably from region to region, and individual eagles may show different food preferences. Magpies, grouse, snakes, and extremes ranging from grasshoppers to large game are hunted and devoured. In severe winters, eagles have been known to kill a deer caught in a deep snow, but their principal winter food is carrion, such as dead livestock, deer killed by hunters, and the now abundant road kills, particularly rabbits.

Is it true, as charged, that eagles kill and make off with livestock, especially lambs and kids? There is a long history of sheepman's mistrust of the golden eagle. Shooting, trapping, and poisoning have gone on for centuries throughout the world.

A climax to the war on eagles came at the end of the Second World War, when Texas sheepmen discovered that eagles could be chased and shot down by airplanes. "Eagle Clubs" were formed in west Texas, and rancher members of each group paid a pilot hunter to shoot off all eagles at lambing time. (Lambing takes place in the open, on dry, rocky hillsides, at a time when transient eagles from the north are still present.)

The pilots combed the Davis, Eagle, and Glass mountains, and many other "rough country" regions. The toll of eagles shot by a single pilot rose as high as thirty-eight in a single day. Probably more than twenty thousand eagles were shot over trans-Pecos (west of the Pecos River), Texas, and southeastern New Mexico between 1940 and 1960. (In New Mexico, bald as well as golden eagles are shot.)

The aerial shoot-offs are now prohibited by law, but "sport pilots," apparently secure in their belief that they cannot be apprehended, are said to have replaced the professionals. "They are supposed to be hunting coyotes," a sheep rancher told me, "but these coyotes have wings!" A few years ago I photographed a pilot hunting over the Caldwell Ranch in the Davis Mountains, where only a few weeks earlier a father-and-son hunting team had died when their plane crashed.

No doubt some loss of livestock occurs, but it has not been possible to confirm the heavy losses claimed by sheep and goat raisers. The fact is that if predation by eagles occurs, it is only a small fraction of one percent of the kid-lamb crop. A few weeks ago I photographed two eagle chicks in Utah sheep country. In the nest were the remains of eight cottontail and jack rabbits, while on the slope scarcely five hundred feet below, grazed fifteen ewes and thirteen small lambs, most of them a few days old! In the sheep country of New Mexico, the Fish and Wildlife Service found only jackrabbit kills by eagles, and in Montana, a several-year study of food habits of over thirty eagle nests revealed no predation of lambs in the midst of a sheep-growing region.

The golden eagle is a persistent species and has managed to survive heavy shooting, relentless trapping, and the widespread use of poison. It is to be hoped that this royal bird with golden hackles —the most admired of all time—will manage to survive into a future where more and more of its habitat is being "managed" for man alone.

PART TWO

REPTILES

With a world-wide reputation as an expert on marine turtles, Dr. Archie F. Carr of the University of Florida has been principal investigator of their migrations for the National Science Foundation. He is currently chairman of the Sea Turtle Committee in the International Union for the Conservation of Nature. This and other research has taken him to Latin America, Portugal, the Azores, and Africa. He is the author of eight books and over sixty articles and papers which have earned numerous scientific and literary awards. His book *The Windward Road* won the John Burroughs Medal and the O. Henry Memorial Award. Professor Carr is the acknowledged expert on the great turtles which range across the world's oceans.

THE SEA TURTLES
ARCHIE CARR

The sea turtles are ancient animals. Their evolutionary beginnings are not well recorded in the rocks, but they certainly existed as far back as the earliest dinosaur times, when there were still no mammals on earth and no birds in the skies. The distinctive marks of the sea turtles are fin-like feet, relatively great size, and a shell in which, during thousands of centuries, some of the bones have been reduced in size and number to give greater buoyancy.

Except when the female emerges briefly to nest every two or three years, and when green turtles occasionally haul out to bask on mid-Pacifiic sand spits, sea turtles spend their whole lives in the water. Some of them make periodic nesting journeys that take them halfway around the world.

The biggest sea turtles are the leatherbacks. They may weigh more than fifteen hundred pounds and are the most highly adapted for marine life of all reptiles except the sea snakes. The shell of the leatherback is no shell at all but a unique mosaic of little tile-like bones covered by a fatty skin instead of by scales.

Most sea turtles are carnivorous. They forage for invertebrates about reefs and rocks and devour drifting jellyfish. The green turtle, however, is almost wholly herbivorous and spends most of its time grazing on submarine pastures of turtle grass, manatee grass, or algae. It is no doubt this diet that makes the meat of the green turtle so palatable.

All the turtles show at least some tendency to mass at nesting time. Together, they travel from feeding ground to nesting beach, often through a thousand miles of open sea with no fixed landmarks to guide them. The guidance mechanisms used are being investigated but are still by no means understood. For example, the most current theory to account for the ability of Brazilian green turtles to make regular landings on Ascension Island—a tiny speck of rock fourteen hundred miles out in midocean —is that they use a sun-compass combined with olfactory perception. This has by no means been conclusively proved, however.

The female ridley turtle appears to nest every year, while the other genera nest on a three-year or, less commonly, a two-year schedule. Tagging of turtles for identification shows that there is a strong tendency for the animals to go back to the same stretch of shore for consecutive nestings. During the breeding migration, the nesting female goes ashore from three to seven times at intervals of about twelve days. Each time that she is ready to lay her eggs, she uses her four flippers to clear away a site well above the high-tide reach, and then with back feet working alternately, she digs an urn-shaped nest hole to the depth that her foot will reach. Into this she drops about a hundred eggs which, according to the species of turtle, range from about the size of a golf ball to a little smaller than

a tennis ball. Then she covers the hole, packs the fill, throws sand and debris about with all four feet to conceal the site, and drags herself back to the familiar safety of the sea. It is known that the incubation period for all the sea turtles is about two months, but the ecology and movements of the first-year young remain a complete and frustrating mystery.

Not much has been learned about the courtship and mating habits of sea turtles except that they take place during the nesting period and are extraordinarily strenuous. Two or more males may often be seen attending one female, and their struggles to fend off one another and to mount the initially coy and elusive object of their ardor makes a great commotion in the water. Once a male has won out over his rivals, his attention to the female is so violent that her shell is often deeply scarred after the encounter.

This zeal of the male sea turtles is used to advantage by turtle fishermen. They throw out wooden decoys made roughly in the image of a turtle, and then harpoon or draw up in big mesh nets the single-minded males as they come courting the wooden female. Until recently the nesting females were regularly taken on shore. This practice more than any other factor has wiped out many rookeries throughout the world and has dangerously reduced population of some of the species.

There are five genera of sea turtles in the world: the ridleys, the smallest; the leatherbacks, the largest; the green turtles, the most edible; the hawksbills, which yield tortoiseshell; and the big-headed loggerheads, the most familiar to fishermen along the coasts of eastern United States. All are essentially tropical in their reproduction, although some loggerheads nest as far north as Virginia. During their postnesting-season travels, many go north. Leatherbacks, for instance, travel into Canadian waters, reach the Sea of Japan, and move far down along the shores of Chile. Ridleys regularly travel to Cape Cod and Martha's Vineyard, and thoroughly chilled young sea turtles are swept up on the coasts of England, Scotland, and the Scilly Isles.

Originally sea turtles were hunted mainly for their meat and eggs. Even now in some parts of the world the eggs are one of the few sources of animal protein for seaside peoples. In other regions, notably in Latin America, the eggs are in great demand as a source of sexual vigor.

An important threat to the future of sea turtles is an increasingly harmful traffic in calipee, the cartilaginous material that is cut from among the bones of the belly-shell. This is the one part of the turtle that is indispensable for the making of clear green-turtle soup, giving it the gummy consistency considered essential by epicures.

Formerly the captured turtles were stored and taken alive to market in order to keep the meat fresh. Now with the high price of calipee, hunters often do not try to save the meat, but butcher the animals on the spot. A lone turtler, instead of having to move a 350-pound turtle to market, simply removes the belly-shell, extracts and cures the cartilage, and takes the resulting three or four pounds of calipee to market in a backpack or dugout canoe. All too often he will slice off the belly-shell and leave the rest of the turtle for the vultures, sometimes so hurriedly that he leaves her alive with her entrails bare to the sun. Although calipee is the *sine qua non* for clear green-turtle soup, it does not have to come from a green turtle. Even the most sophisticated chefs are not able to tell sea turtles apart by their calipee. So the exploitation of all the species of sea turtles has been increased by the demand for calipee.

While the calipee trade was being organized on a worldwide basis, two other turtle products came into prominence. One was turtle leather; the other, turtle oil. The leather is used for expensive shoes and ladies' handbags. Only the

skin of the neck and upper fore quarters is taken. The demand is, on the word of an official of Saks Fifth Avenue, far in advance of the supply. It is so great in fact that on a recent trip along the Pacific coast, my sons saw stacks of hundreds of dead ridley turtles that had been killed by poachers who took away only the skins, leaving the rest of the turtle to rot on the beach.

For millennia, mystical influences have been attributed to sea turtle oil, meat, and blood. In parts of Central America the power of turtle oil to make women beautiful has been believed in for centuries. Turtles also loomed large in the pharmacopoeias of the ancient Chinese, and before Columbus reached America, shiploads of lepers were voyaging regularly to the Cape Verde Islands to try to cure their disease by eating turtle. In Alexandria, Egypt, women still go twice a week to a dockside turtle butchery and drink fresh turtle blood, which they believe will restore lost youth.

All about the tropical world, seaside folk are superstitious about the particular properties of turtle oil. In some places it is considered an elixir, in others a sure cure of syphilis. What the real effect of smearing turtle oil on human skin is, has not been objectively tested. Maybe it does make girls pretty. Certainly the television star now promoting turtle-oil cosmetics is pretty, but I think she got her looks long before she ever heard of turtle oil.

No kind of turtle better illustrates the devastating effect of the recent convergence of demand for turtle products than the hawksbill, from which tortoiseshell has been taken since ancient times. Hawksbills are reef turtles, carnivores that live singly or in small bands and forage about coral walls and heads. Unlike other marine turtles, they do not nest gregariously, but come ashore singly on any small piece of beach in most of the warm seas of the world.

In the old days the shell of the hawksbill was much sought after for such articles as Japanese hairpins, Spanish ladies' combs, and Nero's bathtub. Three decades ago plastic imitations of tortoiseshell began to appear, and the industry, believing it saw a straw in the wind, withered in most places.

Now, however, there has been rebellion against plastic tortoiseshell. Since both calipee and turtle skins have become semiprecious products, it is possible for a fisherman to realize, say, fifteen dollars for a full-grown hawksbill. In the remote places where hawksbills can still be taken, this may represent somewhat more than a fortnight's wages. So, understandably, pressure on the hawksbill has increased to dangerous levels.

I won't go on cataloguing details on the plight of sea turtles. I shall only say that beginning with the precarious status of the Mexican ridley, whose vast nesting assemblages have been reduced from forty thousand females that once came ashore in a single day (this is the only species that regularly nests by day) to a few hundred—with eggs still being carried away in oxcarts and trucks—and looking from there on down through the entire world roster of sea turtle species, there seems no single ray of hope.

This does not mean that the trend of things could not be changed. It could be. All the species of sea turtles could be saved and most of the breeding colonies could be restored; and it would not take heroic measures to bring this about.

There is no doubt at all that techniques of management and culture could be devised that would take the blessings from sea turtles and at the same time insure the continued existence of all the kinds.

Some of the moves most urgently needed are range reconnaissance, exploitation surveys, migration and population studies, international regulation and protection, and pilot culture projects.

Tagging camps should be set up at every locality in which reconnaissance locates heavy breeding. During the past ten years, recoveries of tags, inscribed with a return address and an offer of a reward, and attached to the flippers of nesting turtles, have produced indispensable data. However more extensive tagging operations are needed, to determine the location and extent of the areas to which female turtles return after nesting and to provide information on migratory routes and seasons, reproductive cycles, and year-to-year changes in population levels.

From such information good turtle laws could be devised. If these were then enforced by adequate numbers of vigilant wardens and by international agreements for the control of exploitation, the turtle populations of the world might reestablish themselves in a relatively short time.

Experimentation in the rearing of green turtles in enclosures should be energetically supported. If there is any promise in the sea turtle industry it will probably only be realized through turtle farms. A first step toward developing these would be a pan-tropical search for localities with (a) good sites for hatching crawls, with warm, clear, constantly renewed water of high salinity, (b) a constant supply of cheap animal food for the first-year turtles, (c) extensive areas of submarine spermatophyte vegetation for pasturage or for cut feed for the maturing stock, and (d) freedom from typhoons, hurricanes, and drastic changes in water level.

The most promising places for green-turtle farms are coasts and islands where coral reefs protect broad expanses of shallow sea from heavy wave action. Such territory is widespread in the Caribbean and occurs at many other places in the warm seas of the world. Wherever suitable conditions are found, government support should be made available for small-scale pilot culture projects. To insure a steady supply of hatchlings for such projects the problem of inducing the migratory green turtle to mate and nest in captivity should be studied.

Wherever the necessary conditions prevail there seems no inherent reason why the green turtle should not become a semidomesticated meat animal of great value, supported by aquatic pasturage as cattle are supported by terrestrial grass. Successful development of this culture not only would extend the means of taking food from the sea, but would also quickly take the pressure off wild turtle populations and in this way help save the natural species for the distant future.

A specialist in natural resources problems, William M. Partington has been administrator of the Florida Audubon Society's conservation education center and is now assistant director of the Society. He has done research on pine flatwoods ecology and the reptiles of Palm Beach County and has earned awards for leadership in organizing or promoting several conservation and recreational organizations of South Florida. He lectures and writes extensively on Florida ecology and reptiles. One of his special responsibilties is the conservation of the vanishing American alligator; the chapter which follows is based on many months of study and photography of this subtropical reptile.

THE AMERICAN ALLIGATOR
WILLIAM M. PARTINGTON

Sometime in the near future a poll should be taken throughout the country to discover what five plants or animals the public considers typical of the wilderness areas still found in southeastern United States. Personal favorites, such as cypress trees, wild orchids, panthers, ivory-billed woodpeckers, and Everglade kites would certainly be named, but I'll bet the overall winner by a wide margin would be the alligator.

From early childhood, every American knows what an alligator is. "A is for Alligator" is almost as standard in animal ABC books as "Z is for Zebra," and several generations have been raised on books where alligators had a part, usually as an enduring villain. In spite of this unfortunate characterization, most of us grow up possessing a certain fascination that we never outgrow for these less-than-cuddlesome reptiles.

Before man settled and developed so much of the country from coastal North Carolina to the Rio Grande in Texas, alligators appear to have inhabited almost every fresh or brackish water wetland within this range. John Bartram, the naturalist-explorer, in the mid-1700's and John James

Audubon in the early 1800's, wrote detailed descriptions of amazing concentrations. (It has been estimated that in the 1890's there were still three million alligators in Florida.)

Bartam described a visit to the St. Johns River in northeast Florida that has become an all-time classic. In this untouched region he thought some of the alligators to be twenty to twenty-three feet long, which they may well have been. While fishing in a canoe, he was repeatedly attacked by large specimens and had to beat them off with a club, his only weapon. On returning to the shore, a twelve-footer aggressively followed him but stopped near the canoe. When Bartram came back with a gun, the alligator had become interested in the bass lying in the canoe, and was shot. Another large gator swept some of Bartram's fish into the water while he was absorbed in cleaning them.

Although this sounds fantastic today, when the sight of even a small, wild alligator is rare in most of their range, these tales are probably accurate. Male gators still fight other males within their territories, and the canoe and Bartram may have been (rightfully) regarded as a threat to their domain.

By the late 1800's almost all the potentially dangerous alligators had been killed off, and the animals were becoming rare in many parts due to slaughter for hides, tail meat, oil from the fat for machinery, in defense of livestock, and for "sport." E. A. McIlhenny, a well-educated gentleman from a successful family, spent his lifetime at Avery Island on the coast of Louisiana, where alligators abounded and were largely unmolested. He had an opportunity to study these reptiles from the late 1800's

through the 1930's under conditions such as no one may ever have again.

McIlhenny describes swimming, as a boy, in a bayou where alligators were abundant and large; one that measured 18 feet 3 inches was eventually shot by his tutor at this swimming hole. He and his friends would play games with and annoy slightly smaller gators but were never attacked, although the boys did get out of the way of any alligator that had been sufficiently bothered to run for the water. On January 2, 1890, McIlhenny shot the largest alligator he had ever seen. It measured 19 feet 2 inches, and stands as the accepted record length for this species.

On a few occasions McIlhenny described being attacked by alligators, although he believed that most of them were females protecting their nests or young. Only once was he attacked apparently without reason, and that was by an eleven- or twelve-footer (with a section of tail missing), which he shot in self-defense.

Throughout most of their range alligators become inactive during the winter, retiring to dens dug under banks or to parts of their water holes that they have deepened. Metabolism slows down and there is little need for food since, like all reptiles, their internal temperatures are influenced by their surroundings. Freezes may occur, coating ponds with ice, and there may be difficulty getting enough air to breathe unless the gator can get his nose above the surface before the ice hardens. Alligators have been found dead in Louisiana after freezes, apparently killed by suffocation rather than by the cold. At any rate, the effects of cold weather are certainly a limiting factor in their distribution, accounting

for the fact that they are found along the warmer black-water swamps, streams, and millponds near the Carolina coast rather than in the cooler inland sections.

Studies are being carried on in several states to determine how fast alligators grow and how much they move around. The Florida Game and Fresh Water Fish Commission, for example, has been catching, recording, tagging, and releasing alligators for this purpose, and I have enjoyed some memorable nights accom-panying these operations. One June night was spent in the north end of the Everglades National Park after heavy seasonal rains had flooded the glades. A sea of saw grass extended to the horizon, broken by occasional tree islands, and far-off thunderstorms flashed sheets of lightning. In the early evening, flocks of egrets, little blue herons, white ibis, and wood storks probed the open sloughs and casually flew off to other waters for no apparent reason. Southern bullfrogs grunted from roadside ditches where occasional garfish and mudfish splashed. In spite of high water, several six-to-ten-foot gators unconcernedly floated in the ditches, and an occasional bull gator issued a shaky roar over the swamps. Although Miami was less than two hours' driving distance away, we could have been moved back in time a thousand years. This was not a world of man's making except for the road we were standing on.

The game biologists on this expedition had asked a few adventurous friends along to help them. In order to "land" the alligators, we fastened a strong noose to the end of a cane fishing pole with a couple of clothespins. The next step was to extend the noose over the reptile's head, pull the line tight, and let the cane pole drop into the water to float until the excitement was over.

At first the gators were rather tame and easily caught, possibly because they were accustomed to visitors in the park. After a couple of captures, however, the others seemed to become more wary and were harder to approach either by boat or from shore.

We moved to another pond which was really a borrow pit where rock had been excavated for making the road. The sides had grown up, giving a wild, natural appearance. Several alligators were spotted by the headlamps, their eyes reflecting a bright orange-red glow. The small aluminum boat was launched; one man held a noosing pole in the bow while the other sculled with a single paddle.

A particularly large gator, too big to pass up, came into sight, splashing with his jaws and apparently feeding on something that kept him preoccupied. The

men easily slipped the noose over his head, but then all hell broke loose.

The gator dove, tried to lose the rope by snagging some submerged rocks, and pulled the boat wildly about the pond. The single paddle was useless except to head the boat in the direction the gator wanted to go. Eventually a line was thrown out from shore, and the boat, men, and alligator were recovered, in that order. This specimen was barely short of twelve feet—too heavy to weigh or to wonder what the sex was—and because of its size it had to be a male, probably one of the biggest left in the Everglades.

As a result of these studies and other reports, we can put together some facts about alligators, although continuing research is needed if we are to save them from extinction in the few areas where they still exist as native breeding animals.

In most places alligators mate during April or May, possibly into June depending on the weather and the region. Sexual maturity of both sexes is reached at about six feet in size (approximately six years old), although females may accept larger males more readily than those the same size.

Males seem to outnumber females by seven to three at time of hatching, but this ratio gradually diminishes. Like human children, the young males may be more adventurous and prone to getting themselves in unfortunate situations. By the time they have reached maturity, there are about six males to four females in both Louisiana and Florida.

During the breeding season the males do most of their calling, both in defense of their territories and to attract females who may answer with a growling sound. The male call, or bellow, is given while in water by inflating the body with air, throwing the head and tail upward, and forcing the air through the throat and slightly opened mouth. The skin on the sides vibrates, causing waves and splashes of water, and musk is released from the two glands at the sides of the lower jaw. This creates quite a spectacle and a sound that carries for miles over flat marshes. As with calling frogs, the open water may amplify the roar.

Both adult males and females move around more during the breeding season than at other times, leaving obvious trails through the marshes, and then return to rather restricted home grounds for the rest of the year. Like most wild animals, adult alligators have individual ranges that they tend to adhere to, although severe floods, droughts, saltwater intrusion, change of food supplies, hurricanes, or human alteration of their habitat will cause population shifts. Occasional "adventurous" gators will suddenly move several miles for no obvious reason.

The actual mating takes place in the water, with the male on the female's back, clasping her with his fore and hind legs. His tail is bent down, and the female's sideways to facilitate fertilization. Each act lasts several minutes and may be repeated during the several days that the two stay together.

The male then continues to move about to other females, and if aggressive bull gators are encountered, terrific battles may ensue. Most old males carry scars ranging from missing toes to feet to amputated tails and gouged eyes.

The female, if she has left her water hole or den, returns to it. Some of her young of the previous year, as well as those of other years, may still be staying there with her. However, this may be more a matter of selecting a mutually convenient spot by this time since within a month her attention will be focused on making a nest for her next batch of eggs.

Some females rebuild previous nests, and some "gator hummocks" in the Everglades National Park are estimated to have been in use for five hundred years by succeeding generations. These old nesting sites are composed of compacted plants and muck, and living ferns, broadleaved shrubs, and trees become established on them.

At present, perhaps because there are fewer gators to compete for suitable sites, most females build new nests each year. Some will even start nests which they abandon for other sites. If possible, a female selects a relatively high area, although raised nests are built on flooded marsh. She then breaks off adjacent vegetation in an area about twenty feet in diameter and makes a pile a couple of yards across and about two and a half feet high. If the material is fairly dry, she may make a hole at the top, to which she carries aquatic plants and mud. The whole nest is packed down by crawling over it repeatedly. The entire construction process takes only a couple of days, and when it is finished she is ready to lay.

Now she crawls on top, pushes out a deep nesting hole with her hind legs, somewhat as turtles do, and drops her eggs into the hole. These may number from twenty-five to sixty-eight, depending on the size of the female, her condition, mating success, etc., although the average is about three dozen. These are hard shelled, white, and measure about 1⅔ by 2⅔ inches. After laying she covers the eggs with litter and packs it down again by crawling back and forth over the nest. (Old accounts tell of ninety to two hundred eggs in a single nest in different layers, which may have been estimates, faulty observation, or possibly community nests.)

While building the nest, the female may be easily frightened; but after laying she will usually stay close by when not hunting and may even attack a human investigating the nest. Nevertheless, a certain percentage of eggs are robbed by raccoons, opossums, hogs, or other predators. A recent threat to alligator populations has been the sudden rise in water levels in the Everglades at laying time or shortly afterward. Spring droughts may induce the female to build a low nest, which leaves the eggs vulnerable to drowning when the glades' waters rise. As with most reptile eggs, the shells are porous to allow exchanges of oxygen and carbon dioxide, and only a slight degree of dampness is tolerable.

Composting within the nest creates heat which is highest at first, often over $100°$ F., but during the normal nine weeks of incubation the internal temperature may drop to $80°$ F., considerably below the usual southern summer temperature. Poorly constructed or neglected nests may require longer incubation periods, and if the female is taken away, her nest will probably fail.

During dry weather, she wets down the nest and may add new material as the pile erodes or compacts. Throughout most of the alligator's range, hatching takes place in August.

As soon as the young hatch, they start grunting inside their closed nest. When the mother becomes aware of these demands she proceeds to bite away a large hole in the side, permitting the young to

escape. Her trail by this time is a relatively open path, making the water easy for the young to find, but even on this short trip the usual predators plus hawks or herons may gobble up a few.

After absorbing the remainder of their egg yolks and losing their umbilical cords, the young start snapping at everything small enough for them to overcome at this 8-to-9½-inch size. This may include disabled tadpoles, fish, or even leftovers from the mother's meals, but shrimp, snails, and insects are the usual staple items. Although the mother may actively guard her progeny, the modern alligator, even with young, is rarely dangerous. Only the females that have seen people often enough to overcome their man-shyness are prone to attack. Since the mother may go off on her own hunting trips during the nesting and "baby care" periods, groups of young alligators are often found apparently abandoned.

The young grow fast, especially in the southern part of the range where they enjoy a long active season. By fall they are over a foot long, and by the next mating season they measure about one and a half feet. Herons, turtles, fish, raccoons, otters, and even other alligators prey on them whenever they can. Probably only one baby gator in seven grows to maturity; about 85 percent of a wild alligator population is immature (baby to six feet long).

Due to poaching for hides, loss of habitat, and human fear or indifference, the alligator has become a comparative rarity over most of its range, except in some parks or wildlife refuges, and most conservationists are very much concerned for their future. Throughout the original ranges, perhaps more than 99 percent of the alligators have been destroyed. Why should anyone care about this potentially dangerous animal? Of course it has some place in our history and folklore, but what good is an alligator and who would miss it?

Most readers who have come this far will have their own answers, but maybe I can supply a few more thoughts for your use.

To be practical, wild alligators (unintentionally) assist all wetlands wildlife and fish during the droughts that have become characteristic of our mismanaged wetlands in recent years. Some gators will travel to canals or other man-made water holes, but a certain percentage, especially mature females with young, will stay on in their deepened water holes and dens. These become survival areas for fish and other aquatic organisms, and provide places for wary land animals to take a sip or to get a snack. When the water rises again, small aquatic creatures spread out and help to repopulate the marshes. Wildlife officers and biologists are convinced that the alligator, where native, is *essential* to the survival of a well-balanced marsh wilderness.

Alligators are important in controlling populations of all marsh life, and they are one of the few animals besides otters that will eat the hard-scaled garfish (which devour some game fish). Old-timers will tell how predictably good the bass fishing was at active gator holes, and how the fishing went down after gators were killed off.

In the Everglades National Park, alligators abounded until they were reduced by droughts and poaching. During healthier and wetter times they helped to keep waterways open by their movements and thus assisted in keeping a flow of water to the estuaries where sport and commercial fish bred or matured. The park's estuaries are well known to be essential nursery grounds for shrimp, one of Florida's most important seafood industries. Whole plant communities within the park were influenced by alligators, and reduction of the animals plus less water has caused salt intrusion and allowed salt tolerant plants to move inland. Upland plants have become established along former waterways, and so the whole natural landscape has changed for the worse.

Alligators deserve a place as wild, self-supporting creatures because they belong to one of the oldest groups of air-breathing vertebrates on earth, starting some 200 million years ago during the time of dinosaurs. Productive marsh, swamp, and river systems have been characteristic of the tropics and subtropics throughout the ages, supporting the original alligators and their descendants. In our technologically advanced age it would be disgraceful if we failed to provide the simple protection and management these dramatic reptiles must have.

The alligator's salt- and brackish-water relative, the American crocodile, is more slender and agile. There are probably less than one hundred of these shy reptiles left in the United States, (limited to southernmost Florida), although the same species is still fairly abundant in Latin America. There is only one other kind of alligator—a smaller species found in China—and this is probably even closer to extinction than the American alligator. It *is* possible to save our alligators. They can make remarkable comebacks if we preserve their wetlands, protect them from slaughter for their hides, and if enough people care.

Five years as herpetologist of the American Museum's Central Asiatic Expeditions gave Clifford H. Pope a lifelong interest in the Chinese language and culture as well as a base for his professional career: curating, research, and writing about reptiles.

In addition to long service at the American Museum and Field Museum, Mr. Pope is a fellow of the New York Zoological Society, and a past President of the American Society of Ichthyologists and Herpetologists. He is the author of one hundred bulletins, technical papers, and popular articles, as well as eight books which include such well-known titles as *Snakes Alive, The Reptile World,* and *The Giant Snakes.* When his sons were young, reptiles were the favorite house pets. Cliff Pope's lifelong effort to change the public attitude toward unjustly maligned species led him to choose the water snake for the subject of this chapter.

THE COMMON WATER SNAKE
CLIFFORD H. POPE

Every familiar animal has its image for man, and that of the innocuous common water snake is neither a good nor an accurate one. First, it is very often confused with the dangerous cottonmouth, although to the experienced eye there are many differences in both appearance and behavior. Second, the common water snake defends itself vigorously, putting up an even more alarming show than the cottonmouth. When closely pressed or actually seized, this harmless species not only emits a foul material from glands at the base of the tail but may defecate as well. The resulting odor is highly offensive. Third, the common water snake is mistakenly believed by fishermen to beat them to the catch. Fourth, this aquatic species lacks the beauty of some snakes. Old individuals appear to be dull brown on the back and sides, the pattern being obscure. Only the young are attractive in color. Thus we have a reptile that is thought to be venomous, exhibits alarming and disgusting behavior, and often lacks beauty.

Yet for a lonely small boy living in the backwoods of northeastern Georgia at the turn of the century, this snake had an entirely different image. First, it was one of the only two kinds of snakes that he could readily catch, various other species being scarce. Second, it was the first snake that he dared to catch, and even then with dark misgivings. A book had informed him that no cottonmouths lived in his elevated foothill area, but nearly everyone had warned him that a little boy who played with snakes always wound up in a coffin. Third, the ferociousness of the common water snake added to his excitement. He does admit, however, that when the bite of that first individual drew blood, there were moments of wild doubt.

As time went on and the boy grew, the sport of wading up streams to catch this and the other water snakes became a cherished pastime. In the hot summer days there was no place more pleasant than the partly shaded bed of a stream with the clear water cooling bare feet, the bright sun overhead, and teeming wildlife all around. The magic of those days vanished forever as the boy matured, but the interest in snakes has never flagged, thanks largely to that unpopular species.

How does the common water snake stack up among other snakes of the United States? There are barely fifteen widely recognized groups or types of snakes in this country, and the water snakes are perhaps as familiar as any except the king snakes, garter snakes, racers, and whip snakes, and the venomous pit vipers and coral snakes. Among the ten species of water snakes, ours stands out not only because of its unequaled geographical range but also because of its adaptations, including marked variation in form and coloration. Its range extends from southern Ontario and extreme southern Quebec to the Gulf of Mexico, and as far west as eastern Colorado and eastern Texas. Obviously it thrives under widely different climatic conditions. It is well adapted to lowland life yet it is common to 3,000 feet in the Great Smoky Mountains National Park, and ascends to 4,800 feet there on occasion. Along our southern coasts it lives in salt marshes where it differs in size and habits, and has even become predominantly a striped rather than a crossbanded or spotted snake. Archie Carr writes of fishing in the surf at Naples, Florida; although he was a hundred yards off the beach he noticed that a common water snake was indulging at the same sport hard by.

The common water snake is an evolutionary success. It is probable that the Indians lived in harmony with it, and existing close to nature, readily distinguished it from the cottonmouth. If European man had not arrived, the common water snake might have remained in tune with the Indians indefinitely. The coming of modern technological civilization, however, with the consequent disturbance of the watercourses and the pollution of waters, created the greatest threat the common water snake has ever faced. Destruction of habitats spells final doom to wildlife, which can survive the slaughter of numbers of individuals.

In spite of all the damage man has done, this reptile holds its own remarkably well, and may abound where other large species have been all but eliminated. I recall finding one some decades ago on the campus of the venerable University of Virginia, where a tiny stream gave barely enough protection. So when all water courses are at last purified, more wildlife areas established, and the

rate of human reproduction reduced, the common water snake may remain one of the exciting elements of the fauna and continue to alarm wading boys and girls, not to mention fishermen. By that time the angler may have learned to allow it to remain a picturesque and even useful element of the sportsman's surroundings.

Water and its immediate vicinity have many advantages for animals, as the abundance of fishes and aquatic invertebrates well testifies. Snakes have not passed up the opportunities, either. Water offers a place of retreat, harbors abundant food, and maintains a relatively uniform temperature, this last being of special importance to cold-blooded creatures. It is easy for a snake to be at home in this element. A streamlined body and undulating movements make the snake a natural swimmer. Moreover, the eyes are well protected by a sealed covering, the breath can be held a long time without causing distress, and the smooth skin withstands soaking. Little wonder that water snakes of various kinds are a conspicuous part of the fauna of the well-watered regions of the northern hemisphere.

Although the common water snake abounds in various aquatic situations, we may take as typical a sluggish stream flowing through open Virginia country with abundant vegetation crowding the overhanging banks. Early in September a female three feet long gives birth to fifty young. Before birth they had received some materials necessary to growth via a simple placenta that foreshadows the more complex and efficient one of mammals. The parent should be congratulated because the average number of young is about twenty-five,

though a brood of ninety-nine is on record. Such fecundity must account for the female's being noticeably larger than the male and must be a factor in the survival of this species. The snakelings average eight and a half inches in length and are vividly crossbanded in contrast to the mother whose bands can be detected only when the skin is wet. She shows no interest in the brood but continues to feed and to take sunbaths on the log projecting over a deep pool.

It takes her about fifteen minutes to swallow any large frog that she comes across, even though it weighs a quarter as much as she does. Having only needle-like teeth slanting toward her throat, she cannot chew, nor can she readily kill the frog before devouring it whole. She is also fond of sluggish fishes but, contrary to popular opinion, does not compete with her greatest enemy, the two-legged, almost hairless mammal who preys on the active "game" fishes. If this mammal would only let her alone she might promote his sport by the elimination of some of the sluggish fishes that compete for food with the active ones. Incidentally, after giving birth she will take no more interest in sex, except perhaps briefly in the fall, until the following spring. If in the spring she fails to find a mate, she could still have another brood in the late summer; some snakes are known to store sperm for years. The two-legged mammal can be glad that *his* mate has no such ability.

Due to her size, appearance, formidable behavior, and wariness, this mother is better able to survive than her tender young. These, though quick to defend themselves, make toothsome morsels for various mammals and large birds. A big bullfrog can swallow a young common water snake whole, and hungry king snakes lurk in the vicinity of streams. Rapid growth, however, helps the young pass through this hazardous stage. In the first year they add about four inches to their length and make the same proportional gain the following year. During hibernation the rapid growth ceases. The third year finds them maturing sexually and surpassing twenty inches.

Students of reptile life have recorded many additional facts about this snake; a complete summary, yet to be published, would fill a thick volume and be useful solely as a reference work for other herpetologists. This brief essay can merely hope to dispel a bit of the bad image that the common water snake has created in the fertile but fickle mind of man.

Before the scientific age ushered in a new approach to the study of animals, snakes had given rise to literally tens of thousands of absurd beliefs and tales; little objectivity was discernible in the incredibly complex man-snake relationship, a state unrivaled by our concept of any other animal. This bad image of the common water snake is in part a survival of this extreme subjectivity, which the scientific approach has failed to eliminate. With increase in objectivity goes a rising interest in snakes and the consequent development of a pet market. The common water snake is protected by its image; but who can say that it won't outlive those species whose appearance and behavior make them popular?

Carl F. Kauffeld was an assistant in the department of herpetology at the American Museum and then curator of reptiles for the Staten Island Zoo, of which he became director in 1963. Over the past thirty years he has built the reptile (especially rattlesnake) collection into one of the world's finest and best known. Despite administrative duties, he has continued research on pit vipers in general and rattlesnakes in particular. He is a prolific writer, being author or coauthor of three popular books and over a hundred scientific and popular articles on snakes and their ways. A fellow of the Herpetologists' League, he is an honorary member of five herpetological societies in this country and abroad.

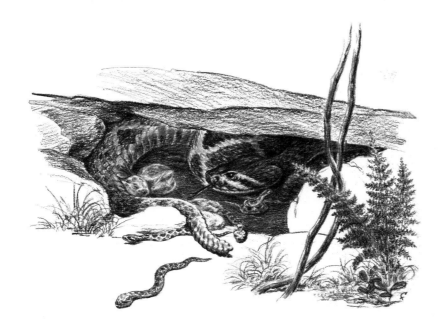

THE RATTLESNAKE

CARL F. KAUFFELD

It is an unusual graveyard . . . unusual because it is hidden in a woods of longleaf pine saplings with here and there lofty loblolly pines, live oaks, and dogwoods in bloom. Spanish moss, blown from the oaks, festoons many of the pines like gray funeral drapery. The doleful notes of mourning doves mingle with the happier songs of robins, cardinals, and mockingbirds, while a red-bellied woodpecker hammers out a tattoo.

Few of the graves can be seen from the sandy woods road because of close-growing trees; most are nearly obliterated except for deep depressions in the ground. Long devoid of markers, they are riddled with rodent burrows. On some, the debris of decorations are strewn—Styrofoam funeral forms, wires from wreaths and artificial flowers, broken glass jars, and clay flower-pots. Some of the graves still retain badly faded, often water-stained type-written labels under glass in cheap metal frames. Others have crudely inscribed headstones which seem much older and more weathered than the dates would indicate. Still others are well marked and clearly inscribed, and a few are even covered by stone slabs.

The names that I could read tended to be flowery and the spelling fanciful, for this is the burial ground of black people. Not a breeze stirred as I stepped into the clearing that marks the site where Clarance Washington and Charity Ford are buried; both graves are relatively well kept, and the inscription on the stone is quite readable. In South Carolina, even as early as March, the sun can be burning hot at midmorning, and it beat down on me now as I read the two tombstones. I turned back into the woods where shafts of sunlight slanted through to the blackened floor—blackened from fires that had charred the mat of pine needles and leathery live-oak leaves, and seared the trunks of longleaf pines. The ground was littered with twigs and broken branches, sometimes entangled with vicious, wiry briars to trap the unwary.

Not twenty-five feet from Clarance and Charity I saw a huge diamondback rattlesnake, loosely draped on the ground with only its head drawn back slightly. He watched me with shining-black, lidless eyes. Not a muscle twitched and his long rattle remained silent.

Greeting him in the fashion his dignity demanded, I said, "Good mawnin' to yo', suh," in what I hoped was the proper accent to use in greeting a southern gentleman. What a beauty! Over the years I have come upon dozens of eastern diamondback rattlers in the wild; the sight of them is always startling and dramatic, but this rattler seemed to be one of the most impressive. Had it been less fine a specimen, I would have left it and gone my way, but this one I had to have for our zoo.

Unfortunately I had only one snake hook and a single large sack with me. It was going to take considerable maneuvering to bag this big fellow, for I had no intention of pinning the head and grasping him in my hands. The pinning method has long been abandoned because it is too shattering an experience for the snake and too dangerous for the collector.

Apparently my handsome beast had crawled out of a rodent hole several feet away and had no escape route close at hand. I considered carefully what I should do. A sapling cut with my pocketknife could serve as a stave to hold the bag open on the ground while I guided him in with my hook. I took my time cutting a stick, keeping a watchful eye on the snake. He still hadn't moved—not even to flick out his long, black, forked tongue. He was truly a magnificent brute. The beautiful design of dark rhombs, light-edged and light-centered, was especially bright and sharp. This is the ruptive pattern which makes these snakes blend so wonderfully with the crisscross lights and shadows of their surroundings. His head looked enormous, and I knew that curved fangs, at least three quarters of an inch long, folded back now against the roof of the mouth, could lay me in a cemetery, too, if I did not keep out of their way.

What fascinating creatures rattlesnakes are! Long acquaintance with their many races only increases my admiration for them. They are the ultimate in snake evolution, and their patterns and mechanisms for survival have been so successful that in many parts of the New World, including certain of the United States, they are the most common snakes. Thirty-two forms exist in this country, and almost as many more in Mexico. They dwindle out toward the tropics with only one or two species in Central and South America, but in North America, including Mexico, they have differentiated and proliferated like the numerous car models turned out by the automobile industry.

Their highly intricate and elaborate apparatus for making lightning-fast injections of poison is shared with all other viperine snakes. The venom is manufactured and stored in glands and injected through the hollow fangs that act like hypodermic needles. It is of course designed for killing prey which consists mostly of small mammals—rats and rabbits in the case of our diamondback. When used in defense against larger animals, such as man, greater quantities of poison are required and the effect is more gradual. The venom does not start to spread until it becomes diluted under the skin. Then it travels through the lymph system to the heart and other organs, causing damage that results in collapse, difficulty in breathing, extreme pain, and sometimes death.

The remarkable heat-sensitive pits of the rattler that look like a second pair of nostrils (one depression on each side of the face) are a more exclusive feature but still shared by all other pit vipers, such as the cottonmouth and copperhead. These facial pits are range-finders —so accurate that a blindfolded pit viper can find its mark with a forward thrust of the head and erected fangs quite unerringly. Besides helping the snake to detect warm-blooded prey by sensing heat, they contribute to its smelling and hearing ability. (Without external ears, the rattler is unable to hear sounds in our range of hearing; instead, it depends almost entirely on ground vibrations.) Because of its adaptable sight, along

with other senses, it can hunt at night as well as by day.

The rattle of our snake—that strange series of interlocking links that increment from the end of the tail twice a year when the skin is shed—belongs exclusively to rattlesnakes. Its strident sound can shatter the stillness of the woods with seeming menace; but actually it is a sign of fear—fear of being stepped on or otherwise molested. That a rattler sounds a warning from gentlemanly instincts is, of course, absurd, and if the snake is sufficiently disturbed to realize danger, it will not rattle. Because I hunt rattlesnakes, I usually see them before they see me. And since I am careful not to arouse them too much, they seldom rattle before I make an overt move in their direction.

Remember always that the snake you see (without contact) is not to be feared; it will not attack you. In fact, it fears *you* more than you fear *it*—and with better reason. Given time and opportunity, most snakes will crawl away into some hiding hole or, failing that, merely remain where they lie coiled. (People who have been bitten by rattlesnakes have startled them and caused them to strike in defense.)

Altogether, the three essential specializations—the erectile fangs, the thermosensitive pits, and the rattle— make rattlesnakes so highly mechanized that they seem to be a product of man's ingenuity. In fact, they are quite improbable! Still a marvel in our technological age, they must have seemed supernatural to the mechanically simple people of bygone centuries. Whatever the evolutionary causes are that produced these snakes, it is obvious that the pattern has "survival value," and thus is duplicated over and

45

over again in a multiplicity of forms. This is called "adaptive radiation," and the rattlers have adapted and radiated and differentiated with vigor.

As with most of our native snakes, rattlesnakes usually mate in the spring. Where the species congregates at den sites to hibernate, the sexes are already convened and find each other easily when they emerge. Otherwise, excepting fortuitous encounters, the male must trail the female by scent, which is probably left by her musk glands. Courtship is rather elaborate, consisting of chin rubbing by the male along the female's back, body contact by undulations—sinuous and voluptuous—and twisting and intertwining of the tails. The intromittent sex organs in all snakes and lizards are located in the tail. Full cooperation of the female is necessary, for the male has no means of holding her. (No female snake was ever raped!) Courtship may be quite prolonged, and when copulation is effected it may last for hours. Sometimes all stimulation fails to arouse the female sufficiently and the male must crawl away, frustrated and exhausted.

Many snakes, including some if not all rattlesnakes, indulge in a curious behavior display which consists of intertwining the fore parts of the bodies vertically and swaying back and forth as they strain against one another. For some time this was believed to be courtship, until it was discovered that the individuals so entwined were always males, and that they were engaged in a sham battle, like arm wrestlers. It was dubbed the "combat dance" and was construed as a struggle to establish territory.

All rattlesnakes are born alive but they are not truly viviparous since there is no placental attachment of the young to the mother. Because the rattlers' transition from egg-laying (oviparity) to bearing-alive (viviparity) is comparatively recent, perhaps within a million years, some young still have the egg tooth—a special chisel-like, temporary structure that projects from the snout. This is used by the egg-born forms to slash their way out of the leathery shell of the egg.

Today the evolutionary trend in rattlesnakes is continuing toward viviparity and some species already show rudimentary placentas. Live-bearing has the advantage over egg-bearing in that eggs can desiccate or rot from too little or too much moisture; they can be captured and eaten more easily by predators, and on the whole are more vulnerable than the young retained full-term by the live-bearing female.

Like most snakes in the United States, young rattlers are born in the late summer or early fall, the dates being greatly influenced by local climatic conditions. Occasionally there are fall matings, the young are not born until the following spring, their development being interrupted during the female's hibernation.

At birth the snakelings are extruded from the mother, wrapped in transparent membranous sacs from which they break out in a few minutes. Although they are born fully equipped with fangs, venom glands, and highly active venom, they do not eat until after they have shed their skins for the first time. This is the initial molt that all species of snakes go through the first week or two after hatching or being born. Most rattlesnakes have one to twenty-one young but others have many more. The Mexican west-coast rattlesnake takes all prizes for fecundity—

as many as sixty young; forty to fifty are not uncommon.

Rattlers have been enormously successful and are found from eastern mountains, southern pinelands and forest-swamps, from central prairies and southwestern deserts to high altitudes in Arizona, California, Mexico, and New Mexico. They have managed to occupy virtually every habitat niche, even persisting at times where man has caused massive disturbance to their habitat as in parts of Florida and Texas. Some have evolved amazing adaptations to special environments. The sidewinder, for instance, has a lateral-looping gait that enables him to cross shifting desert sands easily. This method is so efficient that it has developed independently in several desert snakes of Africa and Asia.

Excepting snakeless Alaska and Hawaii (and Maine and Delaware which have snakes but no rattlers), every state in the Union harbors at least one species of rattlesnake, and many have three or four. Arizona tops them all with seventeen species and subspecies, but of course this does not mean that all seventeen can be encountered in any one area. They are as diversified in their choice of homes as Arizona is diversified in terrain and vegetation: deserts and mesas, high forested mountains and bare stone mountains, canyons and plateaus. There are desert forms like the sidewinder, the tiger, the Mojave; and tableland forms like the prairie and the Hopi. The western diamondback lives in both desert and tableland. There is even a distinct race living in the Grand Canyon; and there are forest forms like the Arizona black, and the black-tailed which lives in more open country.

Then there is a handful of very special species that have become marooned on forested mountaintops of isolated ranges such as the Huachucas, the Chiricahuas, and the Santa Ritas of Arizona, and the Animas of New Mexico. Here the little ridge-nosed rattlesnakes and the even smaller rock and spotted rattlers seem to be survivors of an age when uninterrupted forests, made possible by water from melting glaciers, covered the Southwest. These snakes have been isolated by shrinking forests and encroaching deserts as surely and effectively as they would be on islands in the sea. "Mountain-island" rattlers are especially interesting; most of them are less than two feet long and they are very distinctively colored and marked. Their vertical range starts no lower than 5,000 feet and goes as high as 8,000 and 9,000 feet in the Southwest, and to 14,000 feet in Mexico. Other species like the black-tailed and southern Pacific rattlers have a much greater range vertically—from 2,000 feet, or even sea level, to at least 8,000 feet—and they are wider ranging latitudinally as well.

The size differential in rattlesnakes is considerable: the smallest rarely exceed eighteen inches; the largest may be over seven feet, with the majority falling in the three-to-five-foot class. Undisputed giants are the eastern and western diamondbacks; both closely related species have been known to reach seven feet, and six-foot specimens are not uncommon. The combination of size and the potency and quantity of venom they can inject at a bite places them among the world's largest and deadliest snakes. While the very small forms can hardly be considered dangerous or deadly to man, the generally inoffensive nature of all rattlesnakes makes accidents rare and deaths even rarer. Far more people die of bee and wasp stings in the United States each year than of snakebite.

But let us return to our diamondback in the graveyard who has yet to be caught and bagged. Here I was confronted with a far different problem in a much different habitat than when I hunted the little mountain rattlers in Arizona with such great delight and occasional frustrations. I knew I would have to lift this six-foot giant away from the branches and brambles onto the more open ground where I was standing. The main problem was to prop the bag open without the handy devices I usually have with me. The stave held the bag open but obstructed the opening. Ordinarily, such a large rattler can be made to back into a sack held open by two hooks or a net frame, but lacking these accessories, I would have to proceed as best I could.

Not a sound broke the stillness as I stepped toward my prize. All this time the rattler had maintained his stoic immobility, but as I moved toward him he whipped his massive body into a defensive coil with one mighty contraction. His head was drawn back on the S-curve of the neck; the forked tongue was now fully extruded, waving slowly first up, then down, drawn back into the mouth, then out again. With tail held high, his rattle sounded off. The noise seemed deafening when it split the silence. As my friend Horace Phillips remarked later, "Bones are not the only things that rattle in that graveyard!"

Leaning forward as far as I could, reaching toward him gingerly with my arm outstretched, my four-foot hook seemed all too short. I worked the point of the hook gently under him at mid-body, lifting slightly to test the balance, and then swung him carefully over the branches and brambles to set him down in front of me, a good four or five feet away. How heavy he was!

He made several lunges at me. I could see the bluish-white interior of his mouth and, for a few seconds, the fully erected fangs. He was a very angry snake, as well he might be at having his peace and quiet so rudely disturbed. The rattle was a blur as it whirred with fury, and he made further protest by charging the air liberally with sweet-smelling musk sprayed from glands at the base of the tail. Some find the odor of this musk offensive, but I find it rather pleasant—possibly from pleasant associations. Apparently my diamondback was not to be tricked, cajoled, or otherwise made to enter the sack. Constantly backing away, he withdrew without uncoiling. His head was drawn back and facing forward, ready to strike out straight ahead or to right or left.

All my preparations were futile. The stave I had cut to hold the bag open was quickly a failure. I had tried to attach the hem to the top of the stick, but at every approach the snake would strike at the sack and knock it off. Finally I managed to cover him with it, and using the stick and the hook, manipulated the opening over his head and neck and part of the upper coil of the body. This seemed to have a calming effect. The rattling diminished somewhat and he lay more quietly. Urged by judicious prodding with the hook, he began to back farther into the bag, always swiveling his head toward me. I was careful not to hurry him, for a too sharp or sudden jab might cause him to come out with a rush—all the groundwork gone for nothing. As it was, he did strike out at me several times from the bag, but each time seemed to withdraw deeper.

At last so much of him was within the sack that I gave him a final prod and he whipped the rest of his bulk completely in. Carefully I placed the handle of the hook on the ground over the sack to keep the opening closed. Then I moved the stick backward, pushing the snake as far as I could to the bottom to provide maximum slack for tying a knot in the neck of the sack. This I succeeded in doing, always using the utmost care not to let my hands touch the huge bulge of the snake. Many a collector has found out the hard way that the rattler can and will bite through a bag.

Heaving a sigh, I straightened up and took a deep breath. I confess my legs quivered from the strain. I looked at my watch and decided that the entire operation had taken anywhere from twenty minutes to a half hour—certainly not a speed record for snake catching—but I congratulated myself for a job well done under difficulties.

There was still a little less than a mile to walk and carry the rattler to my friend's house where I was staying, but that would be a pleasure. Unlike most of his kind, the snake stopped rattling as soon as he was in the bag and lying undisturbed, but when I picked it up he started his angry whirring and berated me all the way home.

This is the story of the most recent rattlesnake I have caught; it happened less than two weeks before the time of writing, and I hope it will not be the last rattlesnake for me. In fact, I hope most fervently that there will never be a "last rattlesnake" anywhere, ever.

PART THREE

MAMMALS

A Nebraskan, Ronald E. Smith headed the biology department at McCook (Nebraska) Junior College and since 1957 has been chairman of the department of biological sciences at Buena Vista College in Iowa. As corollary duties, he directs a 160-acre reserve and is writing a handbook for a course, which he gives annually, on the biology and ecology of the marine waters around Jamaica, West Indies.

During graduate work in Kansas, 1955–57, as a member of the State Biological Survey, Mr. Smith studied the life history of the black-tailed prairie dog. This research resulted in a comprehensive bulletin (two editions) and the following account of a most engaging animal.

THE PRAIRIE DOG
RONALD E. SMITH

I could not believe my eyes! Twenty-six clumps of prize peonies in full bud had been cut off about two and one half inches from the ground and neatly arranged on the northeast side of the remaining stubs. As I knelt to examine the mischief, an elderly lady next door hurried over to announce that Herk was responsible, that she had tried to drive her away with a broom, but that Herk would not be deterred. Normally, our prairie dog in-residence would have greeted me up the block, expecting to be carried back to our yard. I went to the house to look for her. Upon opening the door, I was stunned to find that the drapes behind the sofa had been cut off eleven inches up from the back of the sofa. It had been a busy and exhausting day indeed, for the prairie dog was in her nail-keg burrow asleep on her back with forefeet folded over her chest and hind legs pulled close to the abdomen.

The nail keg was hers and inviolate; she vocally resented any indication that we might even touch it. So, despite my agitation, I sat down on the floor a few feet away and called to her. (She never failed to answer vocally and with a grand salaam when called by name.) After a bit, she came stalking

53

out and I took her to the front room and showed her the drapes. Usually when scolded she approached with incisors showing and head cocked to one side. One could grasp her teeth with a thumb and forefinger, and a satisfactory relationship would be reestablished. But this time she sat up on her hind legs and barked and chattered at me with what could easily be interpreted as indignation. She repeated this performance for a full ten minutes outdoors when I indicated my displeasure at the condition of the peonies. Afterward, she stalked across the yard, up on the back porch, and through her private opening in the screen to the sanctity of her nail-keg burrow.

Although for the rest of the evening she answered when we called, she would not come out. Finally, after television was turned on, she marched into the front room, making an obvious detour around me, and settled on a pillow by herself to watch the movement on the screen. (Her usual T.V. watching position was in the crook of my left arm on her back, feet up.) At last, I approached her with index finger and thumb together, which she grasped with her incisors, and after some chatter and tail-bobbing she climbed up to rest on my arm.

Prairie dogs always keep weeds and grasses clipped off around the burrow systems so that they cannot conceal predators. But Herk had never before (and has never since) attempted to trim things. What possessed her to make the yard and drapes predator-proof on that particular day is, of course, a mystery.

Mysteries, however, were not unusual with Herk. During the six years that she lived with us, we were constantly amazed by her actions. No explanations on my part ever convinced my wife and friends that our prairie dog did not have great intelligence.

As a biologist, I am opposed to confining wild animals as pets. But because I was engaged in fieldwork on these animals, I decided that I might gain some insight into their behavior by keeping one at my home to observe. Therefore, the second spring of my study I waited for the first emergence of the young from the burrow system, about six weeks after their birth. On their very first trip out they are so uncertain, and seemingly so bewildered by daylight and everything around them, that they are easily caught by just running them down. By the second day, however, this method of trying to catch them is a waste of time. They learn rapidly.

The behavior of prairie dogs in their dog towns has attracted the attention of many people. In the middle 1800's explorers, trappers, and pioneers crossed the plains west of the Missouri River and east of the Rocky Mountains. Letters and diaries mentioned the gregarious prairie dog with highly exaggerated accounts of their social structure and behavior. They are "attention-getters," and it is not strange that certain myths came to be associated with them. For example, persons all the way from South Dakota to Oklahoma, living in close proximity to prairie dog towns, have informed me confidently and with apparent authority that prairie dogs build up the burrow entrances and pack the mounds before a heavy rain. These rodents, therefore, were weather forecasters. The facts are, however, that mounds are repaired and packed only *after* rain when the soil is workable. Heavy rains are often preceded by sporadic, light showers which give the prairie dog a chance to work on his mound. He is not preparing for any subsequent torrent.

Prairie dogs live in dog towns that may have a population of from fifteen to five thousand. They seem to enjoy being in close proximity to each other; they gather in groups on the mound or to sun themselves. Laboratory animals nestle or huddle together at night. Herk knew nothing of dog-town life, but she seemed content if she had close contact with her human friends.

When I offered my thumb and index finger to Herk as a sign of friendship, it was a substitute for the prairie dog's "mouth contact." In nature a mouth contact is effected by one prairie dog turning its head slightly and touching its open mouth (incisors) to that of another prairie dog, after which they may graze together, groom each other, or go in opposite directions. Often when a prairie dog is on its mound and another runs to the mound, the first dog makes mouth contact as the other arrives. In one stage, young prairie dogs move about making mouth contact with every prairie dog they see. Animals in captivity often act as if they desired such contact, and in this case the desire seems to be satisfied if a person grasps their incisor teeth with his fingers.

Herk was fond of being scratched or even brushed; in return she "groomed" the hair on my forearm or nibbled at the skin on my hand. Grooming (one prairie dog using its teeth to go over the fur of another) is obviously more than just getting rid of external parasites. It probably creates a pleasant tactile reaction, for laboratory animals free of external parasites continue to groom each other. Young dogs seem particularly fond of being groomed and of grooming, and

adults of both sexes indulge the young in this activity.

A prairie dog town is a noisy community. Being gregarious by nature, the prairie dog has many ways to communicate with his kind. These vocalizations are a part of his behavior toward intruders and are well known to those familiar with dog towns.

The alarm bark indicates animals or objects not necessarily considered dangerous but irritating by their presence, such as a man, cattle, traps, instruments, and vehicles. The prairie dog runs to its mound and crouching over the burrow emits a two-syllable sound—*tic-uhl, tic-uhl, tic-uhl*—the first syllable of which is of a higher pitch and shorter duration than the second. The bark is accompanied by a vertical flick of the tail; frequently all that can be seen of the prairie dog is its head and tail. The frequency and intensity of this bark is greatest during the first two or three minutes; thereafter the frequency slows to about forty barks a minute and may continue for as long as an hour and a half.

On hearing this bark, all prairie dogs in the immediate vicinity sit up and look around; if they, too, are suspicious of the object or animal, they run to their mounds and join in the bark. Some prairie dogs, however, utter the alarm call so often that associates pay no attention. The old female who established the hour-and-a-half record could not get the others to look up from their routine activities whenever she instituted the alarm bark. She barked at everything—horned larks, cattle, rabbits, large lubber grasshoppers, and me.

The predator warning bark consists of the same two syllables as the alarm bark, but because the second syllable maintains a high pitch the two barks are recognizably different. The dogs do not wait to perceive the danger themselves, as with the alarm bark, but dash for their burrows. Prairie dogs reaching the safety of the burrow entrance may emit the typical alarm bark as long as the predator is near. The predator bark warns of soaring birds and the badger. Interestingly, a prairie dog will feed within fifteen to twenty feet of a vulture on the ground, but if the bird is flying, and especially if the shadow of the soaring bird passes across the area, the prairie dog perceives the bird as dangerous and emits the predator bark. A prairie falcon sitting on the ground, however, does alarm the prairie dogs. They watch it from their mounds and bark excitedly all the time it is there. As for nonpredator animals associated with the prairie dog, they are tolerated or ignored.

An amusing call, difficult to interpret without anthropomorphizing a bit, is the "all clear" call. When it is emitted, the prairie dog always throws its forefeet high into the air—often with such force that the animal falls over backward or leaps into the air—and brings them down in the manner of a grand salaam. This is also a two-syllable call—*aeeee-ou*—the first syllable uttered in a high pitch as the forefeet are thrown into the air, and the short guttural second syllable as the forefeet drop to the ground.

This call is heard after danger is past, hence the "all clear" interpretation, but it is repeated again and again on warm, clear, sunny mornings just after the prairie dogs come out of their burrows. At this time it is contagious and goes the rounds of all who are already out. During feeding in late morning this call may be given for no apparent reason, but

perhaps as a greeting. When Herk heard my admittedly poor imitation of this call, she immediately answered in true prairie dog style.

Certain prairie dogs seemed antagonistic toward thirteen-lined ground squirrels, and before giving chase emitted a low-pitched snarl. A few individuals in the laboratory also uttered this sound when they were being handled.

Tooth chattering consists of gnashing the teeth together rapidly and is accompanied by occasional low, muffled barks. Animals in the laboratory frequently did this while asleep, and animals in the field have been observed "chattering" while being groomed by another prairie dog.

Young prairie dogs being handled for the first time occasionally scream; apparently this is a fear reaction. I once heard such a scream one evening when a badger was chasing a prairie dog. When this scream is given, other prairie dogs bolt down into their burrows.

Laboratory animals frequently bark in their sleep, and on occasion it was necessary to wake our Herk in order to quiet her. I have had three prairie dogs in-residence, and each so barked.

In early morning, on the sunny side of the mound, when the sun is just high enough to warm the mounds, a prairie dog frequently spends ten to twenty minutes stretched out on its belly, forelegs straight ahead, hind legs straight behind, sunning itself. There is much yawning and stretching, but the position itself is not changed.

In Kansas prairie dogs are above ground by five thirty in the morning in July, but in January they rarely appear before ten. They spend from ten to twenty minutes sitting on the mound, looking around, and greeting (mouth contact) other prairie dogs. They then move out to feed, and after from thirty minutes to an hour return to the mound to stretch out and sun themselves. Following the initial feeding, especially in spring and summer, considerable play activity takes place among the young and between the young and the adults. At sunset, prairie dogs come in from the outlying areas and feed closer to the mound. They begin to enter the burrow one by one; fifteen to thirty minutes later all are below ground and the dog town is quiet. The complete silence emphasizes to an observer how noisy these gregarious creatures really are.

Sleeping positions vary, but two seem to be preferred. The position most observed is a sitting one with the forefeet crossed over the chest and the head bent down between the hind legs, giving the animal the appearance of a furry ball. Also highly favored is lying on the back, forelegs crossed over the chest or sometimes all legs relaxed with no definite position assumed and the head resting on the body of another prairie dog.

Prairie dogs eat grass, but about one fourth of their diet consists of plants unimportant as forage for livestock. In late June and throughout July, prairie dogs eat the seed-heads of foxtail barley, grama grass (both heads and leaves), buffalo grass, cocklebur leaves, and at times, aristida awns. All through the summer they eat grasshoppers and a few other insects, always head first.

In August, seeds and leaves of various low-growing plants found on the mounds, such as white pigweed, Carolina geranium, spurge, and yellow wood sorrel add variety to their diet. In autumn and winter, dry buffalo grass, grama grass, and aristida grass comprise the main part of the diet. In December, they occasionally eat clumps of catcus (*Opuntia*). In January, February, and March, the prairie dogs dig for roots of grasses and forbs. In April, quantities of the darkling beetle, *Eleodes hispilabis,* are found around the burrow openings and in stomach contents. Later in April and in May and early June, peppergrass is consumed in large amounts and often makes up half the diet.

Farmer-ranchers and rodent-control personnel have observed that range rodents are more numerous on depleted and weedy ranges than on ranges of good vegetative cover; they wrongly regard these rodents as the "cause" instead of the "result" of range depletion. Certain animals, like certain plants, increase with the disturbance of the climax and decline as the climax is restored. The prairie dog is one of these animal weeds. Overgrazing by cattle is primarily responsible for the disappearance of range grasses. Room is thus made for the annuals with their fleshy roots and larger and more numerous seeds. With this increased food supply, the prairie dog population increases.

Undoubtedly, in times of drought, prairie dogs may help cattle destroy the range completely. But under ordinary conditions, herbivorous small mammals may speed up plant succession by their preferential food habits; they eat plant species typical of early successional stages—plants not eaten by cattle. Cattle, like other grazing animals, do not graze the range evenly but in favored places. The prairie dog town is always in such a favored place. In earlier days these favored places were created by the buffalo. When cattle are removed from a prairie dog colony, the grass cover increases in density, despite prairie dog activity, to the point that the prairie dogs must abandon the area as the vegetation becomes unsuitable as a habitat for them.

In feeding, a prairie dog cuts vegetation at its base, stands upright with the food in one paw, and eats from the basal portion distally. In this way, spiny plants, such as the cocklebur, can be eaten without injury to the mouth. Frequently only a few bites are taken, the rest discarded, and a new stalk is cut. In the case of our house pet, we found that Herk quickly developed a taste for many foods not available to her relatives in dog town. Among them were breakfast cereals, popcorn, potato chips, jello, and ice cream. She also enjoyed green salad with mayonnaise, and broccoli with sour cream dressing—but she would reject both if they were not properly topped off with the correct dressing.

Prairie dogs enjoy sunshine and warm weather, but like many other animals are unable to tolerate temperatures much higher than 100° F. During consecutive days of extremely high temperature, they show no inclination to aestivate but concentrate their feeding and above-ground activities in early morning and late evening. They come out at all hours of the day but only for a few minutes at a time; then they return to the comparative coolness of the burrows.

Before I started work there, the Barber County, Kansas, dog town had been used by high-school boys for after-school target practice and on Sundays by persons who considered themselves "varmint hunters." Therefore, at the approach of a car or person, the prairie dogs disappeared down the burrows and remained there as long as the cause for alarm remained. I put up no-hunting signs, and within two weeks the prairie dogs were so used to my comings and goings that my approach caused the alarm bark from only certain individuals. I could walk to within ten feet of a prairie dog before it would run away a few feet. Three of them developed the habit of flattening out in the roadway, and I either had to get out of the truck and frighten them away or drive around them. Some prairie dogs live-trapped for the first time would jump at me with teeth showing and tail bristling, whereas others would crouch in the corner of the trap in apparent fear. When handled for the first time, most of them tried to bite, and when successful, they continued to gnash the incisors instead of withdrawing them and biting again.

Any prairie dog that was live-trapped became a repeater. Many had to be released three and four times a day. Having sprung the trap, they ate all the grain and waited for me to release them, after which they ran off about ten feet and began to feed on grass.

Equipment or other objects left in the dog town are summarily inspected. They approach the object cautiously in a more or less crouched position with tail bristling, sniff at the object, eventually touch it with their nose, and then turn and walk away, paying little or no more attention to it.

They dig their permanent burrows in spring or autumn, and frequently make exploratory burrows two or three feet long in summer. Only one prairie dog digs at a time; he may dig the entire burrow. Sometimes one dog, but more often two or three together, will construct or repair mounds. After a rain there is great activity in mound building throughout the dog town. Burrows are often excavated at a time when it is impossible to pack the mounds; the loose earth is then thrown out in a pile. Before a prairie dog tamps the earth, he cleans the burrow. He pushes the debris under himself by means of the forefeet and then with his hind legs kicks it as far as it will go. He carries or pushes the debris and soil to the proper place and then on all fours, with body, neck, and head rigid, and shoulders hunched, he forcefully tamps it down by ramming his nose into the moist material. When working together, one prairie dog may dig out debris while another scrapes up soil and grass from the surrounding area, and yet another does the preliminary packing. Then they may all work at packing for a while, with one dog giving the finishing touches to the mound. Both males and females work at constructing mounds. No one individual seems to be responsible for building and repairing a mound. The hot summer sun bakes the packed mound of mud and grass into a hard, long-lasting structure that even the wheel of a car will not dent. Mounds vary from a foot to three feet high and are from three to ten feet in diameter, depending on the age of the burrow and its location. Burrows that extend straight down six or more feet have rim-type craters; burrows which have a sharp incline have dome-type craters, and burrows on the fifteen-to-twenty-degree slope have piles of earth showing little or no attempt at construction of permanent mounds.

Most prairie dogs do not breed until they are two years old. The breeding season of prairie dogs lasts from two to three weeks. In Kansas it starts about the last week in January, but varies depending upon the severity of the winter and availability of food. The young are born in late March or April; the gestation period is twenty-eight to thirty-two days, the average litter being four. The newborn young weigh about sixteen grams and are seventy millimeters long. At first completely helpless, by the twentieth day they have hair over the body and at five weeks their eyes are open. Small prairie dogs appear above ground when about six weeks old and are weaned at seven weeks of age.

The population of a prairie dog town is greatest in May and early summer, lowest in January-February. By January the composition is roughly one-third each of juveniles, yearlings, and adults. The ratio of females to males is 62 females to 38 males per 100 among yearlings, and the ratio of adult females to adult males is 59.41 per 100.

On young-of-the-year prairie dogs the fur is fine, soft, and rather sparse. After the juvenile molt, in July and early August, the fur is also soft and somewhat sparse. In early October the juveniles undergo the regular fall molt resulting in a thicker, longer, more buff-colored fur. Most hairs are black at the base, followed by bands of buff, cinnamon, subterminal buff, and a terminal black tip. Mixed with these are others entirely black. The spring molt begins the last of April.

Not many years ago it seemed probable that prairie dog towns were destined to disappear from our western plains. Fortunately, however, there were people who were concerned lest a species indigenous to the United States become extinct. As a result of their efforts, prairie dog towns still exist in some western plains states today. Continued concern and an understanding of their importance in the shortgrass prairie habitat may yet save this rodent for the enjoyment of posterity.

BEARS

Stuart L. Free, senior wildlife biologist and leader of the Big Game Research Project in the New York Conservation Department, graduated from Cornell University in 1954 with a B.S. degree in wildlife conservation. After serving as lieutenant in the United States Army, including a period in Greenland, he entered the conservation department as an assistant game research investigator. Most of his work has been on the white-tailed deer and black bear, which has led to his selection as cochairman of a big-game technical session of The Wildlife Society (Northeast Section) and of the Northeast Deer Study Group.

Mr. Free's published papers include about fifteen titles on big game, deer, and bear. He is especially interested in developing an aging method for the latter species. For relaxation, he engages in hunting, fishing, and photography.

THE BLACK BEAR, FRIEND AND FOE
STUART L. FREE

Nearly dead silence reigned over the wooded area as the gun was slowly raised, sighted in, and fired. There was a sharp crack of the powder charge and a resounding thump—the unmistakable sound of a direct hit. Then came the slow exhaling of breath by the more than one hundred people watching. The place was a summer campsite in the central Adirondack Mountains; the target, a marauding black bear; the gun, a special device designed to fire a syringe dart loaded with an immobilizing drug. Unfortunately, the year-round stomping ground for Big Bruin had become the summer recreation area for thousands of folks.

Bruin was a female that parked her three cubs on the outskirts of the camp while she searched for food. At first the stolen groceries, broken refrigerators, and inquisitive pokes into tents were accepted as exciting adventures with which to regale the folks back home. But as the bear continued her daily visits, she became bolder and almost indifferent to the mixture of cheers and groans, curses and laughter, that followed her. Her one objective was food: *any* food—in boxes, in tents, on picnic tables, in garbage

63

cans, refrigerators, or even snatched from campers' hands. She drove several families away from their picnic tables and devoured their dinners. While her unwilling hosts watched resentfully, she licked her chops and then rudely dashed all the dishes, glasses, and pans to the ground with one sideswipe of her paw.

Finally, once too often, Bruin poked her nose through a tent entrance, sniffed, and entered. Startled by an outside noise, she clawed a hasty exit through the back wall. That did it. The irate owner complained loudly, and the call went out: "Bring the dart gun! This bear must go!" Actually she had been a dangerous nuisance for some time. Dangerous because people, not familiar with her unpredictable nature, approached her as a friend, a pet, or a huge toy. Being truly wild, she relied for survival on her muscles of steel, her tense, cat-like agility, and her cunning. Her ability to associate people with food, however, proved her undoing.

This was the reason she had been "shot." When the dart penetrated her body and the special drug was released, Bruin had relaxed and dropped. It was then no problem to carry her, immobilized, to a large trailer and transport her to an area that did not have a ready supply of tourists with ham sandwiches and potato salad.

Her three cubs were left to establish their own homes; they were six months old and big enough to make their way. In spite of her bad habits, Bruin had taught them to stay outside the campground and to avoid people. They had learned their lesson well for they were not seen again that summer. In another year, however, when they were fully grown, they would probably discover that food and humans go together. Like their mother, they would begin to plun-

der, followed by the same cheers and groans, curses and laughter.

Records show that although Bruin would no longer be concerned about her offspring, she was likely to find her way back to the place where she had been captured. Her bear's instinct for locating "home" was well developed and could guide her for many miles. For instance, a New York camp robber, caught in July, was moved fifty-six miles before being released. Thirteen months later, he was back again. A bear in Michigan was transported ninety-six miles, but eventually was recaptured within six miles of where he had first been taken.

One hungry vandal, in upper New York State, broke into a boys' camp in the middle of the summer, attracted by all the food on hand to keep active boys in good spirits. He was caught, marked, and moved thirty-one miles in a northwest direction. The next year, still plagued by an appetite for human food, the same pantry raider was caught at a girls' camp less than a mile from that of the boys'. Again, he was hauled off thirty-two miles, this time to the northeast, and released with the rangers' fervent hopes that he would forget his roving ways. But, only three months later, during the hunting season, he was again silently and stealthily sneaking back in a direction toward the camps. This time a hunter caught a glimpse of the black pirate and ended his prowls.

During the spring, summer, and fall, the bear wanders—sometimes in search of a mate, at other times caring for cubs, and always in search of food. Exactly what makes up the size and terrain of an individual bear's home range is still in the gray area of knowledge. What is known is that the bear is a wilderness creature that requires large forested areas

generally uninhabited by humans. (Its travels, however, may include side trips to farms, apiaries, camps, and homes.) Summer journeys seem to be the most restricted; those in autumn cover the most ground. The size of its summer home range is probably five to ten miles in radius, but the fall territory may often be twice as extensive. The distance de-

pends largely on the presence of native foods: the scarcer the food, the longer the travels.

A mature forest usually provides mast-producing trees of beech, black cherry, and oak. Many large beech trees will clearly show the marks of a climbing bear on their smooth, pale gray bark. Following the scratches, one can often look far up and see a tangle of small branches and twigs that resemble a messy, oversize nest of a poor-housekeeping squirrel. This is where a bear has sat, reached out, and pulled in masses of leaves, twigs, and stems along with the rich, flavorful beechnuts. As the animal stuffed himself almost to the bursting point, the inedible scraps accumulated and became a jumbled "nest."

The list of items consumed by black bears is almost endless. They have been known to eat practically everything from aluminum foil to zwieback. Their native foods depend on the season and are limited only by what exists on the range.

Early every fall there comes an insatiable urge for food. Large male bears, weighing four hundred pounds or more, will fill themselves to the point where their stomachs actually touch the ground as they lumber along with swinging stride. The smaller animals pay due respect and carefully avoid any close approach.

Bears are remarkably successful at locating and devouring the type of foods carefully avoided by diet-conscious humans because they produce quantities of fat. The largest male bears carry over 600 pounds, but the heaviest females seldom weigh more than 350. In a general comparison, an 8½-year-old female is equal to a 2½-year-old male.

Bears take up winter residence in a variety of places: in caves, under tree roots, among fallen trees, or in conifer thickets. In Alaska, they may stay as long as six months each year in a den, while in the south they may not den at all.

A person can have a lot of fun in fall and spring by following the footprints of bears. The late-fall tracks will lead

in and out of rock crevices, **up and down** steep rock ledges, through and around tangles of fallen trees and root hollows. The bear walks into many a cave and cranny and backs out, stepping very carefully in his own tracks. Then he cautiously jumps sideways as far as possible and continues on his way searching for another site to investigate.

A den that I once saw occupied by a bear was near the top of a mountain, under a birch tree snug in a hollow among the roots. A medium-size female had picked this shelter as a remote, protected winter home. Little did she realize then that her nursery was right in the middle of a ski area under construction. Nevertheless, the sound of chainsaws, burning brush, and noisy vehicles did not prevent her from staying on and giving birth to two cubs in January.

The sow was observed many times in her den and always appeared fully awake. She was alert enough to give the typical bear warning signal: a sharp exhaling of breath in a loud huff and a threatening chomping of the jaws. There was no mistaking the clear warning: "Keep your distance!" Although the cubs remained hidden, protected by the mother's body, they were far from quiet. Their shrill cries sounded like young pigs, squealing for more milk.

The nearly hairless cubs together weighed about as much as a football (sixteen ounces) at birth, but by late March they were big enough to leave the den with their mother. They stayed with her through most of the summer, continually trying her patience with their mischievous ways. At the slightest hint of danger, however, a warning from her sent them scooting up a tree. Faster than a cat, they climbed to the top of the highest branches, and once up there, they would stay, tenaciously hanging on with their sharp claws. When the danger had passed, they backed down the tree and moved on to their next adventure.

Since no misfortune separated the family that fall, they remained together for the fattening season and on through another winter denning period. Shortly before their long rest, they had ceased to eat and their digestive systems were cleared.

When spring came, they emerged from the den with the same empty stomachs and set to work looking for food. Some of the earliest tender greens, a squirrel's cache of nuts, and a still partially frozen carcass were eagerly eaten. Soon after this, they went their separate ways as each youngster explored for a territory of his own. The female, stimulated by a new urge, searched for a mate.

Female bears can breed for the first time when two years old, during the May to July period. The entire year is spent caring for the young and it isn't until the following spring that the female accepts another mate. If you see a typical nine-year-old female, she could be raising her fourth family including her tenth offspring. Her productivity could continue for several more years.

A black bear's life-span can be as long as thirty years in the wild, but very few actually attain this ripe old age. Once a bear reaches its fifth year, it has a good start. The more it learns about its environment, the dangers, and the food sources, the better are its chances for long-time survival.

Man is still the primary factor that limits the size of bear populations—even to the extent of eliminating them. Where human populations encroach on the bears' domain, the forest is cleared, land plowed, homes, factories, and schools constructed. The wilderness disappears and so must the bears. Even in the remaining wild country, a man may carelessly leave out food and garbage that attract hungry bears, and then he congratulates himself on shooting the "dangerous nuisances." Where people and bears come together, a delicate balance is set up. Unless adequate consideration is given the animal, it will disappear from all but the most remote areas.

If we wish to save the black bear, we must save its environment. Only then will our youngsters have the opportunity to catch a quick glimpse of a furry ball of mischief as a cub goes scurrying after its mother, to spot a bear "nest" in a beech-tree, and to hike through the fall snows looking for bear tracks.

An authority on bears around the world, Albert W. Erickson devoted five years to field research on the black bear and the bobcat in Michigan, and seven years to study of all three species of Alaskan bears as well as furbearers and hoofed game. Since 1965 he has been curator of mammals in the Bell Museum of Natural History and associate professor of ecology at the University of Minnesota. Dr. Erickson has also had experience with the spectacled bear in the northern Andes. With special competence in capturing and marking animals, he has been an advisor to the Norwegian Government since 1965 and has spent much time on polar bears in Spitzbergen. He has published about thirty papers of systematics, biology, and age determination in the bear tribe.

THE GRIZZLY
ALBERT W. ERICKSON

Sixty-five bears could be seen at one time as they fished for salmon in a favorite part of the McNeil River on the Alaska Peninsula. We watched them with elation, knowing that the "hunting" would continue to be good. From time to time we shot one with an anesthetic dart from a syringe gun, then marked and released the animal for future identification in our research project. The brief interruption to their pursuits did not seem to inconvenience or deter them.

Among the bears that frequently came to fish was a big, swayback female with three cubs. One afternoon, a smaller mother also arrived with her three offspring, but when she made a catch, she suddenly left her young, dashed up the bank, and disappeared. The two sets of young bears joined forces and when Swayback turned to them, she was surprised to find that her family had doubled in size. She inspected the six cubs, sniffing here and there, but could not solve the mystery. Manifestly disconcerted, she departed upstream and then swam to the opposite bank, followed by the six small bears.

A half hour or so later, the smaller mother returned, expecting to find

her family where she had left them. She sniffed and snuffed, up and down, back and forth along the bank, and finally crossed the river. Here she picked up the scent trail of the cubs and followed it to them, but they showed no joy at seeing her nor did they make any move to join her. At this point Swayback returned from a brief fishing foray, saw the "intruder," let out a mighty roar, and charged her.

During the melee that followed, a high wail abruptly stopped both mothers. One of the cubs, trying to get out of the way, had lost his balance and plummeted into the tumbling river. Instantly both mothers plunged after the endangered cub. For a moment the frantically pawing little bear bobbed to the surface and then disappeared in the strong current. The smaller mother reached

him first and guided him farther downstream and to the opposite shore.

As mother and youngster moved to a safe distance, Swayback lost interest and lumbered back upstream to the cluster of five frightened cubs. Anxiously she moved from cub to cub, showing an increasing consternation. An hour before, her family had blossomed to six—and now there were only five! Was she able to count? Certainly she was very disturbed. Seeming unable to decide what was wrong or which of the young were hers, she retreated into the alders with all five cubs bouncing along at her heels.

This was the first time that I, or to my knowledge anyone else, had ever witnessed cub adoption by the mighty grizzly. As we had watched the little drama from our vantage point, several questions continued to intrigue us. Is a bear unable to comprehend the number of her young? Obviously the incident would suggest this, although the mother with extra cubs seemed to realize that something was amiss, and the cubless mother had tried hard to find her "lost" offspring. Of most interest was the apparent inability of either mother to separate her own young from the others.

This is contrary to heartrending tales of the past. Possibly Swayback's sense of smell was deficient or perhaps the six cubs romping together had absorbed each other's litter odor and produced a mixture that was confusing to both mothers.

At any rate Swayback kept the two foster cubs, and we saw her large family regularly for several weeks afterward— as long as we remained in the area.

If a mother could not recognize her own offspring, is it any wonder that zoologists often could not identify different brown bears? At the turn of the century, Dr. C. Hart Merriam declared that there were over one hundred species of brown and grizzly bears. The famous zoologist based his classification on body size, pelt color, and cranial characteristics, all of which are highly variable in this group of bears, even within individual families. Later studies confirmed this diversity, but resulted in the now generally accepted view that all one hundred "species," formerly classified as brown and grizzly bears, actually belong to a single species which includes the brown bears of Europe and Asia. Thus such bears as the renowned grizzly and the giant Kodiak bear are only racially different.

Which species of bear is the largest? This answer is difficult because criteria for determining size are not agreed upon. For a number of years the so-called Kodiak brown bear was considered the largest on the basis of its extraordinarily large skull and hide. Recent evidence has shown, however, that the hides of polar bears exceed on an average those of the Kodiak bear. To further confuse the issue the body weights of the largest of both the Kodiak and the polar bear are approximately the same—hovering around 1,150 pounds!

I have little doubt that the largest bear that I have seen resides in Washington's National Zoo. This immense beast must weigh more than 1,200 pounds. When recently anesthetized for research in cooperation with the zoo officials, six men were required just to roll the animal over. I'm naturally anxious to rig a weighing device to register the claim that the animal is the world's largest. But when this is accomplished, our question will still remain unresolved, I'm afraid, since the monster's father was a polar bear and its mother a Kodiak bear! (Such hybrid crosses, whose offspring are fertile, show the genetic closeness of the polar and the brown bears from which the former apparently evolved. They are still considered to be separate species, however.)

The grizzly bear is as variable in form, size, and coat color as is *Homo sapiens*. Adult males average half again as large as females. The coat color of the grizzly ranges from blond to dark brown even within the same litter. As a general rule, the coastal bears of Alaska and western Canada are quite uniformly medium to dark brown. Interior forms are more frequently mottled and a large proportion exhibit a dark undercoat with light-tipped guard hairs giving rise to the so-called silver-tip grizzly—and a most striking coloration it is. The legs of

71

all grizzlies are generally quite dark. An infrequent, but highly sought, color phase is light blond and occasional specimens are creamy white. Grizzly bears also vary in color according to age and season. Males tend to be darker than females. A distinctive feature of most cubs is a white collar of fur which persists through most of the first summer. After these early months they are, with rare exceptions, void of white fur in marked contrast to all other bear species.

To me, the two most impressive physical features of the grizzly bear are its massive head and claws. The claws may be five inches long—much larger than those of any other bear species. They also differ in that they are heavy and blunt, an adaptation to digging for food. With these tools, bears can tear open rodent burrows,

anthills, and metal containers discarded by man.

Although authorities disagree on the minimum breeding age of the grizzly bear in the wild, records of captives indicate that both sexes generally attain puberty at approximately three and one-half years of age. In the natural state, breeding takes place from approximately late-May through mid-July and the same female may accept several males over a one-to-two-week period. The gestation period lasts about eight months but can be anywhere from 194 to 278 days. This variability is explained by the female's special pregnancy cycle called delayed implantation. The fertilized eggs do not immediately fasten to the uterus wall but lie in a state of quiescence for several months before implanting

and beginning development. Implantation regularly occurs in late October or early November despite the time of mating and thus the wide variation in gestations. Births occur quite uniformly in January or early February while the mother is in her winter den. The normal litter is two, but three is common and four not unusual.

At birth, the cubs weigh a scant ten to twelve ounces, their eyes and ears are closed, and they are covered with only thin, fuzzy hair. They are, in fact, quite similar in development to a human infant born two or three months prematurely. As such they are not able to maintain body temperature and must depend on their mother for warmth as well as nourishment. She emerges from her winter den in April or May by which time the cubs have grown to seven or eight pounds. They will remain with her for one or two years depending on whether she mates every second or third year. (A female will breed in consecutive years only if her cubs are lost or taken from

her during or prior to the next breeding season, a fact long exploited by zoological gardens.)

The winter sleep of the grizzly bear is commonly misunderstood. It is not akin to the deep hibernation of the groundhog whose temperature may fall to near freezing. Rather the bear's temperature drops only a few degrees and the animal remains totally alert and capable of full activity. This "sleep" is, nevertheless, an interesting phenomenon lasting up to half of each year in the extreme north. During this time the bear neither eats nor drinks, which is more remarkable in the case of the female since at the same time she gives birth to young and nurses them for three or four months. The "hibernation" of the grizzly has been studied by capturing bears in Yellowstone Park, fitting them with radio transmitters, and then following their movements throughout the winter.

Although captive grizzlies live to be thirty years old, it seems unlikely that many wild bears, subject to normal mortality and forced to fend for themselves, reach such advanced age. We must admit that the natural factors which control grizzly populations are still unknown. Direct death at the hands of enemies, other than man, is certainly rare and inconsequential. Several times cubs have been known to be killed by large bears, presumably males; I have seen this only once.

As a rule, animal matter is a minor portion of the grizzly bear's diet except in coastal areas where abundant runs of salmon comprise a major food item in season. Even then the bears prefer berries when these become available. Other animal foods include small rodents, insect larvae, and occasionally larger prey or carrion. The bulk of the diet is vegetable, particularly grasses.

Consequently, the grizzly bear cannot be considered a significant predator. The very young of big game animals and occasional adults are killed, but these instances seem unimportant to the survival of the prey species involved or, for that matter, to the welfare of the grizzly. It is not unusual, however, for grizzlies to attack and kill livestock when available, and in a large measure this has been their undoing. Though only a few individuals are believed to develop this habit, the species as a whole has been held accountable and dealt with accordingly. When the grizzly forages upon the carcasses of cattle which have died from other causes, the predator image is further exaggerated.

Bear attacks on man are largely perpetrated by animals that are wounded or startled and thus on the defensive; mothers protecting their young can also be dangerous. For the most part, however, precautionary measures can prac-

tically eliminate the chance of a person getting into difficulties with bears outside of parks.

When camping in bear country, for example, people should dispose of all garbage by burning or removal to a distance. They should also discourage bears from entering a camp area by prominently displaying bright objects or placing a towel or sheet where it will flap in the wind. A further recommendation is to leave considerable human scent in the immediate vicinity. A short walk in the area around the tent is especially advised before retiring or leaving for the day. Camps should always be placed away from game trails. Above all, bears should not be encouraged by feeding since they can make no distinction between proffered food and camp rations. Feeding also breaks down their natural fear of man.

Persons traveling on foot in bear country can usually avoid trouble by exercising a few simple precautions. Most bear attacks have occurred when the animals were encountered suddenly at close quarters. In these circumstances, they react instinctively to what they may assume to be an enemy. Consequently, unless silence is necessary, it is advisable when passing through dense cover to sing, whistle, or make other noise which will alert bears to your presence. A few pebbles carried in a can attached to your belt will serve the same purpose. This is particularly important if you are traveling against the wind. It is also a good idea to wear a bright, light-reflecting garment or hat.

A grizzly protecting any large animal carcass on which it is feeding or has fed should be strictly avoided. Characteristically, grizzlies completely cover such

74

food with debris and then take up protective custody near or on top of the heap. In this situation they are extremely aggressive. When returning to an elk, caribou, or other big game that he has shot, the sportsman should watch for a grizzly that may have taken possession of the carcass during his absence.

Because bear attacks are experienced by so few persons, it is difficult to recommend procedures for defending oneself without a gun. There may be some solace in knowing that few bears press their attack to the death and fewer still eat any part of their victims. More commonly than not the bear breaks away suddenly, perhaps when it realizes that its adversary is a human, or it may desist when the person loses consciousness. Victims have reported that the bear reattacked when they moved or moaned, and urge that the person who has been mauled "play dead" even after the bear relinquishes its hold.

The brown-grizzly bear has been greatly reduced in both distribution and abundance since the advent of modern man. Over most of Europe and Asia only relict populations persist, with the exception of a few areas such as the Russian Kamchatka Peninsula. In America, less than a thousand wild grizzlies now exist south of Canada. Even in the latter, the bear has suffered greatly at the hand of man, but goodly populations still persist in British Columbia and the Northwest Territories. Happily its status is far brighter in Alaska where, except for areas around a few major towns and cities, the species is probably as abundant today as during earlier times.

Because the grizzly is a creature of the open country, in contrast to the black bear of the woodland, the grizzly is the more vulnerable to man. It is also without doubt more aggressive and predatory, a factor resulting in its persecution in livestock country.

The destiny of the grizzly bear is at present of serious concern to many groups and persons. In my opinion this concern is excessive. Certainly the numbers and distribution of the species have been adversely affected by man's activities. It couldn't have been otherwise in view of man's direct competition for the lands it occupied. However, major steps have been taken to assure the grizzly's perpetuation in refuges and national parks and by protective legislation. The fact that the species has a wide range in the northern hemisphere is additional assurance for the future.

In some instances, overzealous attempts at conservation actually endanger the bear. A case in point is on the Alaska Peninsula, which is very likely the finest large grizzly range in the world. Absolute protection of the bear in such situations is to me most shortsighted since, by reasonably harvesting these animals, their economic and recreational as well as esthetic worth can be impressively demonstrated. Unless it is shown that the best use of the Peninsula is for bear management, we are quite defenseless in opposing other uses of this land, such as ranching.

I do not feel that the welfare of the grizzly is best served by considering it a fragile species, except in Europe; rather it should be considered a natural resource which will produce a sustained yield under proper management. This policy, carried out in the surprisingly large number of areas over the world where the species still exists, would insure the future of the grizzly bear.

A specialist on the Arctic, C. Richard Harington obtained his M.S. degree from McGill with a thesis on the history, distribution, and ecology of the muskox. During the I.G.Y., 1957–58, he served as a meteorologist on northern Ellesmere Island, then entered the Canadian Wildlife Service to specialize on the polar bear. Since 1965 he has been curator of Quaternary Zoology in the National Museum of Canada and is carrying out detailed studies of Ice Age animals in the Yukon.

As Dick Harington relates in the following account, his research on polar bears involved spying on family life in winter dens. On one occasion, his "bear dog" led him to a snow slope just as an angry bear started to emerge. Unarmed, and deserted by his "brave protector," Harington departed at his highest speed.

A POLAR BEAR'S LIFE

C. R. HARINGTON

When briefly describing a polar bear's life, it seems best to start at the beginning. This beginning occurs around the Arctic Circle—perhaps along the Colville River in Alaska, on the coast of Wrangell Island, Franz Josef Land, Spitsbergen, near Scoresby Sound in Greenland, or on northeastern Baffin Island. These are a few of the important denning areas in the bear's circumpolar range, and we must focus more closely to find the individual den site.

In early October the pregnant female searches for deep snowbanks on the south-facing sides of hills or valleys. Usually the thickest drifts are situated well up the slopes and to leeward of the prevailing wind in the region. She excavates her den and seldom leaves it before or soon after giving birth—unless her hunger is urgent.

Early in December she enlarges her dwelling prior to bringing forth twin cubs, a male and a female. Only ten inches long, weighing about one and a half pounds and almost naked, they stay snuggled in their mother's thick fur to keep warm. Blind and deaf, they do not hear or see well for another month. During the first few months, the mother suckles them continuously on her fat-rich milk. Polar bear milk has the appearance and consistency of cow's cream —but it smells like seal and tastes like cod-liver oil.

The oval-shaped dens must be quite comfortable—especially the mother's first den, which is small and may become very warm from her body heat. The continued deposits of drifting snow on the roof keep them well insulated.

If we open a small hole in the two-foot-thick roof of the enlarged home in late February (as I have done several times), we shall see that the mother has quickly emerged from her lethargic state and is growling. Irritated and worried by the strange noises above her, she is treading around and around in circles. The two small cubs are cowering, their backs to the wall. Surprisingly, the den is very clean and there is almost no ice on the walls. A little fresh air and light penetrate the ventilation hole that the mother has punched through the end of the room. This opening is about two feet in diameter, and the room itself is eight feet by ten feet by almost four and a half feet high. When we lower a thermometer through a small hole in the roof, we shall find that the temperature is just over $14°$ F., which is $37°$ warmer than the outdoor air.

A month or two later, when the noon sun becomes hot on the slope, the mother breaks out of her snow-sealed den, and soon afterward leads the young cubs down to the sea ice. On their journey, the youngsters play a great deal—sliding, tumbling, and wrestling with each other. As we watch them, the mother prowls, head down, along the drifted leeward margin of some hummocky ice.

Catching the scent of a snow-covered seal den, she crouches motionless before it, and the cubs follow her example. Suddenly, with lightning-like blows of her paws, she scatters the hard upper layer of snow, rises up on her hind legs, and drives both forelegs down with the entire weight of her body. The den collapses and the seal's breathing hole is plugged with snow. She scoops out the "whitecoat" (a seal pup in white pelage) from within and almost simultaneously dispatches it. (Bears are not always so successful at hunting. Their misjudgment, the alertness of the seals, or too-great thickness of snow and ice that covers the seal dens may thwart them.)

If we take a look at the family again toward the end of April, we may catch sight of one of the cubs, about the size of a retriever, sliding down the drifted side of an iceberg. With delight the youngster lands on its rear—all four legs extended. The second cub appears and both run up and slide down, again on their haunches. While her offspring play, the mother is poised over a seal's breathing hole in the ice a few hundred yards away. Because she is downwind of the hole, her scent does not warn the seal, and she can watch for her prey and keep track of her cubs at the same time. Just as the seal starts to come up, she strikes it a stunning blow, pulls it onto the ice, and proceeds to immobilize it with paws, claws, and snapping teeth. The small bears scamper toward her and tug at the flippers, but they eat little of the seal. The mother strips the seal's skin and fat back from neck to tail, as if peeling a banana. In a short time she has devoured most of her kill, and the family departs.

Thus, during their early life on the pack ice, the young cubs follow their parent and are usually attentive during her hunting lessons. But sometimes they become impatient and spoil her efforts. Solicitous of her young, she appears to take such frustration philosophically; yet when extremely provoked she sends them head over heels with disciplinary swats of her paw. By July the cubs have acquired a taste for seal blood and fat, and are usually weaned. However, some mothers continue to give milk for twenty-one months, and their cubs get special treats.

In August or September, when much of the pack ice has broken up, drifted ashore, or melted (depending upon latitude and environmental conditions), the seals are no longer dependent on their breathing holes, and of course they can swim faster than the bears. So the mother and cubs vary their routine by wandering along the coast of an island or the mainland. They sniff continually for scent of washed-up seal, whale, and walrus carcasses, and sometimes make off with meat from Eskimo caches.

The small cubs seem to take pleasure swimming with their mother. It is cooling, instructive, and safe—provided they keep close to her shoulders for protection. When large numbers of adult male polar bears gather at carcasses near the coast, the mother may lead her offspring far inland to avoid danger from their elders and to feed heavily on succulent berries and grasses. The cubs, now approximately nine months old, weigh about 130 pounds and are becoming worldly-wise under their mother's care and guidance.

In preparation for winter the family eat a great deal and grow very fat. Once more, they move into a snow den. This may be in October, or it may be later, especially if they find a good seal-hunt-ing area on the new ice of a fiord, and weather conditions are not unusually rigorous. Their second-year den is larger than the maternity den, although no higher, and sometimes consists of a big room with two adjoining smaller ones. During the winter, the mother and cubs may come out of their den occasionally, depending on weather conditions and physical needs. Sometimes they are seen hunting well out on the fast ice in early January.

In any case, by March the family is seeking the maternity "igloos" of seals, where the delectable "whitecoats" may again be killed and devoured. The bears patrol the coast, and if they happen to discover a patch of grass not too thickly covered by snow, they are likely to eat it to vary their diet.

When August has come again, the cubs are about twenty months old and five feet long and weigh over 400 pounds. We can see them along the coast of a small island completely surrounded by water. Their mother has abandoned them and swum away to hunt by herself on the drifting ice farther north. Both young animals have fed well on a large walrus carcass which they found near one of the rocky, hauling-out areas and have eaten small "salads" of grasses and scouring rushes.

As we watch, the male cub climbs over heavily eroded coastal rocks, while the female is a half mile offshore, cooling herself by swimming and floating in the sea. Soon the two young bears will have to face the long winter without their mother's care or help. It will be a test of their learning, their skill, and their strength. They will separate and through-out the winter, in an almost continuous night, wander over the dark, snow-cov-

ered coasts, taking shelter only during storms. They may starve to death if they have been unable to store sufficient energy in fat, or they may be attacked and killed by adult male bears.

Probably the young female reaches sexual maturity in her third year and the male in his fourth. Their mother can mate again the third spring following the birth of her cubs. (Only if a female loses her young is she able to mate and con-

ceive in the spring after giving birth.) Breeding is at its peak about mid-April, but may last from March to May or even later. Sometimes it takes quite a while in the vast spaces of the Arctic for a male and female to get together.

However, if we can take a look at our mother bear the spring after she has left her cubs, we shall see that she is being followed by two adult males. They have little trouble detecting her trail because she urinates at brief intervals along the way. When the younger of the bears tries to approach her, he is immediately attacked by the larger one. A short, vicious scuffle takes place and the smaller bear is wounded. Although bitten particularly severely in the hind quarters, he persists in trailing the female. The victor shakes himself, rubs his muzzle in the snow, and ambles along, taking his time. When he finally joins the female, she is ready to respond. The two remain close together, wandering around in small circles, touching each other simultaneously with their muzzles.

Not long after mating, the couple part. The gestation period lasts about eight months and the she-bear follows her normal routine of hunting, grazing, and scavenging, until embryonic development (which is probably delayed in polar bears) begins in late September. Then, influenced by internal changes, she moves inland along a steep-sided stream valley, searching its banks for a suitable snowdrift in which to make her new maternity den. In mid-October she claws out a hole near the top of a heavily drifted slope facing south-southeast. Approximately eight hundred feet above sea level, it is less than ten miles inland. Dissatisfied, she leaves the pit with its scattered chunks of snow and begins her final den at a higher level, in deeper snow.

It is worth noting that adult male bears may use a den periodically from September to December or even January. In some cases these retreats are used solely for resting and digesting their food after hunting, or they may be occupied as temporary shelters during very bad weather. Most adult males, however, hunt continually during the winter and

rest only on ice or in convenient snow-drifts.

After the fourth winter, we find our male "cub" again—more than three years old and about six feet long. He has been dozing in the warm April sun on a south-facing slope of an island, but now he starts hunting for seals along a tension fracture in the ice. Surprised by a distant sound, he looks up to see an Eskimo with his dog team three hundred yards away. The bear quickly rises on his hind legs to test the new scent. Then he drops to all fours and moves hesitantly forward, as if curious, to a distance of two hundred yards. Peering and sniffing, he finally concludes that he is in danger. Suddenly he swivels and gallops awkwardly away over a narrow promontory of the island.

The Eskimo cuts his dogs loose from the sled and they shoot forward like arrows from a bow. Almost immediately the still rather inexperienced bear finds himself surrounded by enemies on flat ice with no hummocks for protection. The snarling huskies circle him, dashing in and out and nipping at his hind legs. All the bear can do is to keep turning and swatting at them. Excitedly the Eskimo loads his gun and fires, but in the confusion he accidentally shoots one of his leaping sled dogs. However, the second and third bullets slam into the bear's neck and head, and he slumps down, with clenching jaws. Blood seeps into the snow.

Had this bear lived to a greater age, he would probably have approached his maximum size by the time he was eight years old. Fully adult males commonly measure eight to eleven feet in total length and may weigh up to a thousand pounds. Their muscular development at

this stage is amazing. Females, however, appear to grow little after their fourth year; adults commonly weigh about five hundred pounds and are approximately 25 percent smaller than the adult males.

Little is known about the life-span of polar bears. One, a female in the Washington Park Zoo, Milwaukee, died a natural death at the age of thirty-five, and another lived to an age of forty years in the Regent's Park Zoo, London. From the appearance of some skulls and the degree of tooth wear, a few bears probably attain similar ages in the wild.

Many injuries may be sustained by the white bears as they grow older. Numerous gashes can be received in fights during the mating season; these show up as scars on the pelts, and are much more frequent in older bears. Small septic wounds in the feet are common and have been known to cause inflammatory synovitis and consequent lameness in walking. Arthritis deformans and osteoarthritis are not unusual. Fractures of ribs, wrists, ankles, cheekbones, and lower jaws result from accidents or fights. Decayed and broken teeth are a normal affliction of very old polar bears, and must cause them considerable pain. As far as I know, external parasites have never been found, and apart from intestinal tapeworms and *Trichinella* worms which are often embedded in the diaphragms and musculature of older bears, internal parasites are poorly known. The livers can be poisonous to humans because they often contain large amounts of vitamin A.

In addition to these injuries and infections that plague the species throughout life, the young may be killed by older males; and any bear, on rare occasions, is threatened by wolves and walruses.

Above all, man is the white bear's greatest enemy; not only because he methodically and efficiently hunts seals (the bear's main food), but also because he is the primary predator of the bear itself. Thus man is displacing this animal in its ecological niche as the ruling flesh-eater of the Arctic coasts.

Now that we are aware of some of the bear's problems in living, what are we doing to keep it alive? The burden rests with us. Actually polar bear conservation involves many problems, some of which were considered at the First International Conference on the Polar Bear held in 1965 at Fairbanks, Alaska. Polar

bear harvests, hunting regulations, and life history were among the subjects discussed by delegates from Canada, Denmark, Norway, the Soviet Union, and the United States. Because two of the greatest problems in polar bear research and management are reliable population estimates and major patterns of population movement, the subsequent talks dealt with improvement of aerial polar bear survey techniques, and methods of immobilizing and marking the bears in an effort to find out more about their movements.

There was unanimous agreement that polar bears, which roam widely throughout the Arctic Basin, must be considered an international circumpolar resource, but that, until enough scientific research has been done to provide the basis for more precise management, each nation should take all necessary conservation action for itself. (The Soviet Union prohibits hunting of polar bears; other countries permit it with various restrictions.) One point fully agreed upon was that cubs and females with cubs should be protected at all times.

At a second meeting in Switzerland in 1968, a permanent polar bear committee was formed under the auspices of the International Union for Conservation of Nature, and agreement was reached on a coordinated research plan. The five nations now exchange essential information by means of a yearly polar bear data sheet, and are increasing and redirecting their research to make it more effective.

The international liaison between polar bear researchers and cooperation on field projects in many parts of the Arctic auger well for the future of the polar bear.

OTHER MEAT-EATERS

Ecologist Paul F. Springer entered the United States Fish and Wildlife Service in 1948. He became chief of the Section on Wetland Ecology at the Patuxent (Maryland) Research Center ten years later, was transferred in 1963 to head the South Dakota Cooperative Wildlife Research Unit, and in 1967 was made assistant director of the prairie wildlife research center at Jamestown, North Dakota. While he is primarily interested in birds, especially the ecology and management of waterfowl, he has been deeply concerned with the effects of mosquito control and use of pesticides on wildlife. He has published over fifty papers on these subjects, and his work on the black-footed ferret in South Dakota has made him the foremost authority on this rare species.*

* The research was a cooperative project of the United States Fish and Wildlife Service, the South Dakota Department of Game, Fish and Parks, South Dakota State University, National Park Service, Welder Wildlife Foundation, and Badlands Natural History Association.

THE BLACK-FOOTED FERRET
PAUL F. SPRINGER

The time: a morning in mid-August.
The place: a prairie dog town in south-central South Dakota.

My student assistant made a hurried trip to the phone.

"What should I do?" he inquired excitedly. "Those black-footed ferrets that I am studying are being *buried alive* in their burrow by a prairie dog!"

This *was* a switch! Ordinarily black-footed ferrets eat prairie dogs and take over their homes. No wonder my student was agog.

I suggested that this might not be the first time that a prairie dog had turned on his archenemy and that the young man had better go back and watch for further developments. Nothing happened the rest of the day, however. The prairie dog, apparently satisfied that he had disposed of his foes, no longer showed any interest in the burrow. When my student returned the next day to where the ferrets had been buried, he found that the plugged entrance of the "tomb" had been opened from the inside during the night. The ferrets had left, probably less disturbed by the whole incident than my student.

We found this and other unexpected behavior to be commonplace during a cooperative study of the ferret in South Dakota from 1964 to 1968. It was surprising that almost none of these activities had been reported in the literature since the first account of the species had been written over a hundred years ago. Indeed, during the four years that we studied some thirty-five different animals, we had never seen some of the behavior that has been alleged to take place. (For example, it has been said of ferrets—incorrectly—that they hibernate, that they have a year-round breeding season, that the male helps to rear the young, that the species is especially bloodthirsty and irritable, that it subsists only on prairie dogs, that, like a fox, it leaves scraps of food around its den, and that there are only several dozen ferrets left in the world.) Obviously there has been a scarcity of firsthand observations of ferrets in the past.

Why is the black-footed ferret an animal of mystery? Is it really as rare as reported? Why is it considered endangered and what is needed to ensure its preservation?

It was not until 1851 that the black-footed ferret became known to science. In that year John J. Audubon and John Bachman described the species on the basis of an imperfect skin brought to them from the vicinity of Fort Laramie, Wyoming. During the next twenty years no "official" specimens were taken, and the species became the center of an international controversy. British scientists doubted its existence and publicly repudiated its sponsors in this country. It was falsely rumored that Audubon and Bachman had invented a new species to add glamour to their publication *The Viparous Quadrupeds of North America.*

Only after naturalist Elliott Coues received a number of specimens in response to a special plea in sporting magazines were Audubon and Bachman and the American scientific community vindicated. During the more than a century that has passed, only occasional ferrets have been seen, and few have been captured. The ferret remains a rare mammal even in museums and probably less than two hundred scientific specimens exist in the entire world.

It was therefore an exciting event when, in 1964, an employee of the United States Bureau of Sport Fisheries and Wildlife and my student assistant discovered a ferret in a prairie dog town in Mellette County, South Dakota. Subsequent observations revealed that other ferrets were living in the area. Here at long last was a unique opportunity for a sustained investigation of the life history and ecology of this mysterious animal!

A member of the weasel family, the ferret has a distinctive appearance. Contrasting with its tan coat, whitish forehead, muzzle, and throat are the startling black mask, black legs, and black tip of tail. Some twenty-one to twenty-four inches long, including a five-to-six-inch tail, the ferret is a little longer than a prairie dog but not as stout. The female is smaller and usually lacks the male's black longitudinal stripe in the pubic region. Unlike some weasels, the ferret's fur does not turn white in winter, but becomes paler and longer.

The only native mammal with which it is sometimes confused is the long-tailed weasel that is smaller, brown instead of tan, and lacks the black mask (except in the South) and black stockings. The domestic fitch, descended from the polecat of Europe, Asia, and north Africa, is similar in size and mask and is also confused with the black-footed ferret. This immigrant may be distinguished, however, by its longer, bushier pelage and entirely black tail. (The domestic fitch was introduced into this country for catching rats and rabbits.)

The black-footed ferret is a plains dweller, inhabiting the shortgrass and the midgrass prairie of North America. Originally it ranged from southern Alberta and Saskatchewan to Arizona and Texas. Even today it may occur in places throughout much of this area but in considerably reduced numbers.

Although unknown to early fur traders and settlers, the ferret was recognized and held in special regard by the Plains Indians. To the Sioux it was known as *pispiza-etopta-sapa,* meaning "black-faced prairie dog." Various tribes used ferret skins as pendants on headdresses of chiefs and as sacred ceremonial objects. The ferret was also attributed demonic powers. The Pawnees of Nebraska, for example, believed that if the animal sat up and looked at a person while working its jaws as if chewing, the entrails of that person would at once be cut to pieces and he would die.

During our four-year study in South Dakota, it was confirmed that the ferret is primarily a nocturnal creature, spending most daylight hours underground in burrows constructed by prairie dogs. This apparently is an adaptation to the hot summer climate and to the fact that its prey, the prairie dogs, are diurnal and can be more easily cornered in their burrows during the night. In the northern part of the ferret's range, this underground shelter is essential to survival during the winter.

The ferret is most likely to appear above ground during spring and fall when more moderate temperatures prevail, but signs of its activity are scarce even then. Its tracks do not show up in the hard, dry soil characteristic of its habitat, nor in snow because the latter is infrequent, soon disappears, or is compacted by the wind. Many animals can be traced by their droppings, but the ferret usually leaves its excrements in a burrow. These several factors make the ferret appear more rare than it actually is, even in areas where close, continuous study has shown that the animals are present.

Most of our observations of ferrets were made at night from a pickup truck, using a 100-watt aircraft landing light with a red filter to reduce glare. We found only one conspicuous ferret sign— a trench-like structure made when it digs into a prairie dog burrow that is partly or completely closed. Ordinarily this trench is erased by prairie dogs during the day when they cover the burrow entrance.

Throughout our studies, males and females were never seen in pairs; apparently they come together only for a brief period to breed. In the northern states this probably happens in April. The young, usually four but varying from three to five or more, are born in late May or early June. The mother nurses them in her burrow and does not bring them above ground until early July when they are about one-third grown. From this time until September was the only period throughout the year that we saw ferrets with any regularity. Every night the mother brought her offspring out of their burrow and took them on excursions through the prairie dog town.

On these occasions, she appeared at her burrow entrance after darkness had settled and looked around for several minutes. Then, apparently to be sure that no danger existed, she moved quickly to nearby burrows, descended, and usually came out immediately. When satisfied that all was well, she returned to the burrow containing her young and reappeared after a short time, calling them out with a low, plaintive, "Ungh . . . Ungh . . . Ungh . . ."

At first the big new world alarmed the young ferrets and they would run back into their burrow. The mother kept patiently calling them, but sometimes had to go down after them and bring them out by their necks. When she had them all assembled, she traveled about the prairie dog town with the young obediently trailing in a string behind her. After the tour was over, she relocated them in another burrow and resumed her hunting.

The young ferrets were playful animals and were often seen tussling with one another. By early August the mother was housing them in separate burrows. This was the first time that we saw them hunting by themselves. The adult male apparently never assisted in rearing duties; he probably had no interest and would not have been permitted if he had. In fall the young dispersed and more ferrets were seen then, as they wandered to new locations, than at any other time.

Although occasionally found elsewhere, ferrets are most often seen in prairie dog towns. Because so little was known about ferrets for more than a hundred years, eminent zoologists have been very careful to say, "It is *assumed* that ferrets eat prairie dogs." During our four-year study, however, several of us saw ferrets go down into burrows and come up with freshly killed prairie dogs. One night I saw a ferret take a dead prairie dog down a burrow. (Perhaps the victim had run out, trying to escape the ferret, and had been overtaken and killed.) At any rate I could see part of the ferret by the light of the truck and hear it eating the prairie dog.

Sometime after our studies of six prairie dog towns that were frequented by ferrets and other predators, all of the prairie dogs disappeared. (One of these towns covered approximately three hundred acres.) There had been no trapping, shooting, poisoning, or disease; but droppings and stomachs of ferrets were filled almost completely with prairie dog fur and bones. (Perhaps not all the prairie dogs were eaten; some may have left because of predator harassment.)

Although ferrets take other prey when available—such as ground squirrels, rabbits, mice, ground-nesting birds and their eggs, reptiles, and insects—their principal food, particularly in the north during winter, is the prairie dog. To be so dependent on one species is obviously poor economy. Perhaps the ferret's rarity is due to some sort of self-regulation of its numbers which tends to avoid overexploitation of its food supply. This may result from intraspecific strife, territorial spacing, low reproductive rate, high mortality, or other factors. We don't know enough about the species to be more definite at the present time.

At any rate, we found that the relationship between the ferret and the prairie dog is not as one-sided as is commonly depicted. In a number of instances a prairie dog came within two feet of the ferret and tried to force it down a burrow. Many times a prairie dog would smell the ferret in a burrow and proceed to cover it up. This burial was, of course, only temporary, but it deterred the enemy for the time being. Sometimes I have seen a prairie dog run in front of a ferret, apparently trying to divert its course. Occasionally an exceptionally bold dog would strike a ferret from the rear in a "hit-and-run" manner. The ferret's withdrawal was not always flight but at times an attempt to entice the prairie dog close enough to attack it. Whenever the predator made a sustained charge, the prairie dog turned tail and ran.

Although one of my other student assistants once saw a ferret kill a prairie dog above ground, this is unusual. It is not easy for a ferret to catch and kill an adult prairie dog unless it is cornered in a burrow. Young prairie dogs remain underground day and night and are easy prey while their parents are out of their burrows. But most adults have to be caught at night when they retire to their sleeping dens. Even here an alert adult prairie dog with its sharp teeth must present formidable odds to a ferret trying to get a death grip on its throat in a dark, narrow tunnel.

Many times we watched a ferret descend a burrow, known to contain a prairie dog, but hustle out again almost immediately. In some cases ferrets showed fresh wounds and old scars, perhaps incurred in combats with prairie dogs. Somehow, though, the predators manage to overpower their prey.

On the other hand, ferrets have a number of their own enemies, including badgers, great-horned owls, and domestic dogs. Man is by far the greatest threat. Auto traffic, shooting, and trapping claim some animals, abetted by the ferret's fearlessness and curiosity. However, man's principal influence comes from removal of food by reduction of prairie dogs, usually accomplished by poisoning with 1080 or strychnine. These chemical agents may have secondary lethal effects when ferrets eat dead or dying prairie dogs. (Our studies showed that ferrets will eat fresh prey that they have not killed.)

What is the future of the ferret? Since it is so closely associated and dependent upon the prairie dog, a program for preservation requires the retention of adequate numbers of prairie dogs. This could include setting aside public refuges for both species, encouraging the reduction of private and government-supported prairie dog control, leasing the right to protect prairie dogs on private lands, and transplanting ferrets to new areas.

Man, however, must first decide the number and distribution of ferrets that he wants. He has the technical knowledge and means for saving them. The future of these rare and endangered denizens of the Great Plains is clearly up to him.

Glen C. Sanderson has worked for more than two decades on age and sex determination, breeding habits, and population characteristics of the raccoon. Much of his professional career has been in the Illinois Natural History Survey, and since 1963 he has headed its Section of Wildlife Research. He also holds professorships in Southern Illinois University and the University of Illinois, is head of the Mammal Society's Committee for Conservation of Land Mammals, and is a member of the editorial board of The Wildlife Society. Most of Dr. Sanderson's thirty published papers concern the raccoon. Some, however, include other mammals and the results of his three-month study in Malaysia during 1963 to develop means for tracking rats by radio.

THE RACCOON
GLEN C. SANDERSON

"Jock" was the first of a long line of baby raccoons that my wife and I reared when I was working on a research project at the University of Missouri. He followed us about the campus and was variously identified as a squirrel, opossum, badger—and even a raccoon! One foreign student, confusing "raccoon" with "cocoon," asked: "Is that one of those animals that spin their own silk?" In spite of misidentifications, the black mask and heavily furred, ringed tail make the raccoon more easily recognizable to the public than any native mammal except perhaps the cottontail and the skunk.

The one fact that everyone "knows" about raccoons is that they always wash their food. The second part of the raccoon's scientific name *Procyon lotor* comes from the Latin word *lotor,* meaning "washer." New research, however, has shown that raccoons are *feelers* rather than *washers,* and that repeated handling of food items, with or without water, is exploratory behavior. Two recent investigations found that wetting the palms increases the sensitivity of the raccoon's hands. Finally, contrary to a great deal of literature, a recent study of food "washing" concluded that only *captive* raccoons "douse" their food.

The bushy tail of the raccoon is about half as long as the head and body combined. The five toes on each foot have short, nonretractable claws. Long, slender paws, with naked soles, resemble a child's hands and are dexterous, as a scandalized houseguest discovered. Coming into the bathroom one morning she found the family pet raccoon scrubbing the toilet with *her* toothbrush!

A raccoon's weight depends upon geography, age, sex, season, and, in the case of females, breeding status. In the Florida Keys, the average weight for the adult male is four to five pounds; in the northern states it may be up to twenty-two pounds. During autumn, adult males and nonbreeding adult females nearly double their weight, which prepares them for the long, hard winter. Females that have raised young that year cannot, of course, store as much fat. In Minnesota, raccoons of all ages may lose 50 percent of their weight from November to late March, and when this happens, juvenile mortality is heavy. I have weighed approximately ten thousand Midwestern raccoons during the last ten years, and the heaviest tipped the scales at 26.5 pounds. (Raccoons weighed by hunter's or trapper's imagination, or a pet raccoon stuffed with sweets, do not count.)

When cold weather comes, raccoons often den together to keep warm. I have found them alone, in groups of eight to ten, and once there were twelve huddled together. As many as twenty-three raccoons have been taken from one hayloft; other groups have been found in the attic of an abandoned house, and even under the pulpit of a rural Methodist church that was very much occupied.

The larger groups consisted of all ages and members of both sexes; the smaller units were most often a female and her young.

Raccoons do not hibernate. Their body temperature is the same whether they remain in their winter dens several days or for weeks at a time. And although they are usually nocturnal, on cold, bright days they may peer out of their tree dens and sun themselves on big tree limbs or on top of squirrel nests. Along the seacoasts they come out to feed, not according to time of day, but depending on the time of receding tides, day or night.

During the warmer months they seem to prefer tall grass, piles of driftwood, stream banks, and ground burrows. They also live in coastal marshes and on the Canadian prairies where there are no trees. In Iowa I found the animals living in small caves and crevices.

Not intimidated by man's works, they sometimes den in trees less than fifty feet from a farmhouse, in corncribs, machine sheds, haylofts, and piles of posts and lumber. Wild raccoons are not especially frightened by bright lights, and those used to feeding at garbage cans pay no attention to them. Some of these clever creatures have learned to rap on cabin doors, and at least one of them used to pull the latch in order to enter and receive goodies.

When raccoons are about a year old, they become sexually mature. (Females in the North and both sexes in the South are a little more advanced.) Most males are sexually active from October through May—never for the entire year. Individual sexually active males, however, may be found at any time. In the

northern half of Illinois, mating generally occurs in February, and most of the young are born during mid-April.

Female raccoons ovulate regardless of whether they are mated or not, and each ovulation is followed by pregnancy or pseudo-pregnancy. If a yearling female does not breed during her first heat in the season, she will not do so until the following year.

In the Midwest and farther north, a female rears only one litter annually. She may, however, give birth to two litters in the same year if the first is lost at or near birth. The second of these two litters may be born as late as July or August due to the two successive gestation periods. Other late litters come occasionally from females which do not become pregnant until after the second heat or which abort or resorb their first litters. Because juvenile males become sexually active later than adults and remain so during the time when second ovulations occur, juveniles are thought to sire a majority of the late-born young.

Each raccoon litter may contain from one to seven young with the mode at four. Considerable geographic variation is shown by the average of 2.4 in Maryland, 1.9 in coastal North Carolina—and 5.0 for New York!

At birth, the young are blind and unable to stand; they are lightly furred and the mask and tail rings are only pigmented tracings on the skin. Their eyes open at between eighteen and twenty-five days of age, and their milk teeth erupt in one to two months. If at any time it is necessary to move the cubs, the mother raccoon carries them by the nape of the neck like a cat.

The young depend largely on milk until the tenth week and then leave the den and travel with their parent. (Captive raccoons come out of their nest boxes two or three weeks earlier.) Although the mother weans her offspring by the fifteenth or sixteenth week, she usually keeps them with her until the following breeding season.

Raccoons are the most omnivorous of all North American animals, but they prefer corn, as almost every gardener in town or country knows to his sorrow. (An electric fence is a more efficient deterrent than a shotgun carried by a sleepy owner in the middle of the night.) Crayfish, wild grapes, huckleberries, insects, earthworms, and occasionally ground-roosting small birds are other items on their diet. Most raccoons stay near water, but sometimes they live a mile or more away. In Florida, when no fresh water is available, they lick dew or dig shallow wells in the sand to get the fresh rainwater that is lying on top of the heavier salt water.

Although the slang term "coon's age" means a long period of time, raccoons are not especially long lived. Approximately 60 percent of the raccoons alive, at least in the Midwest, are not yet a year old. An "old" raccoon may live to be seven years of age, but the average life-span is about two years. Some remarkable "ancients" have lived to be twelve.

The raccoon populations nationwide followed a downward trend prior to 1940 and then rose sharply during the forties and fifties. They climbed to an all-time peak in 1962 and still remain at a high level. Very likely more than 14 million raccoons are now in the United States.

What is the reason for this amazing population increase? Is it due to tightened legal restrictions on the harvest? I doubt it for Missouri has tried this and their raccoon population increased no more than Iowa's where there were no added restrictions. Was the national increase due to the drop in popularity of long-haired fur? Not likely, since the harvest of raccoons continued to increase even with pelt prices falling from seven dollars to less than three dollars apiece. Nor does it explain the simultaneous continent-wide increase.

Being hunted in every state of the union is not the only affliction of wild raccoons. They are subject to pneumonia, infectious enteritis, canine distemper, rabies, and leptospirosis. While the incidence of these and other diseases in recent years has not been alarming and has not affected overall population trends in spite of locally severe outbreaks, they are potentially important.

In addition to disease, raccoons harbor a wide variety of endoparasites and ectoparasites. The effects are usually negligible, but if an infested raccoon has other physical troubles, the parasites may intensify the illness. Parasitism and starvation are inseparable. Interestingly, the raccoons that were introduced in the Soviet Union lost all North American helminth parasites except one, but they acquired those native to their new habitat. At least nine species of ticks have been found on raccoons, fewer than on squirrels and rabbits.

The raccoon's feats of endurance and natural resistance to infection constantly amaze me. Many animals recover from injuries caused by hunters or trappers and from the severe effects of crippling accidents. I found one adult male raccoon with both feet cut off halfway to the elbows but living in a den fifteen feet above ground level. Another had a heavy wire around its abdomen and a sharp projection that had penetrated the body wall. I have even known of two blind raccoons which were surviving in the wild.

Probably over two million coons are trapped or shot each year in the United States. In this country the fur is used mostly for trimming cloth garments; that of heavily furred northern raccoons can be sheared of guard hairs to resemble beaver. Europe is the main market for the *coat* pelts that come from the sparsely furred coons of the southern states and some of the thinly haired adult females and young animals from farther north. In 1964, 728,000 raccoon pelts, worth $1,344,000 were exported to Canada, West Germany, and ten other countries.

A minor commercial demand exists for raccoon meat. Coon hunters are not the only ones who know it is delicious when properly cleaned and prepared. In Chicago and other food markets, it costs more than chicken, hamburger, and the cheaper cuts of beef.

For years, I have tried—unsuccessfully—to interest physiologists, nutritionists, and others in the potential value of the raccoon as a research animal. (The scars on my hands spoil my argument!) I believe that in ten years of rigid selection, a fairly tractable laboratory animal could be developed. Psychologists, who want intelligent subjects and do not need to restrain them for shots, surgery, and instrumentation, are beginning to use tame and semi-tame raccoons in their studies.

Several excellent books in recent years have shown that raccoons make interesting pets. States vary in their regulations, and if you are planning to keep a pet raccoon you should first check with the local conservation officer or the state office of the Department of Conservation to make sure that this is legal. Caution: A lone female raccoon may undergo a period of extreme intractability, caused by pseudopregnancy in the spring, and should either be allowed freedom to mate or be isolated while the period lasts. And remember, raccoons are fierce fighters when attacked.

Highly intelligent, curious, and adaptable to conditions ranging from seacoast to mountain, the raccoon has survived and even increased its numbers despite heavy hunting and the pressures of advancing civilization. It is man's close neighbor in all but the most urban and most northern areas of the continent. In pioneer America, the raccoon furnished settlers with food, clothing, and sport. Today it continues to provide us with these essentials and is, in many respects, one of our most interesting native animals.

After growing up on Maryland's warm eastern shore, William O. Pruitt, Jr., became a biologist in the Arctic Aeromedical Laboratory at Fairbanks, Alaska. Later, he entered the Cooperative Caribou Investigation of the Canadian Wildlife Service and was for three years an associate professor of zoology at the University of Alaska. Since 1965 he has held a similar position in the department of biology at Memorial University, St. John's, Newfoundland.

From his research on the ecological and behavioral adaptations of mammals to boreal environments across the continent, Dr. Pruitt has written numerous scientific papers, popular articles which have appeared in *Harper's, Holiday,* and *Scientific American,* and a fascinating book, *Animals of the Far North.*

THE WOLVERINE
WILLIAM O. PRUITT, JR.

It was a raw, wet, and windy day on the tundra in northwestern Alaska when my partner and I were setting out a mouse-sampling plot. I straightened up to ease my aching back and there—much to my astonishment—were three wolverines loping along in single file on the hillside across the creek. Later on in the day, we again saw the family (a female and two half-grown kits) in an area of low willow thickets. We had wolverines all around us, even downwind. One kit energetically dug away at a ground squirrel burrow, making sand and earth fly. I noted that the excavation was indistinguishable from what most people would call "grizzly diggings."

After my partner and I had exposed all our film, we just crouched, watching. Once when the female was a good three hundred yards away, I "squeaked" and she stood erect on her hind legs and listened, turning her head back and forth to locate the sound. After two hours of immobility in the wet wind we were numb and our teeth were chattering. We arose, broke the spell, and returned to camp actually satiated with wolverines.

Probably no animal in the North has had more balderdash written about it than the wolverine. From some of the tales, one would think it a veritable giant. But wolverines are only about forty inches long, from tip of nose to tip of tail, and stand from fourteen to sixteen inches high at the back. They weigh from about twenty-seven to fifty-five pounds and are a blackish brown with a broad stripe of tan or yellow curving from shoulders to the base of the tail. (The shape, distinctness, and color of this band are highly variable.) Most have a patch or two of white on the throat or chest.

Wolverines have broad, flexible paws which they use to manipulate objects and their food. Their tails are rather bushy and are used to express their emotional state, much as a dog uses his tail.

A wolverine seems to have only two gears—dead stop and full speed ahead. Their normal gait is a bound or lope with all four feet hitting the ground at about the same time. This gait is an adaptation for moving over snow. Indeed, wolverines seem more closely associated with snow than are other mustelids. Their range is limited to those parts of the northern hemisphere with a continuous winter snow cover. During the snow-free season they seem strangely subdued, but with the arrival of the winter snow cover they are in their element —able to travel far and fast. Wolverines have three-to-four-hour cycles of activity, which alternate with corresponding periods of sleep.

I once observed a wolverine bounding over the soft snow around Grove Lake in the Northwest Territories. The lake is well named, and the trees, huddled along one steep side of the lake, act as a giant snow fence. I sank to my waist in the drifts. The caribou floundered through or

avoided that side of the lake, but the wolverine skimmed over the surface like a hare. On that same trip we followed a wolverine trail from the air. He moved in a straight line for some twenty miles. His trail did not deviate for bare, rocky ridge or snow-filled gully but kept its heading like a straightedge on a map.

The wolverine eats anything it can get. Since it is neither large nor swift, it usually feeds on carrion, ground squirrels, birds and eggs, insects, berries, and similar fare. The wolverine, like other successful northern animals, is an opportunist and takes whatever country meat it can obtain. Thus if it encounters a caribou wounded, exhausted, or mired in deep snow, it will use its great strength to subdue the food supply. Likewise, if it encounters a bit of bait providentially furnished by a trapper, down it goes. A cabin, reeking with food smells, is similar

fair game. One of the most valuable survival attributes of the wolverine is his ability to starve. The North is always "hungry country," especially in the wintertime, and the wolverine's ability to go without food for days or even weeks, plus his great mobility, enables him to live where species of lesser endurance would starve to death.

The wolverine has an extremely large home range, on the order of 50,000 to 75,000 acres. Like other members of the Family Mustelidae, it stakes out a vast area for itself by means of scent stations. Under the roots of a fallen tree or in a rocky cave or talus slope the female digs a den and here she has her young—usually two or three, but as many as five have been reported. The kits are very pale in their nestling pelage, with yellowish-white bodies and dark heads. They nurse for eight to ten weeks and

then are weaned to the adult diet. They stay with the mother for two years until they become proficient at hunting and food-getting. They are not sexually mature until four years old. Breeding takes place in midsummer, but there is delayed implantation of the blastocyst until January. At this time regular gestation starts and the young are born in late March or early April.

Probably no man today knows the wolverine better than Peter Krott, an Austrian forester who raised many wolverines in Finland and Sweden. His scientific papers in his book *Demon of the North* are a gold mine of valuable information on wolverines. Krott found them

fascinating animals to have around— playful, gentle, inquisitive, mischievous, and patience-trying. A great deal of our information on their behavior and early life comes from Peter Krott's pioneering work.

My only experience with a captive wolverine was when I was a graduate student at the University of Michigan. "Intrepidus" was our official mascot and lived in a small zoo at the Museum of Zoology. He had been captured after babyhood, but by the time I knew him, he was quite old. Treppy was gentle and actually dignified, very much like a well-loved hunting dog. He could be fed by hand but would move away from petting. This behavior was unlike Krott's wolverines which had been captured as nurslings.

In the popular literature there are many tales, almost legends, of the redundant ferocity, strength, cunning, and destructiveness of the wolverine. However, after Peter Krott's experiences and my familiarity with Treppy I know they are not innately fierce. Of course, almost any animal, including the wolverine, will fight if cornered.

We have seen that the wolverine requires a huge home range to make a living in the hungry country in which it lives. We also know that it marks its home range with urine and secretions from its anal glands. And if the wolverine encounters a food source in its range, whether caribou carcass, trap set, trapper's cabin, or cache, it puts its signature on the windfall. Since the scent not only is detected by other wolverines but is also repulsive to other animals (competitors), it is biologically effective. Remember, the wolverine is a member of the Family Mustelidae, a group that includes such famous scent-makers as the skunk and the mink.

I also mistrust the tales of the wolverine's cunning and ability to avoid traps. I know of one Alaska trapper who takes wolverines regularly and with impunity. The fact of the matter is that most trappers today are not highly skilled. The native peoples of the North live in a broken culture with many of the old skills forgotten. Most of the white trappers have entered the craft, not in childhood, but in later life and have never had the opportunity to learn the real complexities of the art.

I believe the stories of the great strength of the wolverine, for I have dissected some specimens and have marveled at their tremendous muscle development. All the Mustelidae are rather single-minded (and simple-minded) critters. If a scent intrigues a wolverine it will use its great strength to reach it, no matter how long it takes.

This is one animal that many Alaska mountaineering expeditions have reported at very high altitudes; expedition after expedition often sight wolverines far above the last plants well into the zone of permanent snow and ice.

An interesting comparison can be drawn between the wolverine track in the snow and the published tracks attributed to the yeti, or Abominable Snowman, in the Himalayas. The similarity of the tracks plus the wolverine's penchant for venturing into the permanent snow and ice zone have led me to conclude that the yeti is a large, perhaps undescribed, species of wolverine. Other facts make this a logical assumption—the scarcity of wolverines, their ability to travel far and fast, the few supposed sightings of the beast standing on its hind legs on a distant hill. The peculiar loping gait of the wolverine could be confused through the shimmering heat waves with a bipedal creature running with its knuckles hitting the ground. In short, I suspect the Abominable Snowman to be none other than the wolverine.

My fondest recollection of a wolverine is of the time one ran across the snow-covered Richardson Highway in front of my jeep, in the heart of the Alaska Range. The animal bounded up a steep slope and turned, erect, to look back at me. What a sight he made, with the grand snow peaks of the Alaska Range forming a glittering backdrop! He was the very spirit of the wilderness.

Alan B. Sargeant entered the United States Bureau of Sport Fisheries and Wildlife in 1962; after working for a year on animal control problems he was assigned to research on the life history of the red fox in Minnesota. The study was supported jointly by the bureau and the Bell Museum of Natural History at the University of Minnesota. Utilizing newly developed radio telemetry techniques, the project furnished much of the information in this chapter.

Mr. Sargeant has published a number of articles on such subjects as pocket gophers, automatic radio tracking, and the mammals of Itasca State Park, Minnesota. Since 1967, he has been a research biologist in the Northern Prairie Wildlife Research Center at Jamestown, North Dakota.

THE RED FOX

ALAN B. SARGEANT

Few mammals are more widely distributed or well known in North America than the red fox. This species occupies such diverse regions as the Arctic north and arid plains, both deciduous and coniferous forests, and is successful in urban, agricultural, and wilderness areas. Although no one habitat is typical for the species, it seems to be most abundant in farming country. And it has the ability to learn and adapt, which is essential for its success in such places in spite of intense efforts to trap, hunt, poison, dig from dens, or otherwise reduce their numbers.

All red foxes are not red. Although the species is typified by its brilliant red coat with white throat, chest, and belly, its white-tipped tail, and varying amounts of black on its ears and feet, a variety of color phases occur. These include the "cross fox" with darker fur down its back and across its shoulders, the "silver fox" with its dark coat and silver-tipped guard hairs, and the "black fox" which is as dark as its name implies. In some areas, a genetic mutation is frequent; this is the "Samson's" or "cotton" fox, which is a red fox without its sleek guard hairs and thus its coat consists almost exclusively of the dull wooly underfur. All color variations, however, have a white tip on the tail, and animals of different color phases may be born in the same litter.

My experience with red foxes comes primarily from studying their habits and movements in east-central Minnesota with the aid of newly developed radio telemetry techniques. We attached miniaturized radio transmitters around the necks of individual foxes, and were then able to follow the activities of the animals simultaneously and continuously from an automatic tracking system developed at the University of Minnesota. The small collars containing the radio transmitters weighed less than one-quarter pound. Each radio had a different frequency and was capable of sending radio signals for many months. These signals, received from directional antennae up to two and a half miles away, allowed remote determination of each fox's location, travels, and certain habits.

In order to secure foxes for radio-tracking, we first had to find them. Their presence is often betrayed by their tracks and trails, scattered fecal deposits, or dens containing pups, and the strong, sweet smell of their urine. They are not frequently seen even when numerous. I recall asking a farmer if he had noticed any foxes. He said that two had been killed the previous years but there hadn't been any around since. He was surprised when I told him that at this time and during the previous six months I had been following by radio a vixen that traveled on his farm almost nightly and frequently slept in a wooded swamp behind his barn.

In central Minnesota, red foxes breed in late January or in February, and after a gestation period of approximately fifty-two days, whelping occurs. Generally a litter will consist of four to seven pups, although I have examined gravid vixens with one to eleven embryos. The pups are born in underground dens during late March or April. The dens usually have several entrances, the main one being marked by a large mound, and are characteristically located on slopes in woods or open country. The same dens are frequently used year after year.

When pup foxes are four to five weeks old they are weaned, and come above ground apparently for the first time. During their first ten weeks, their life revolves exclusively around the den, and food is brought to them by their parents. They can often be seen playing outside the den but they dash into it for protection when disturbed.

The vixen seem to be more strongly attached than the dog (male) to the pups. In fact, the dog of one radio-tagged pair was not known to visit the den at all, yet he was an integral part of the family since he had lived in the area with this vixen for over a year. (Seemingly, like humans, some fathers are less solicitous than others.)

Considerable amounts of food accumulate at fox dens. This may include remains of rabbits, birds, mice, snakes, fish, poultry, garbage, and even eggs. The softer parts are usually consumed by the pups, but decaying, uneaten parts, particularly heavy bones and feathers, and frequently whole-food items are scattered about. The pups urinate and defecate around the den and this, combined with the decaying, uneaten food soon gives the site a characteristic appearance and smell. This, perhaps more than any other feature, typifies a fox den.

106

Generally, red fox pups will use three to five different dens during the spring. The first change in location seems to take place shortly after weaning but it may occur at any time, particularly if a den is disturbed. A person or other large animal simply walking up to a den will frequently result in its being abandoned. The new site may be in the same vicinity, but I have observed moves of nearly a mile.

As the pups grow, they extend their activities and when approximately ten to twelve weeks old they use dens much less intensively. As each week goes by, they travel over an increasingly larger area—a relatively few acres in mid-June, half a square mile by mid-July, and a square mile or more by mid-August. By mid-September the pups are occupying most of the parental territory.

The adults spend comparatively little time with their offspring once they are weaned, although the vixen will frequently bed near the den. By the time the young have given up heavy use of

den sites, they may encounter their parents only briefly during the day or night. However, these meetings are sufficient for the adults to continue any necessary training. On one occasion in late June, a vixen accompanied one of her pups on a trip while leaving another behind. The young foxes seem to have a thorough knowledge of the home area and do not stray even though they are apparently left unattended much of the time.

In September some pups begin to disperse. Not all pups leave at the same time nor even during the same season, and the first departure may occur during any month of the fall, winter or perhaps later. Males are typically the first to start out and they move the farthest. One male pup traveled thirty-five miles between late July and early September and crossed a major river. Another left the den in mid-December and was killed a few days later eighteen miles away. Female pups do not seem to leave as early as the males and may remain in or near the parent area. Most records available

107

on the dispersal of female pups show them being killed less than ten miles away from home. However, some pup foxes, both female and male, are known to travel over one hundred miles.

In all seasons there are certain foxes which are travelers. The number of these transients is particularly large during fall and winter when the pups are dispersing. The wanderers, adult and young, are especially vulnerable to trapping and hunting because they are in unfamiliar country. Trappers may capture twenty or more foxes in a small area during the fall and winter, most of which are probably foxes on the move. Fox hunters using hounds often hunt the same territory repeatedly. They have told me that after killing foxes, they give the area a rest for a week or two. Then they return and can be reasonably certain that other foxes will be there.

Underlying this transient segment of the population are the resident foxes. These animals compose the social families which characteristically remain on the range until they are killed. A family typically consists of a vixen and dog that produce pups and care for them. Since some offspring, particularly females, do not disperse during their first year, a family may include more than a pair. One radio-tracked trio consisted of a vixen which had pups, a vixen without pups, and a dog. This group lived in the same neighborhood during and after whelping of young, and remained together until the following winter when the barren vixen was killed.

The activities of our radio-tagged adults were confined to relatively fixed territories. Each family occupied a separate area and each family member traveled rather thoroughly throughout its

home range nightly with seemingly little regard to season or weather conditions. By following the movements of a single adult for a few nights, we could determine where the entire family lived over a long period of time. I have seen places occupied by the same group for more than a year and a half, with little change between summer and winter.

The territories of adjacent families butted up against each other with virtually no overlap. They are somehow defended from neighboring and transient foxes, although the boundaries did not seem to be patrolled nor did I ever detect foxes of different families there together.

When a family of foxes is killed, neighboring or transient foxes invade and take over the vacant tracts. Thus, where foxes are suffering heavy mortality through hunting, trapping, or for some other reason, there is a constant readjustment in the size, shape and location of red fox territories.

The size of the areas occupied by different fox families in the same region is approximately the same. It is related to the population density, and the fewer the foxes, the larger it is. I have documented territories which ranged in size from one to almost four square miles. A fox population of one family per square mile is relatively dense, while one family per three square miles is moderate.

Red foxes move primarily at night and rest during the day. Generally, activity starts about sunset and ends around sunrise. The animals spend most of the night traveling, although there are many exceptions. A fox proceeds rather steadily throughout its territory, spends little time in any one place, and returns around daybreak to bed in the area used the previous day. Commonly, family members visit many of the same places during a night, but they are seldom together. I know of no instance where a pair traveled together for even a few hours, although they occasionally bedded in the same locality. Exceptions occur, however, particularly during the breeding season.

As a rule our radio-tagged foxes covered from eight to twelve miles each night. The greatest distance that any fox was known to travel in one night was approximately twenty miles—when a vixen made two trips throughout her territory and finally returned to bed near the site she had used the day before.

At the time of whelping, the mother restricts her movements. One of our radio-tagged vixens made infrequent short forays from the den during the first three days after whelping. But after this period she made nightly trips, frequently going over a mile away but returning once or twice during the night.

Much of a fox's travel seems to be related to defending its territory rather than to hunting. The animal must patrol its range regularly or perhaps lose it to neighboring or transient individuals. Thus, hunting and traveling are interwoven and it is incorrect to assume that simply because a fox is going through a woods or field that it is hunting.

When a fox has made a "kill" or otherwise found food and has eaten, it continues on as though nothing has happened. Other "kills" may be made and cached for future use. Often the victims, such as moles, shrews, etc., are unappetizing to the fox and are simply dropped and left. The number of prey killed and either discarded or cached is unknown, but frequently a fox will kill considerably more than needed for survival. Uneaten food is typically placed in a small hole in the snow or soil and covered. I have observed "sign" in the snow which indicated that a fox had paused while walking, pushed part of a rabbit into the snow and, using the nose, covered it and then departed. A small depression six to eight inches across was the sole evidence that a cache had been made.

Red foxes are said to be opportunists, taking food in proportion to that which is available or abundant; however, this is not entirely true. Certainly they take advantage of whatever may be periodically available and they have a varied diet. Nevertheless, some prey is selectively hunted even when it is scarce. I have seen foxes which were devoting much time to hunting cottontails and were successful in spite of the very low number of rabbits. Whenever they are present, the cottontail and meadow mouse are the two major prey items in the diet. During the winter, foxes are primarily carnivorous but in summer they are more omnivorous, often feeding on insects and berries.

The red fox has been and will continue to be a controversial species because of its diverse relationships with man. It is useful to the farmer because it subsists largely on rodents and insects that are often considered farm pests, but at the same time it may prey on the farmer's poultry, lambs and piglets. Its pelt is of economic value, yet it is a carrier of rabies. Hunters praise it as a sport animal, but they berate it because it preys on certain game birds and mammals. Regardless of your feelings toward the red fox, few will deny its right to exist or its beauty, and most people will take pleasure from simply seeing one.

Charles Henry Douglas Clarke researched birds and mammals of the far north for the National Museum of Canada before becoming mammalogist for his country's national parks. In 1944 he entered the Ontario Department of Lands and Forests. From biological research he transferred to game management and became chief of the department's Fish and Wildlife Branch.

Dr. Clarke is a Canadian member of the Great Lakes Fishery Commission and a fellow of the Arctic Institute of North America. At various times he has been a governor of that institute, president of The Wildlife Society, and Canadian External Aid adviser in wildlife to the Natural Resources Ministry of Kenya. Doug Clarke's special interests are ecology, animal populations, and the predator which he describes in this chapter.

THE TIMBER WOLF
C. H. D. CLARKE

It is almost certain that the first sign you'll ever see of a wolf will be its tracks. At least it was that way with me, in 1928, when I walked through the wild land of Ontario ahead of our senior axman, Henry Bell. After a mile of flinty ground we came to the ford of Coldwater Creek and there, in the bare sand, were tracks—reasonably fresh tracks—beaver, moose, bear, and wolf. I felt a surge of fulfillment—I had arrived! The wolf tracks made the occasion. They were huge, clear, wet, and a sure sign of wilderness. I could see that Henry, for all his long lifetime in the bush, was just as exhilarated as I was. Henry was an Indian.

Over vast areas where they once lived, wolves are gone. In Mexico, parts of the United States, and some countries of western Europe, wolves still exist, but they are hanging on by a thread. Wolf country today is Canada and the Soviet Union, and we are not given much information about Russian wolves.

At first sight any wolf looks like a large German shepherd dog. No two wolves look exactly alike, nor do any two shepherds. Most of the wolves in North America are dark gray in color, but in the most northern Arctic regions all wolves are pure white, and in the northwest many are pure black. Many wolves have dark, or even black, mantles, in a predominantly gray pelt, and in the fringes of the high Arctic much more whiteness is found than farther south. All these variations, and more, may be found in shepherd dogs.

Weights also vary with individuals and by regions, all the way from forty pounds to one hundred and forty. The extremes are rare. Males are bigger than females, and the wolves of the northwest are bigger than those farther south and east. Seventy pounds may be taken as an average weight for the whole range.

For all their superficial resemblance, wolves may be told from shepherd dogs at a glance. A wolf is so long in the leg that you cannot fail to notice it. His chest is deep, from top to bottom, giving him a touch of the greyhound look and a little of the greyhound speed. His face is gray. His muzzle, though wide, looks pointed because of his broad head. His feet are big. When he runs, his tail sticks out almost straight, but most of the time he carries it down, even between his legs.

Contrary to popular belief, wolves are not fierce nor do they look fierce. Research workers handle wild wolves without using drugs. In Europe many tales were circulated about people-eating wolves. However, it is now generally accepted by knowledgeable people that these wolves were rabid, and no rabid animal is a proper indicator of the disposition of the species. In North America, we have had no comparable outbreaks of rabies, and for years, the late Jim Curran, editor of the Sault Sainte Marie, Ontario, daily *Star,* had a standing offer of a reward for an authentic instance of a

wolf attack in Ontario. In the end he concluded, "Anyone who says he's been e't by a wolf is a liar!"

In short, treat a bear with respect, especially one with cubs, and most particularly a grizzly. But wolves? Enjoy them, they're fun! To see them is a real challenge to your woodsmanship.

On the Arctic tundra, and to a degree in the western mountains, you can find dens and thus keep packs under observation. In the east they are rarely found. Once we asked a group of trappers if they had ever seen wolf dens, and the only affirmative came from an elderly Indian. When he was a very small boy his father led him to a den and told him to take a good look because he might never see another! They are very secretive creatures, indeed. One day, I stumbled on a little beaver pond quite close to a highway. It was evident that a pair of wolves was living there for the whelping period. They played a lot, but wandered not at all, and they had a deer on which they were feeding that would last them for weeks.

North of Toronto in Algonquin Park, however, the wolves have lost some of their privacy because of the ingenuity of the research teams who are determined to replace wolf myths with facts. One team got the idea of playing recorded howls to which the distant wolves immediately responded. The responses allowed the scientific "interlopers" to take a couple of bearings and find out where they were. It was not long before it was also discovered that wolves would answer a human howl. The voice of a wolf can be imitated because, unlike that of the coyote, it is within the normal human range.

Using such techniques, the researchers were able to determine that the wolves in their area numbered about one to every ten square miles and that, contrary to the hunters' ancient cry of "wolf menace," wolves do not contribute to the balance of nature. Even when there is an abundance of prey available for the killing, wolves continue to be very economical eaters. In Algonquin Park they completely consumed the whole carcass of most of their kills—80 percent, in fact—and often left nothing but a patch of hair and a grease spot. I am afraid the wolf that has satisfied his hunger curls up and sleeps when he should be hunting in the interest of the "balance of nature."

More interesting is that in virgin territories where neither game nor wolves are often molested, the population level of wolves does not rise. In fact, it is no different from that in areas where wolves are frequently trapped.

In Algonquin Park, wolves were protected from hunters for five years. At the beginning of this period, the ratio of young wolves to old wolves was high because trapping had been heavy, and few lived very many years. At the end of the period, the total number of wolves was virtually the same, but the ratio of young to old had declined.

During these years of research, a number of wolves were tagged. Some were given collars with tiny radio transmitters. By means of tracking, trapping, and telemetry, it was determined that there was no significant emigration or immigration. The packs numbered from about six to ten wolves and ranged from fifteen to thirty square miles in the summer and fifty to sixty square miles in the winter. Only one wolf tagged from any pack living entirely in Algonquin Park wandered outside its boundary. The litters aver-

aged five; however, survival of the young was poor. Apparently the pups must compete with their elders in some way even when the food supply is adequate. For when the period of protection ended and more adults were removed by trapping, more young continued to live. The decreased number of pups surviving in a protected area and the increased number surviving when the population is subjected to losses is a part of the automatic control that keeps the population numbers stable.

This phenomenon of population stability has been confirmed by other research groups. The number of wolves on Isle Royale, a protected national park in Lake Superior, has varied little since they have been studied and are comparable to the one per ten square mile population in Algonquin Park. The wolf packs observed for years in Mount McKinley National Park by Adolph Murie remained about the same and bitches did not breed every year.

Even when living in protected areas like national parks, wolves do not always have their own way. Subordinate wolves must defer to dominant wolves. And, rarely, a prey species may retaliate. Not too long ago, a man attracted by ravens came across an astonishing scene which he showed me. Dead on the ground, side by side, lay a wolf and a beaver. Obviously the big rodent had been "logging" a short distance from its pond when it was ambushed by the wolf. But it was not an instant kill. In a final spasm the beaver had whipped around, sunk its incisors through the femoral artery in the wolf's leg and held on—to the death.

Wolves in Canada that are not protected show no tendency to occupy completely cleared farmland even when patches of bush contain plenty of deer. Apart from this, they occupy all of Ontario. This is in spite of a bounty, first paid in the eighteenth century, and still in effect. It cannot be shown to have affected the size of wolf populations at all. Neither have occasional poisoning campaigns in the past. Wolves react intelligently to poison baits, and are the last to show any diminution in a control program. Ravens, eagles, Canada jays, fisher, marten, wolverine, and lynx will all disappear first.

For a long time the answer to all shortages of game was to persecute wolves, and it is perhaps because the per-

114

secution has been so ineffective, yet so consistent, that Ontario hunters now realize that major changes in deer and moose numbers have gone on independently of wolf numbers or anything done to keep down wolves. Moose are now superabundant. Out of an annual surplus of more than thirty thousand, less than half are taken by hunters, and uncontrolled increase is obviously dangerous for the moose. Deer in Ontario are at the northern limit of their range and periodically suffer heavy die-offs. It has been shown that these losses have nothing to do with wolves but are related to critical snow depths and cold in winter. Furthermore, they can be mitigated by intensive management of winter range to produce a maximum amount of browse.

The wolf has always had a bad press. Several times in recent memory, deer have died from malnutrition in severe winters, and unless they were on a "wolfless island," wolves were blamed. Very recently, in an area where deer were in the initial stages of recovery from a succession of bad winters, and wolves had moved in, a conservation officer attempted to cut the pressure on the deer by removing a few predators. Strange accounts of wolf predation arose because the officer had been using deer killed in widely scattered highway collisions as bait for his snares. A misguided sportsman thought the carcasses were all wolf kills, and his gory photographs were widely circulated.

A famished thirty-pound coyote that wandered into a city became, with the aid of a short-focus lens, an eighty-pound timber wolf. Newsmen are not only at the mercy of their informants but are often required to bring in a sensational tale. Corrections are never made. It is said: "We newsmen do not chew our cabbage twice."

Fortunately the image of the wolf is beginning to change. People who once feared and hated wolves now delight in listening to them as they answer a "howl" in Algonquin Park on a summer's night. They have been able to see and hear for themselves some of the results of wolf research. Books about wolves by such writers as Lois Crisler, Farley Mowat, and Rutter and Pimlott have further increased understanding and interest.

Consequently, an attempt to set up a new round of wolf persecution recently provoked thousands of people in the United States as well as Canada to protest by mail, telephone, and telegraph. Many of them were pacified when an official statement declared that wolves would be unmolested in such places as Algonquin Park, and although hunted freely elsewhere, they would be controlled officially only where damage to livestock was demonstrated or a study showed that wolf pressure on deer herds was excessive.

Farmers are taught and urged to protect their own livestock. The bounty, even though it has never hurt the wolves, is under criticism to the extent that its years may be numbered. Bounties have been abandoned in most parts of Canada, and though at first they gave way to official poison campaigns, these, too, are being dropped.

Who knows? Maybe Canada will one day be known as the Land of the Wolf!

As a seven-year-old schoolboy in Manhattan, Richard G. Van Gelder decided on mammalogy as a career, and he earned a Ph.D. at Illinois in 1958 for work on spotted skunks. Meanwhile (1956), he entered the Museum of Natural History and two years later was made chairman of his department. He has participated in or led expeditions to many lands and was successively lecturer and assistant professor at Columbia, 1958–63. He is now president of the American Society of Mammologists.

For relaxation, Dr. Van Gelder writes books, such as *Biology of Mammals* and *1001 Questions Answered about Mammals* for adults, and *Monkeys and Apes* for children. His hobbies are diversified: listening to baroque music, collecting stringed instruments, growing tropical house plants, reading dictionaries, and building a country home with his own hands.

SKUNKS
RICHARD G. VAN GELDER

"Imagine a mixture of strong ammonia, essence of garlic, burning sulphur, a volume of sewer gas, a vitriol spray, a dash of perfume musk, all mixed together and intensified a thousand times." This description of a skunk's scent came from the pen of the famed naturalist Ernest Thompson Seton, a mephitophile who once spurned the thought of eating a skunk because it was "too much like eating a baby." But Seton should have tried roast skunk, as I have; he would have found it very tasty.

In the two decades that I have been studying skunks, my travels have taken me to all parts of their range, from thirteen thousand feet in the Andes of South America to sea level in Massachusetts, from far north in Canada to the pampas of Argentina, and from the coniferous forests of Colorado to the deserts of central Mexico. They have bitten me, and I have bitten them; they have shot at me, and I have shot at them; and although I have never lived in their homes, they have lived in mine.

And through it all, I have never been sprayed by a skunk—they always missed!

I had my first real chance to be sprayed when I was working at the Bronx Zoo in New York as a teen-ager, and was given a skunk to handle and to make tame for use in the Children's Zoo. It had been given to the zoo by a woman who had had it as a pet and who had assured the zoo that it had been "descented." The skunk, despite my handling, turned out to be a bit of a rotter, and after biting me several times, finally chewed up a monkey that shared "Noah's Ark" with it and was exiled to a pen with a number of other skunks. A few weeks later, the keeper went into the cage to net a skunk to be exchanged with another zoo, and as the net dropped over my late friend, it turned around and fired with both barrels. They had to close the small-mammal house for a week until the odor diminished. Somehow word got around that I had a way with skunks, but I never thought so.

My college career almost ended with a skunk, when I made my first attempt to skin one for scientific study. I knew from books that the scent was contained in two glands that are alongside the anus, and that I should be careful in that area. But the skunk had been frozen and was not well thawed, and besides, my scalpel slipped. I was working in the basement of the veterinary building at Colorado A & M College, an area already rich in odor, but I soon became aware that my skunk was adding an aroma that surpassed all others. I tucked my unfinished trophy under my arm, turned on the exhaust fan, and ran for it. I buried the evidence under a garage and prayed that the odor would disappear, but they ran me down by telephone and I denied everything.

With more experience I learned how to remove most of the skunk odor from my hands or from the skunks themselves when I was skinning them—a cup of ammonia in a bucket of water—but even so, a mephitologist gets a little sensitive about being smelly. One year I traveled through the western United States and Mexico collecting skunks and examining specimens at museums. I had just broken camp in northern Arizona one crisp November day and was on my way to study at the Museum of Northern Arizona in Flagstaff, when a skunk ran across the road. I leaped from my car with a pistol loaded with .22 dust shot and gave chase. Dust shot has about the same effective range as a spraying skunk, perhaps a dozen feet. I often wish a movie had been made of our battle, as we ran about through the brush, stopping to exchange ineffective shots, and then continuing the chase. I finally got him when he ran out of ammunition before I did, cut out the scent glands, threw the carcass in the trunk, washed my hands in ammonia solution, and raced off for Flagstaff. I had had the windows open in the car for the two-hour drive, and I arrived just as the museum was closing. I rushed to the receptionist and asked to see the curator about examining skunks in the collection, and when she went off to find him I caught my breath—and what an odor of skunk! When the young lady returned, I started to make amends for coming in to look at skunks and also smelling like one, and said, "The odor of skunk is—"

"Yes, isn't it terrible," she interrupted. "We have two of them living under the building and they let go last night."

I was saved again.

There is a prevalent idea that if you can pick up a skunk by its tail, it cannot spray, but most mammalogists do not believe this, because one of the more fa-

mous ones once put it to an experiment
—and got well sprayed for his curiosity.
However, I now believe that there may
be some truth to the old legend after all.
A few years ago I carried a mother
skunk and her four half-grown young in
two small garbage pails on the back seat
of my car from northern New Jersey
where they had been caught, through the
heart of New York City, to the American
Museum of Natural History's Kalbfleisch
Field Research Station on Long Island.
While I was painting spots on the backs
of the young ones so I could recognize
them later, the mother escaped and headed for the woods. I rushed deep into the

woods ahead of her, and then got my
students, who had been interested but
distant observers, to drive the skunk
slowly toward me. I stood stock-still,
with my legs apart, and when the skunk,
tail high, walked beneath me, I reached
down and snatched her into the air. I
fully expected to get both barrels right
in the face, but nothing happened. As I
carried her back, by the tail, to the garbage pail, I could see the muscles
around her anus working away, but no
odor came out. There are two little nipples out of which the spray emerges, and
these must be everted through the anus
before the skunk can spray, and I suspect
that when the skunk is lifted by its tail
by surprise, it cannot point the nipples
out and spray. But if the nipples are
already sticking out of the anus and the
animal is lifted by the tail, watch out!

Defending by means of scent glands
is characteristic of all three major kinds
of skunks, the spotted, striped, and hog-
nosed. There are slight differences in the
pungency of each, and some mammalogists claim that they can tell them by
odor, and even express preferences for
different kinds. Although I also agree
that there are differences, I have only
been right about 75 percent of the
time when I tried to guess, by odor alone,
which one of three kinds I might have
in a trap.

The spotted skunks (genus *Spilogale*)
are the smallest of the three genera, and
one of the two species, the pigmy skunk
(*S. pygmaea*), measures only ten inches
in length, including the tail. Six more or
less parallel white lines down the front
part of the body break into short stripes
and spots on the rump in the spotted
skunk (*S. putorius*), which gives them
their book name. Locally they may be
known as civet cat or hydrophobia cat

119

(shortened to 'phoby cat in some places). They are the most weasel-like of the skunks, with slender bodies and quick movements. They are also the only skunks that are good climbers. Even in their psychology, the spotted skunks are much more like weasels, and while their defense is probably equally effective as that of their larger relatives, they are much more wary. From keeping them in captivity, I came to the conclusion that the front half of a spotted skunk is colored disruptively for camouflage, but the white-plumed tail is a blatant warning signal.

Many a night when I went to the outdoor cage to feed my animals in the dim light from a distant window or from a pale moon, I couldn't find them. It was ridiculous to think that I was unable to see my animals in a 15-by-15-foot cage, but it was only after I had jumped and

shouted and banged a tin food dish that I could scare them enough so that they flipped up their tails—that bright flag I could see easily. When these little skunks are threatening, they sometimes rise on their front legs and take a few steps toward you, and if this is intended to startle you, it certainly works.

The common or striped skunk (*Mephitis mephitis*) is the animal we generally think of when "skunk" is mentioned, and, indeed, in most parts of the United States and Canada, it is the most common member of the skunk tribe. Unlike its spotted relative, the striped skunk seems very secure in its manner of defense, and his temerity extends even to automobiles, which accounts for the large numbers seen dead on roads.

For the most part, striped skunks are tolerant animals not only of man and other animals but also of their own kind.

When winter comes in the north, the skunks are protected by a good layer of fat and move into their dens—sometimes as many as twenty to a single burrow. Although they do not actually hibernate, they may remain in the dens for as long as three months, metabolizing their fat. But if the burrow entrance is not blocked by snow, they may come out and wander about. (In northern United States the mating season starts toward the end of February, and the males, especially, wander widely.)

Very little is known of the life history of the hog-nosed skunks (genus *Conepatus*), which range from southern Colorado southward throughout South America as far as the Straits of Magellan. These, the largest of the skunks, get their names from their big, naked snout with which they root in the ground in search of insects and their larvae. The ones that live in the United States have solid white backs and all-white tails. But farther south there is a variety of color patterns, with many of the animals looking very much like the striped skunk, except that they never have a white line on the forehead. The rooting behavior is strongly developed, even in the very young. One summer, on the pampas of Uruguay, I extricated two nursing babies from a burrow. They had their eyes opened but could scarcely stand, and only one could produce a very faint musk. But when I tossed a handful of fresh dirt in front of them, down went the noses as they rooted around in search of the grubs they had never seen or tasted.

One of the peculiarities of some of the South American hog-nosed skunks is that they are immune to the venom of the rattlesnake group of reptiles—despite the fact that they live high in the cool Andes where these snakes do not occur. There is evidence that spotted skunks may also have a high degree of immunity. Skunks are further protected since one of the chemicals in their musk seems to work as a repellent to rattlesnakes, as well as a lot of other animals.

Skunks are sometimes kept as pets, but are often a disappointment to their owners, as they are less affectionate than a dog and sometimes more aloof than a cat. I have only known one that was a really fine pet, and she was intelligent enough to count and obey some orders. When climbing a flight of ten steps—and this is heavy work for a skunk—she would obey a command to come down only if she had not ascended more than five steps. If she was higher, she would scramble on to the top, disregarding the command.

By their specialized defense, skunks have capitalized on the intelligence of other mammals, for one experience is usually enough to teach man or some other predator to leave alone any creature with strongly contrasting black and white marks. Skunks are probably more abundant today than they were before the arrival of Europeans in North America, and they are one of the larger mammals that manage to survive in close proximity to man. Overall, they are beneficial to man in their control of insects. And in a world where man seems intent upon eradicating all the animals he can, it is nice to know that one kind is thriving. But it is also disheartening to think that one reason why skunks are successful is that they, alone, are able to shoot back.

James Hatter was the first wildlife biologist to be employed by British Columbia, and he became chief biologist in 1951. He was promoted to assistant director of the Fish and Wildlife Branch in 1962, and to director the following year. He also served as assistant professor in the University of British Columbia, on a part-time basis, from 1950 to 1956. The author of numerous articles on game administration and management, his professional interests have become focused on "communication and the need to improve public understanding of the factors that determined the presence and abundance of wildlife." Long interested in the cougar, he was among those forward-looking persons who advocated its removal from the provincial bounty list and its official recognition as a game animal.

THE COUGAR (MOUNTAIN LION)
JAMES HATTER

In 1917 King George V awarded the Albert Medal for valor to an eight-year-old boy and eleven-year-old girl on Vancouver Island. A picture of these children occupied a prominent place in our home. Mother was the family nurse at the time they had defended each other against the attack of a cougar.

It was a September afternoon in 1916 when Doreen and her playmate, Tony, told Mother that they were going to look for their pony about half a mile from home. As they trudged along the trail, carrying their horse bridle, the sun filtered through the autumn-colored leaves, a red squirrel skittered into the brush, and a Steller's jay shrieked. Suddenly the children stood stock-still with terror. A few feet ahead of them crouched a mountain lion. It sprang at Doreen, knocked her to the ground, face downward, and began to tear at her clothes. Young Tony jumped on the cougar's back, overbalanced the animal, and Doreen was able to scramble to her feet. Both children pounded at the beast with their fists and the horse bridle. Blind in one eye and momentarily confused, the lion hesitated and then leaped on top of the boy, biting into his back and head.

Screaming at the attacker, Doreen thrust her right arm into the lion's mouth trying to prevent further harm to Tony, whose head was now covered with blood. The lion clamped its mouth shut on her arm. Frantically she dug the fingernails of her left hand into the animal's one good eye. The pain and temporary total blindness caused the lion to release its hold on her arm. Both children again flailed him. Scared and bewildered, the cougar retreated and ran under a log.

Although Tony's scalp was badly torn and both children were bleeding profusely, they managed to reach home. A hunter immediately returned to the scene to find the animal lapping blood where the struggle had taken place. It was in a starving condition and nearly blind.

This story of the children's bravery had much to do with my early admiration for the men who hunted the cougar to "protect deer and other wildlife from destruction." In later years I was to learn more about this animal which has suffered so much from the glamour associated with protection of human life, domestic stock, and wildlife.

The rugged terrain of the West has become the last holdout for this large predator which once occurred widely over the North American continent. Now it is found only from the southern-most tip of South America to the Peace River region of British Columbia. A considerable amount of this vast area is still wilderness which has provided protection from the impact of mankind and lessened his ability to destroy this interesting member of the cat family, second in size in the western hemisphere only to the jaguar of extreme southern United States and Latin America.

In British Columbia, the cougar is probably as numerous as anywhere on the continent. But a predatory animal is never as abundant as species upon which it feeds, and there is much for us to ponder about this ability of the weak to outnumber the strong. Like all large carnivores at the top of the food chain, the cougar does not reproduce prolifically. It breeds at two years of age and produces up to five young every two years. Usually, not more than three young are found with the mother after they leave the den and begin hunting.

In early life the kittens are spotted and are attended only by the mother. At birth they weigh about a pound and are perhaps twelve inches long, but as adults they may reach two hundred pounds and, in the case of an adult male, extend more than eight feet. The female is smaller.

Two little cougar kittens given their freedom about the home of one of our predator hunters appeared to communicate with each other by a sound that can best be described as a whistle. There has been much argument about the sounds made by the adult cougar. I never really believed that it screamed until I lived in the old graduate house at Washington State University. Across the road was the college mascot, a large male cougar who paced his spacious pen and screamed periodically. A fellow student, trying to explain these noises, commented that he knew how the cougar felt—lonesome and in need of a female companion. (We cannot, of course, positively interpret the behavior of a wild animal in this way.)

The cougar is not particular in its meat-eating habits. Deer is a favorite

food item, especially in winter, but the diet may include a long list of items from horsemeat to small birds. It has also been known to eat its own kind. A large male is able to kill heavy animals such as cattle, horses, elk, and moose, although its biting span is only three to four inches. Following an attack from the side the prey is usually bitten in the neck just behind the ears. In smaller creatures, such as deer and sheep, the spinal column is injured, and combined with the weight of the attacker the victim is brought to the ground. The same technique appears to be used on large domestic animals, and on moose and elk, although more difficulty is experienced and unsuccessful attacks are probably common.

Despite its strength, it is doubtful that many cougars live more than ten years under natural conditions. Intestinal worms, ticks, and fleas may infect the animal, but their greatest enemy is starvation. John Lesowski, a conservation officer at Williams Lake, B. C., with many years experience hunting cougar, has observed that young cougars in particular may starve to death when snowshoe hares are scarce. When the "rabbit" population crashes, animals that have become dependent upon this food during years of abundance in places where big game is not plentiful may suffer from acute malnutrition. One starving cougar was found in a haystack, and another under a school bus.

This long-tailed cat is not as well adapted to cold temperatures and deep snows as the lynx and bobcat which have short tails and are more thickly furred. During cold winters in central British Columbia, ears and tails of young cougar may become frozen and shortened.

The cougar establishes a territory or home range over which it travels in search of prey. Territories vary in size but may extend over fifteen or more square miles. Movement away from this "home range" is usually by young animals setting forth to establish their own territories. It is among these young "travelers" that losses most often occur.

Upon occasion a cougar has been known to fight and kill its own kind, but for the most part, there is very little strife, as they tend to disregard one another by some kind of mutual avoidance reaction. This behavior is believed responsible for the spacing of individual territories and therefore the automatic regulation of numbers.

Few people have ever seen a cougar in the wild and even fewer have had the opportunity to witness its attack on prey. In winter, the story of the stealthy approach and the attack may be read in the snow. Once a cougar gets into a good position for the final plunge, chances of making the kill are high. It is before this, during the initial approach, that the intended victim is most likely to escape. Either the predator is detected or circumstances prevent an approach within attacking distance. The cougar does not engage in a lengthy chase, and unsuccessful attacks usually terminate quite quickly.

If a healthy cougar ever attacks a human, it is probably because the person panics and runs. This is an exciting challenge to which the predator automatically responds. However, with increasing age and/or physical handicaps, a lion may no longer be able to successfully overpower an animal the size of a deer or elk and may therefore attack small domestic animals, such as the family dog and even an occasional human being. It is interesting that the attacks on

people are usually poorly executed. The animal is apt to approach hesitatingly, as if it were uncertain just where to bite such an unusual creature as man.

In the past fifty years there have been only eight instances in British Columbia of cougars attacking humans; it is most exceptional behavior when it does occur. Newspaper writers realize that the cougar is looked upon as a rather sensational animal and unfortunately tend to dramatize its ability as a killer.

Condemnation of the cougar as a livestock predator was widespread in early America. As a result, bounties were paid for its destruction, almost from the earliest days of settlement. The bounty system has not only been subject to fraud but it has resulted in nonselective destruction of cougar over much of the animal's range. Under the impetus of the bounty system, areas of comparative abundance were hunted with more enthusiasm than districts where a single elusive livestock predator remained at large. The bounty system has, for the most part, been replaced by the more effective use of professional hunters employed by wildlife agencies to attend to complaints in populated areas and destroy particular animals. Our slowness to admit to the waste and ineffectiveness of bounties has paralleled our reluctance to accept the cougar as a worthy inhabitant of our forests and wilderness lands.

As the facts surrounding predator-prey relationships accumulate from the many excellent studies by wildlife scientists, we have little reason to be proud of the manner in which we have persecuted the cougar in the belief that we were practicing conservation. As our knowl-

edge advances and with every new study, we are forced again and again to the conclusion that predators are not important in determining the ultimate numbers of deer, elk, or other big-game animals. The cougar does, however, contribute to stability and quality of the deer herd: first, because it disperses them over the winter range, thus lessening losses due to competition for food in restricted winter habitats; second, because it tends to prey on individuals that are less alert or for some reason less fit to survive. (The hunter, on the other hand, is not selective in removing the weak or less fit—he wants the biggest and the best.) Biologists firmly believe that the mountain lion has contributed to the evolution and long-term survival of the large ungulate animals upon which it preys.

Here is an animal worthy of protection and management. However, its future will likely continue in jeopardy unless wilderness reserves are established to protect it and legislation devised to award it the protection of a big-game animal throughout its range. Overcoming my early fear and condemnation of the cougar, I have found it personally satisfying to have participated in the removal of bounties and finally to have been among those wildlife administrators to elevate the cougar to the status of a game animal in British Columbia. It is noteworthy that all experienced cougar hunters with whom I have come in contact in British Columbia hold cougars in high regard and have enthusiastically sought greater recognition for them.

Hunting this elusive animal for sport is exciting. The distant baying of hounds as the dogs bark "treed" is not easily forgotten, especially when physical endurance is required to follow the hounds over rough terrain. Many British Columbia cougars grace the records of the Boone and Crockett Club trophy competition. It is preferable that this fine game animal be hunted for sport and appreciated as a trophy and as an interesting creature of the wild rather than destroyed as an obnoxious predator.

Between college years at Yale, William G. Sheldon spent summers on scientific expeditions of the United States National Museum to western Canada, and in 1933 he joined a search by the American Museum for the giant panda in interior China. Since obtaining his Ph.D. at Cornell University in 1948, he has been Leader of the Cooperative Wildlife Research Unit at the University of Massachusetts.

Dr. Sheldon's research in life histories of birds and mammals has led to publication of numerous articles and the definitive *Book of the American Woodcock,* for which he received the Special Act Award of the Bureau of Sport Fisheries and Wildlife. He has also won the John Pearce Memorial Award from the Northeastern Section of The Wildlife Society. One of his "favorite" mammals, the bobcat, is his subject in the following account.

THE BOBCAT

WILLIAM G. SHELDON

A silver trout flashed from the bottom of the crystal-clear water and made a splash in a vain effort to take the fly I was casting. The setting was a beautiful small lake in the pristine wilderness of interior Nova Scotia. As the sun dipped below a rim of virgin hemlocks I made another cast from the bow of the canoe. Soundlessly, like a shadow, an animal appeared on top of a granite boulder on the shore. Within two hundred feet of the canoe, that ghost of the woodlands, a large bobcat, had come out of the trees to drink. He stopped and stared at me. Then, in an instant, he melted back into the forest. This was the first bobcat I had ever seen, a vision I can never forget.

Many men have spent a lifetime in the haunts of this picturesque predator without having ever seen it. I have been fortunate in seeing several and have studied their habits and behavior by tracking them in the snow.

In the early folklore of New England, tales of the wildcat and its prowess as a fighter are legendary. Wild in nature and of ugly disposition if cornered, this shy, secretive denizen of our wild lands has shown remarkable tenacity in surviving in the face of burgeoning human populations and often relentless persecution by man.

Not to be confused with its northern relative the Canadian lynx, which has longer hair and ear tufts, larger feet, and a black tip on its stubby tail, the bobcat, sometimes called bay lynx, varies in color from reddish brown to light gray and is streaked with black. The black on the tail tip appears only on the upper surface. A mature male may weigh as much as forty pounds and the females around fifteen to twenty pounds. Although the Canadian lynx appears larger, its weight approximates that of the bobcat.

The lynx confines its range to the evergreen forests and mountains of Canada and Alaska, whereas the bobcat has a range encompassing all the United States, southern Canada, and northern Mexico. I have seen these wildcats in the deserts of the Southwest, where they seem as much at home as in the deep snow and subzero temperatures of the North.

In late February or early March in the Northeast while snow still covers the ground, male and female consort during the breeding season. (The famous naturalist Bachman records that the caterwauling of the male bobcat during breeding is very loud and virtually indistinguishable from the cougar.) If the female does not find a mate, she may come into heat repeatedly. It is therefore not surprising that throughout the range of the bobcat, kits may be born in any month of the year. (In the Northeast very small cats with milk teeth have been killed in late October suggesting breeding in April or May, two months after the season.) To give birth, the female seeks a den in a rock ledge, under an uprooted tree, or in a hollow log or tree hole. Her usual number of kits is three or four, although litter sizes of seven have been recorded. The kits' eyes open in about two weeks, and soon thereafter they crawl to the entrance of the den to cavort and play much like fox pups. Later in summer and fall they follow their mother and stay with her often until midwinter, when they have become efficient hunters on their own. The extent of the parental duties of the father is not known, but it is suspected that he may breed more than one receptive female and remain independent of the family. Contrary to sentimental tales of the father helping to wean the kittens, he probably devotes all energies after the mating season to a celibate search for food.

The voice of bobcats is very much like domestic cats but intensified in volume several times. It spits, growls, hisses, purrs, and caterwauls. Cats I have kept in captivity usually growled, laid their ears back, and glowered at me with their intense yellow eyes whenever I approached the cage.

Most people do not think of cats as good swimmers. My observations, however, indicate that the bobcat is buoyant, fast, and will swim simply to get from one place to another. In January 1955 in central Massachusetts when the temperature was below zero and over a foot of snow covered the ground, I saw a medium-size bobcat, chased by two hounds, swim across a swiftly flowing small river and climb a tree on the far side. During the summer of 1967, I learned that a fisherman killed one with an oar while it was swimming between two islands in Quabbin Reservation, Massachusetts.

Unlike foxes, raccoons, bears, and a few other carnivores which are omni-

vorous like man, bobcats eat only meat. I have learned a good deal about bobcat food habits in the Northeast from following cats in the snow and examining the stomach contents of over one hundred turned in for bounty. Like most mammals these wild cats feed on animals which are abundant and can be readily caught. The bread and butter item of cats in the southern part of their range is the cottontail rabbit, and in the northern section the snowshoe hare. Many other

mammals as well as birds are preyed upon, including gray, red, and flying squirrels, mice, deer, porcupines, woodchucks, domestic cats, wild turkey, ruffed grouse, and a variety of smaller birds.

Although bobcats are chiefly nocturnal, they occasionally hunt during the evening, early morning, or even at midday in the winter, when food may be scarce and difficult to capture. In years of snowshoe hare abundance I have observed concentrations of bobcat tracks in thick spruces where these lagomorphs abound. In other years cats extend their hunting to mixed forests of hardwood and softwood. Being opportunistic hunters, they often catch squirrels of different kinds, an occasional grouse, and mice in open fields.

Do bobcats kill porcupines with impunity? Most carcasses of bobcats examined from New Hampshire had one or more porcupine quills but none of the cats seemed to have noticeably suffered.

They apparently flip a porcupine over with one of their strong forepaws and attack the rodent on its vulnerable underside. One cat had two quills which had pierced the stomach wall, but seemed to have been in good condition. Several quills in other cats were emerging on parts of the face where they appeared to have been diverted by the bones of the skull. It would be hard to prove that a bobcat has ever died from attacking a porcupine. Although an inexperienced young cat might receive a lethal dose of quills, it would crawl into a hole before dying and not be found. One old male bobcat, even with its hind quarters nearly paralyzed from bird shot, was able to kill a porcupine. Quills had pierced both front legs, face, and chest, but it was a good meal!

Feral domestic cats are taken by bobcats but not always as a prey item. There is one apparently well documented record of hybridization between a large black domestic tabby cat and a wild tom bobcat. This occurred at the ranch of N. Melkowski six miles west of Byfield, North Dakota. Their domestic tabby frequently hunted in the breaks south of the ranch. In early June she produced a litter of seven kittens. Four were like the mother, coal black, long tails, but unusually large feet. The other three had bobtails, large feet, tufted ears, and were colored gray like young bobcats. Unfortunately, the entire litter was killed by a domestic tomcat on June 27 when the kits were about two to three weeks old.

The bobcat is not a serious deer predator but will not hesitate to attack a deer which may be weakened by winter starvation, or other infirmities such as old age or gunshot wounds. In tracking bobcats which hunt stealthily and depend on their sight in making stalks, I observed many dashes made after deer, but in most cases these "attacks" were futile. If a bobcat does not catch its prey in the first chase, it quickly gives up.

None of the North American cats can outrun a healthy deer that is not hampered by crust and deep snow. Deer are taken by stealth. Two kills found in Massachusetts were small deer passing under a rock ledge which offered a vantage point for a waiting bobcat. Bobcats jump on the back of a deer and severely bite its neck until it collapses. In contrast, Canadian lynx have been observed killing mountain sheep by pouncing on their backs and biting their eyes out. Cougar kill deer and elk by using their strong forearm to grasp the head and wrench it back, breaking the neck of its prey.

The sense of smell, which is probably not as highly developed as in other carnivores, plays some part in the bobcat's prowess as a hunter. I have observed places in the snow where bobcats have waited, crouched on top of a stone wall or near a burrow entrance until a cottontail rabbit emerged.

The bobcat has become a prized game animal in many areas in the East. Successful hunters, using trained hounds, must have fortitude and stamina. This wild cat is more reluctant to "tree" than a cougar, and many a hunt requires miles of rigorous travel. Even the most skilled hunters rarely get a bobcat; it is a sport that calls forth high ethics among sportsmen.

It is deplorable that this secretive and colorful furbearer yields a bounty in many states. In cases where an occasional bobcat may take toll of such vulnerable domestic animals as sheep, it should be eliminated by limited and local control measures. The bobcat is one of the few symbols of wilderness still remaining in more settled parts of the country. It is a valuable resource which we should be forever vigilant to preserve.

BROWSERS AND GRAZERS

Caleb Glazener became a biologist in the Texas Game and Fish Commission in 1940. From 1946 to 1955 he directed the Wildlife Restoration Division, and was then made assistant director of the Wilder Wildlife Foundation. He is also professor of wildlife management at the Technological College in Lubbock, Texas.

Mr. Glazener is a fellow of the Texas Academy of Science and has served as vice-president of The Wildlife Society. His research has been primarily on geese and other aquatic birds, the wild turkey, and white-tailed deer. This has resulted in about thirty-five technical and popular publications, of which his forty-page chapter on the Rio Grande turkey, in *The Wild Turkey and Its Management,* is notable. Caleb Glazener has a lifelong familiarity with the peccary and has chosen it as the subject of his chapter.

THE COLLARED PECCARY

CALEB GLAZENER

The pickup skidded to a stop and two of us jumped out and sprinted toward the deer trap, hoping to prevent the escape of a big white-tailed buck. We were about halfway across a dense stand of waist-high grass when an explosion of sound and motion erupted around us. An undetermined number of peccaries sprang up, grunting, snorting, and running headlong in all directions. They possibly were as scared as the two fellows who had awakened them.

That experience made me question the stories my great-grandmother told me about peccaries. Like most Texans, she called them by their Spanish name, *javelinas* (ha-va-lee-nas). She told about bands of one hundred or more of these vicious wild pigs. Supposedly, they were always on the lookout for lone, foot-traveling humans to attack on sight. So quick and furious was their charge that even the best hunter had time for only one shot before climbing a convenient tree. The ferocious band always surrounded the tree, squealing in anger and clacking their teeth throughout the night before moving away. Later stories emphasized the disastrous consequence of crippling one of a band, or of catching a squealing pig.

Subsequently, as a farm boy in South Texas, I heard and read many contradictory stories about the disposition and behavior of peccaries. Later, as a wildlife biologist with the Texas Game and Fish Commission, I learned about them through personal experience.

Most peccaries in Texas are over the South Texas Plain, the lower end of the Gulf Coast Prairie, and the southern and western edges of the Edwards Plateau. But there are some in the Big Bend and along the Pecos River. Preferred habitat includes stands of prickly-pear cactus, desert shrubs, or "chaparral," and mesquite.

At times I have seen fifty to seventy-five peccaries daily for several weeks in succession. Again, the same locality revealed none for two weeks or longer. One October afternoon a big boar galloped up to U. S. Highway 83 south of Catarina, Texas, and ran parallel to my car for nearly one hundred yards before turning back in the direction from which he had come. At sunrise on another day, my wife and I saw a lone animal cross U. S. Highway 290 ahead of us, a few miles east of Fort Stockton. We watched it trot steadily on through a sparse stand of short brush until it disappeared in the distance.

Peccaries do much of their feeding at night, beginning at dusk and stopping about sunrise. How constant it is through the night I do not yet know. Through late spring and summer I have watched small bands move each morning from their night feeding areas to their bedding sites. In cooler seasons and on ranges where they are not molested, they feed at various hours of the day. In fact, during a four-day, subfreezing period in January 1962, one band foraged throughout each day—possibly because it was warmer then.

Foods vary with the seasons. Late in the usually mild South Texas winters, succulent grasses and forbs attract peccaries to roadsides and openings in brush or woods. From May through August, as berries, wild grapes, mesquite beans, Mexican persimmons, and other wild fruits ripen and drop, they become successive centers of attention for foraging bands. Through all seasons, regardless of what else may be available, peccaries shift intermittently to prickly-pear cactus, taking both the leaf pads and the ripened, purplish-red fruits, called tunas. The latter they bite off one at a time, apparently ignoring their clusters of tiny spines.

In feeding on leaf pads, the animal first breaks off a segment of one or more pads, either by pawing it with a forefoot or by biting and pulling. Once the pad is on the ground, the peccary pushes it back and forth, first on one side and then on the other. This operation—performed jointly with feet, nose, and mouth—removes some of the long, sharp spines. The peccary then bites off a portion, chews it vigorously, and swallows it, including any remaining spines.

Feeding bands, I have watched, moved slowly and in irregular order. Individuals would be fifteen to twenty yards apart at times, but younger ones tended to stay closer to their mothers. On reaching a ranch road, or even a public road, the band would normally follow it for some distance and feed along the road shoulders or in the borrow ditches.

Peccary bedding habits also vary with the seasons. On a summer day in Brooks County I came upon six adults sleeping under the shade of a dense live oak

motte. They were in scooped-out sandy beds, spaced about two feet apart. I've also frequently seen them on the Welder Refuge at the edge of a creek bottom sleeping underneath a thicket of shrubs and grapevines. In the summer they may sleep on top of a thick layer of leaf litter. In the winter they burrow underneath the litter, sometimes singly, sometimes by twos, threes, or fours. On occasion they lie alternately head to tail, parallel, after the fashion of domestic hogs. In the Big Bend, peccaries bed down in caves or under overhanging ledges, where, incidentally, I've found quantities of hair and great numbers of fleas.

Time and again I have approached close to feeding peccaries, moving slowly, quietly, and upwind toward them. So long as I remained motionless when one raised its head, it took no notice of me. Movement or sound at close range brought immediate lifting of heads, alert flaring of ears, and erection of hair along their backs. Noses began twitching, and sniffing became audible as they tested the air for my scent. Shortly, each animal faced in my direction and their musky odor came strongly to my nostrils.

If I were exceptionally close when they discovered me, there was always that warning sound of their snapping teeth, then either a slow turn and an orderly drifting away or a sudden wheeling and headlong flight. The latter reaction was invariable if my vehicle rounded a bend in a brush-bordered road and took a band by surprise. Under such circumstances I've watched individuals attempt to crash through impenetrable walls of shrubbery, only to be thrown back by a mass of interwoven branches. Sometimes a second desperate lunge at the same spot followed, before the startled animal turned to an opening through which it could escape.

Peccary musk comes from a gland under the skin along the midline of the rump, just forward of where the tail should be. Secretion is through a duct, the opening of which is slightly rimmed and readily visible when a startled animal is facing away from a person. At such times, while hair on the back stands erect, that along the rump tends to flare outward and leave the opening of the duct exposed.

I have seen newly born peccaries in every month of the year but more commonly in midspring and midfall. At those times, several age classes of young might be found in the same band. Although there are normally two pigs at birth, there is frequently only one survivor after a few weeks.

A sow and her young apparently communicate and maintain contact by a combination of scent and sound. When together, they do much sniffing at each other; when separated, the pigs constantly grunt, whine, and squeal. The tawny little ones suckle at any given opportunity, either while the sow is on foot or while she lies to rest. Herd activity, including frequent dashes to escape real or suspected danger, seems to keep the pigs hungry, as well as limiting their body fat.

On two occasions in Brooks County, I caught small peccaries by hand, letting them squeal to see what the herd would do. I staged each chase in a nice, wide clearing, my pickup readily accessible if needed as a haven from a resentful sow. However, in each instance the band of adults and other young dashed away without so much as looking back. On another occasion, I found remains of a pig—both hind feet, one kidney, and some hair—in and under a wolf trap. All other sign was blotted out by the numerous tracks of a coyote that must have enjoyed an unexpected meal. In this instance, another sow obviously deserted her young under threat of danger.

Another time I drove between a day-old pig and its mother. When I stepped down, the youngster came right to me, sniffing at my boots. The anxious mother circled nervously some yards away, alternately advancing and retreating. She kept up an almost constant castanet-staccato snapping of her teeth, suggestive of intermittent bursts of machine-gun fire. The pig punctuated its exploration of my boots with a series of soft grunts and squeals, each one causing the sow to begin another partial approach. When I finally got into my car and backed away, there was a quick reunion, accompanied by further sniffing, grunting, and squealing.

I learned, too, that it is not necessarily suicidal to wound one of a band of peccaries. A first shot crippled an adult female, and a second one was required to stop her squealing. Her companions, meantime, all left at top speed, without any hesitation. However, a squealing female being taken from a live trap brought a band on the run—forcing the trapping crew to jump up on the trap and remain there for quite a while.

Even when dogs approach them, peccaries usually try to escape. But if the dogs press the chase and overtake a fleeing band, there follows a dramatic change. One such event I witnessed ended at a clump of thorny lotebush. Five adult peccaries turned at bay there, heads out and teeth snapping furiously. Two experienced dogs spread right and left, barking lustily from a distance of several feet. A third, inexperienced and unobserving, checked himself too late. There was a dust-blurred flurry of violent action, a lightning-fast chatter of snapping teeth, and the dog was ripped and torn. He did not live long enough to profit from his experience with cornered peccaries.

Fighting occurs between individual peccaries, too. Many times I have heard out in the brush sudden outbursts of angry squealing and the sharp cracking sound of teeth. Solitary old boars are fairly common, frequently displaying torn ears and other battle scars. They have presumably been defeated and driven out of their bands by younger males.

One night in 1963, students at the Welder Refuge heard sounds of conflict in brushy cover near the headquarters site. Through use of flashlights they spotted two struggling boars. One had his canine teeth fully embedded in the right side of his opponent's neck and was straining for even deeper penetration. By the time I arrived, only the loser remained, bleeding freely and moving with difficulty. The next morning we followed his erratic trail about a hundred yards before losing it in the dense brush. Four months later the complete skeleton of an adult boar was found another hundred yards away. We assumed that the crippled combatant had managed to travel that far before dying of his wounds.

Peccaries captured while very young can become fascinating subjects for those who wish to study them. However, they are not suitable playmates for children, for as they approach maturity they become more temperamental and increasingly hazardous. In fact, there is hardly an appropriate place for a hand-fed, semidomesticated peccary outside of a zoo. I have never known one to come to a happy end. One "pet" developed a selective taste for chickens in the ranchyard and had to be disposed of. Another apparently tried to bite the hind foot of a horse and received a kick that left its neck in a permanent kink. Two, kept as college mascots, severely wounded the school's president in an unprovoked attack.

One pair of orphaned pigs brought to the Welder Refuge knew only to snap, bite—and squeal. When offered rubber nipples on bottles, fingers, or food, their response was the same. Another young male would lie for hours alongside a boot belonging to the student who fed and cared for him. Gradually he came to accept other persons if they fed him and permitted him to make all the overtures in getting acquainted. It was a mistake, however, for a stranger to attempt to pat him on the back or head. Even though his teeth had been "tipped" to remove their needle-like points, his bite was quick and painful. We finally penned him for the protection of visitors who ignored warnings about his resentment of their advances.

There has probably been as much controversy about the eating quality of peccary meat as about their temperament and behavior. In my opinion, properly braised and seasoned cuts from a young female are distinctively delicious, and any cut from a boar is distinctive to the point of unpalatability. This, too, is based on my experience. Therefore, when visitors begin asking whether peccaries are good to eat or whether they are vicious and dangerous, my initial reply is usually, "Do you want me to tell you the truth or what you expect to hear?"

With doctorates in zoology from the universities of California and Michigan, Lloyd Glenn Ingles taught biology, and from 1952 to 1965 was department chairman and head of life sciences at Fresno State College. Upon retirement he was given the Outstanding Professor Award by the California State Colleges.

Dr. Ingles is recognized as a top-rank naturalist of the Pacific Coast, being author of over eighty papers and three books. The latest, *Mammals of the Pacific States,* was published by Stanford University Press. His specialties are the ecology of pocket gophers, the California gray squirrel, and the Audubon cottontail. For relaxation, he makes nature photographs in color for showing at international salons. "Doe-face," the story of a mule deer, is a product of professional observation at his leisure-time cabin in the Sierra Nevada near Yosemite National Park.

DOE-FACE, THE MULE DEER
LLOYD G. INGLES

The stillness of the Sierra morning was broken by a loud crash in the willow thicket. A large gray mountain coyote suddenly emerged and bounded away in short jerky gallops. Close behind it ran Doe-face, an angry, big-eared, wide-eyed mule deer doe. Her hair bristled, her tail was erect, and she snorted "Schfew!" furiously several times. Beside her pranced her last year's fawn— now two-thirds grown. When the coyote reached a safe distance, it paused and looked back hungrily for a few moments. Then it trotted, with lowered tail, on into the forest. The "villain" often accused of killing deer had been routed.

It was the middle of June and Doe-face had just returned to her summer range in the red fir forest of the Sierra Nevada. On the way back up the mountains, she had shed her gray winter coat and was now a bright reddish brown. She was obviously pregnant.

As the remaining snowbanks in the high country melted, she spent most of the daylight hours chewing her cud as she lay in a dense clump of little firs on the warm southern slope. It seemed as if she were always hungry.

Every day about 4 P.M. she would amble over to a chinquapin bush to nibble its light green new growth of leaves. One night she ate twenty-two half-grown snow plants down to the ground. Another night she almost completely devoured a mushroom the size of a washbasin. After three weeks, her sharp-pointed triangular tracks were all over her home range.

She disappeared on the fourth of July. For three days no one saw her. When she returned one evening, it was quite evident that she had fawned. Although I watched her closely during the daylight hours for the next week, she never betrayed the location of her young. However, late one afternoon something appeared to be moving in a patch of ferns at the edge of the meadow and my binoculars revealed the large pointed ear of a tiny spotted fawn responding to annoying insects. The fawn was about two feet long and lay very quietly with its head and neck outstretched on the ground. As long as it lay still, its camouflage made it almost invisible.

My large German shepherd dog passed along the trail without sensing the little fawn only five feet away. A few moments later, he was yelping and running down the trail, hotly pursued by Doe-face. Nothing less than a mountain lion or a bear would have dared to face those sharp prodding hooves. A doe with a newly born fawn seems to have a special fund of courage.

Was there another fawn? If so, Doe-face would have certainly dropped it in a different place; a pair would be more likely to attract attention and would be in more danger if one were discovered. It was not until the second of August that we learned she had twins. When we first saw them, both were butting her udder vigorously for the rich milk. (Although the fawns actually begin to browse after they are a week old, they continue to nurse heavily for at least two months.)

Doe-face had little fear of us. She would come close to our cabin to eat watermelon and other fruits that we left out on a nearby log. The fawns, however, were always shy; they watched from about fifty yards' distance and would bounce away at any unusual movement or noise. As the fawns grew, they browsed farther away from their mother, their spots became dimmer, and they gamboled about chasing each other over the forest floor.

One night late in October, I heard a great commotion in the forest about two hundred yards from our cabin. A deer was screaming and another was snorting loudly and rushing wildly about. It was cloudy—no moon—not even starlight. The cries and thrashings were quick and frightening. The next morning I went into the woods to investigate. The female fawn was dead. Its body had been partially covered by the killer with pine needles and litter. One shoulder and front leg were missing. Viscera was strewn about on the bloody ground. Tracks of a mountain lion and one or more cubs in the soft earth told the story. They would doubtless return to finish their meal.

A few days later the first big snowstorm started the mule deer on their long annual trek down the great mountains to their winter feeding grounds in the brush-covered foothills forty miles away. Doe-face and her fawn were among them. They traveled along the age-old trails of their ancestors. But these routes were well known to hunters and the season had not yet ended. Many times Doe-face and her faintly spotted fawn were

panicked by the crack of a high-powered rifle aimed at mature bucks. Finally, however, they came through the long gauntlet of fire to spend the winter with the other surviving mule deer on a range about one-seventh the size of the one-hundred-acre coniferous forest and meadow of their summer home.

The breeding season began about the last week in November, and there was a noticeable restlessness among the deer of the migratory herd. The bucks had been rushing around for some time rubbing the dead velvet off their antlers and polishing these weapons as they swung their heads viciously in the tough manzanitas and brushy ceanothus. Now was the time for each buck to try to prove his dominance. Sometimes there was just a clashing of antlers as one lone buck dared to challenge another with a harem. Sometimes blood was drawn, but usually such contests were little more than pushing and shoving matches until one buck had had enough and would run away leaving the other with perhaps half a dozen does. Battle to death rarely occurs unless the antlers of the two become permanently locked and the duelists starve to death.

By the first week in December the ancient routine was well under way. The dominant buck followed the small harem about, frequently checking each one for communicative sex scents. Occasionally he would charge off after a flanking lesser buck. By the first of the year, most of the receptive does had been bred. It would be about two hundred days until the birth of the young fawns—nearly all fathered by the strongest, most virile of the surviving bucks.

By the first of the new year the bucks had begun to lose their antlers, though some carried them until March. Testicular hormonal changes caused decalcification at the base of the antlers and there was nothing left to hold them on. As the skin grew over the wound, it made patches of velvet. The bucks became as docile as does and formed small groups which often remained together as they moved slowly up the mountains to the summer range. They no longer seemed interested in the does or their offspring. There were no more contests or combats.

Sometime after the antlers were shed, the bucks began developing new ones. Secretions from the hypophysis, a ductless gland at the base of the brain, started the growth of bony knobs under the skin. Even in mature bucks, they were only an inch long by the end of April.

As the rising temperatures pushed the snow line farther up the mountains, the bands of mule deer started back to their summer home. They drifted slowly up the slopes, browsing leisurely on the new growth of the ceanothus, manzanita, and mountain mahogany. There were no hunters now.

When Doe-face arrived back in our cabin area, we knew for the first time the sex of her last year's surviving fawn. He was a little spike buck, nearly two-thirds grown. His unbranched antlers were about as long as his ears and were covered with velvety skin richly provided with blood vessels to carry the food to the growing bony antlers until about the middle of September. Then the blood supply would automatically cease; the velvet would die and have to be rubbed off.

By mid-June, Doe-face already had another set of twins and a new annual cycle had begun. For Doe-face and her kind, the annual trek up and down the great mountains is a way of life, as it was for their ancestors. Their peculiar genetic constitution compels them to live as they do. Another herd of mule deer living farther down in the foothills looks almost exactly like the migrant deer, but they lack this instinct to move up and down with the seasons.

Doe-face is a large doe—standing about forty inches high at the shoulders. She belongs to a subspecies known as the California mule deer, or granite bucks. Farther north and east of the range of the granite bucks lives another, even larger subspecies—the Rocky Mountain mule deer, or lava bucks. Southeast is a smaller mule deer called the burro deer. Across the San Joaquin Valley in the Coast Range live the black-tailed mule deer.

Each of these races has its own distinct physical characteristics, and all differ in behavior as well. Where the geographic ranges of these subspecies overlap, however, the animals interbreed and their features intergrade. Because they interbreed freely, biologists consider all the races to be a single species of mule deer (*Odocoileus hemionus*).

East from Oregon and the Rocky Mountains is a distinctly separate species —the white-tailed deer (*Odocoileus virginianus*). The mule deer differs in having much larger mule-like ears and a black-tipped tail; the antlers of the buck branch dichotomously—that is, the points do not come from a single beam.

Contrary to the belief of many hunters, the number of points on a deer's antlers is only a rough indicator of a buck's age. It is a much better gauge of its physical condition. Very old bucks,

twelve years of age or more, may have low, long, wide-spreading antlers with only one or two points. With teeth worn nearly to the gums, these decadent deer, although they have so far successfully eluded the predators and the rifles, cannot live much longer.

Migrating animals frequently have special problems of survival. In the case of the mule deer of Doe-face's tribe, there are two serious ones, both created by man. First, the winter range of the deer in the foothills is being rapidly cleared away for ranches, with the cattle, sheep, and horses taking most of the available forage.

Secondly, mountain lions, coyotes, and bobcats are still being removed by traps, poison, and hunting, especially from the winter feeding grounds. The result is that locally there may be too many deer returning to the summer range, especially in national and state parks where they are not hunted. The killing of Doe-face's female fawn was an age-old predation that actually benefits the species by holding the population down. Hormonal means of population control are also known in deer and other animals. However, where the lions and other predators have been reduced or eliminated, the feeding grounds are often overbrowsed. The range is damaged and the deer have to be removed or starve to death.

What is the answer? Hundreds of research biologists, their universities, conservation departments, and other agencies are determining natural and artificial methods of population controls, for Doe-face and her migratory kind must be perpetuated for posterity.

147

Richard J. McNeil has specialized in deer since joining the Michigan Conservation Department as a biologist in 1957. He obtained his doctorate degree in 1963 from the University of Michigan with a study of white-tailed deer population and economics. Later he assisted New Zealand authorities in establishing a research program on the introduced red deer.

Dr. McNeil is now an assistant professor of conservation at Cornell University. In addition to teaching classes, he carries on an extension program via radio, television, and printed media to inform the public concerning white-tailed deer. He is also conducting a sociological study of hunters and fishermen, attempting to identify and describe them and to measure their attitudes.

CRIPPLED DOE

RICHARD J. McNEIL

The trapdoors were closed. Lee Queal and I approached quietly, walking down a gentle slope and into the old meadow. A few shaggy junipers stood around the trap site and only a cricket interrupted the quiet, warm evening.

We peered through a crack in the Stephenson trap, an ungainly wooden box, nine feet long, with drop-doors at both ends. Perhaps this time our corn and molasses had attracted something bigger than the raccoons, opossums, and squirrels which were forever springing our traps and the wasps which had found them to be almost irresistible nest sites.

A large deer—a doe—was lying quietly inside. Quickly we arranged our tools nearby and spread our net in front of the door. A reef on the rope to open the door, a few kicks on the side of the trap, and suddenly a deer and two men were thrashing around in the net. The doe's impact carried us several feet from the trap. We quickly immobilized her legs and worked the net off her body.

We blindfolded the doe and she immediately became much calmer. A quick pinch with a pair of pliers and she wore an aluminum tag in her ear.

The little strip of metal bore a number, 514627, and the legend "Please notify Mich. Dept. Conservation, Lansing."

Normally it took only a few minutes to put tags and a colored plastic streamer in a deer's ears and a numbered collar around its neck, to make a few measurements, take a small sample of blood from a vein in its ear, and then release it. But this doe was different. Somehow in the trap she had torn her skin for about ten inches along her elbow. So after placing the first identification tag in her ear, we set about repairing the injury. The wound was clean so we carefully sutured it shut with about a dozen little metal clips, aligning the edges of the wound carefully and hoping that our somewhat makeshift surgery would be adequate.

We finished our work as quickly as possible, but it had taken nearly a half hour. The sun had gone down and the summer air was turning chilly. We stepped back, lifting off the blindfold as we released the doe's legs. We hoped she would move off quietly and, indeed, she lay there a moment as if she had no fear. But then she scrambled to her feet. She fled across the field with terrific bounds, and with each leap we worried that she would tear loose the sutures.

Almost every night we drove the old trails, shining our spotlights over the meadows and into the woodlots. And each time we searched especially carefully in the open field where the big doe had been trapped. After several weeks, when summer had gone and the dry oak leaves rattled on dormant branches, we became resigned. She must not have survived. No doubt the sutures had not held, or the wound had become infected and the doe had died.

Then one dark night our spotlight picked up a big doe with a white collar. There was no mistaking the black "7" on the collar. She grazed slowly between the junipers, finally turning and showing us her injured side. No scar was visible; the healing had been excellent. And only a slight limp, visible when she ran, betrayed her history.

After that she lived regularly in her rather small home range in the oak woodlot and the juniper meadow. She had a fawn with her most of the time. Probably she was one and a half years old, and had had her first fawn that spring, since food conditions were good in southern Michigan. We had not examined her teeth while we were handling her because we wanted to excite her as little as possible. If she were one and a half, she would now be losing her deciduous, or baby, teeth, replacing them with the permanent molars and premolars which would gradually wear away during her lifetime.

She was eating much coarser and harder foods now that summer was ending. Instead of grazing in the meadows, she spent the cold evenings browsing more on the twigs of the dogwoods and aspens. Dawn and dusk found her in the oak woods, searching for acorns on the forest floor.

November was the breeding season. The antlers of the bucks had reached maximum size in September and then began to harden. The furry skin, called velvet, died and peeled away in long shreds. More velvet was lost when the bucks began thrashing bushes and small trees during times of sexual excitement. The necks of the older bucks were swollen with fluids and the bucks presented imposing sights as they began a season of wandering in search of does.

Several times we saw bucks following and pestering the crippled doe. After avoiding them for many days, she probably came into heat about mid-November. She would be receptive for perhaps only a day, and after mating, the buck would leave. He would then look for another doe in heat, following her scent in the air or on the ground until he found her or until another buck drove him away.

Young bucks, only half a year old, were also playing sexual games, even occasionally trying to mount a doe or another fawn. Although a few female fawns would become pregnant, the young bucks would not become sexually mature for another year.

We saw the crippled doe frequently, almost always in the juniper field, or in the nearby woods. Her fawn was nearly as large as the doe by now and had lost her spots when she shed her summer coat.

Autumn was a good time for the crippled doe. Food was still plentiful. There was no hunting on the George Reserve until later, although occasionally a poacher would be found prowling around the seven-foot fence surrounding the area. Outside, the bucks were moving in search of does, and many bucks fell victim to automobiles on autumn nights.

As the days grew shorter and the weather colder the crippled doe spent more time in the shelter of the woodlot, or down in the swamp where there was less wind and she could maintain her body heat more easily. Her gray winter coat had long hollow hairs over a fine underfur and provided such good insu-

lation that she could bed down in the snow all night without any snow melting or ice forming. She bedded down in a different spot each night, sometimes in the warm swamp, but often on a hillside under a lone juniper tree. She wandered more widely now, browsing on hardwood twigs and digging for acorns through a foot of snow. Her fawn still accompanied her most of the time.

The bucks lost their antlers in late December or early January. As the antlers were dropped, mice quickly began gnawing on them, and only rarely did remnants last until spring.

Our trapping work continued, and down in the swamps where the snow became most heavily crisscrossed with tracks, we also set snares. Not snares to kill or capture, but self-attaching collars which would be placed around a deer's neck as she walked along a trail. We put out fifty of these collars on our two square miles and eventually a dozen deer, including the crippled doe's daughter, were wearing blue plastic collars with numbered discs dangling from them.

The deer which had gone into the winter sleek and fat gradually became more angular in contours, as fat deposits under the skin and around the heart and kidneys were drawn upon. The acorns were all eaten by now, and only woody twigs and the thorny junipers were available for food. The woodlots were silent, except for the chickadees and blue jays. At night an occasional red fox padded silently across the old field, digging here for a mouse, smelling an old rabbit track there.

Winter is a grim season for deer. On the George Reserve, deer were harvested then, under State Conservation Department permits. Deer drives were held, with dozens of people walking through the swamps, pushing the unknowing deer to the spots where the shooters were waiting. The dead deer were brought in for autopsy and butchering, and we were pleased that the crippled doe wasn't among them.

Starvation was no problem in southern Michigan, but food was scarce in the winter, and hungry deer were less able to escape from marauding dogs which often chased them on the crusted snow. And lungworms, present in almost all the deer, imposed an additional stress during the winter.

Late in the winter we found the daughter of the crippled doe dead in a swamp. Her body was frozen into an icy pool and half buried with ice and snow. Perhaps a poacher had shot her, or her lungworms had caused a verminous pneumonia, or she had become exhausted and then chilled after being chased by dogs. Her life-span had been eight short months, even then longer than for many deer.

With the coming of spring, snow began to melt, and the crippled doe, attracted by the bare patches on the southern slopes, fed more in the daytime. As more snow disappeared, so did the danger from free-ranging dogs. New life burst forth and the deer gorged themselves on the fresh green sprouts, many getting diarrhea from the quick change in diet.

As the ponds thawed, pickerel weeds and water lilies began to grow, and the crippled doe spent many mornings up to her belly in the water, immersing her head like a moose and pulling up the rich green plants. She was five months pregnant now, with twins as we later found out. She ate prodigiously, both in recovering from the winter period of semistarvation and in response to the demands of the growing fetuses inside her. Her winter coat was very shaggy now, as bunches of long gray hair began to fall out. By mid-May she had her summer coat, a red one, much thinner than her winter coat. She looked especially sleek and healthy in the evenings, and she appeared almost coppery-colored in the strange lighting at sunset.

The bucks, too, looked fine in late spring. Their new antlers were starting to grow, and by the middle of May the antlers on some had begun to branch.

In late May, about six and a half months after she had mated, the crippled doe delivered her fawns. For a few days she had isolated herself in a small brushy area. Then suddenly one evening when her eyes glowed green in the beam of our spotlight, there was a second pair of eyes glowing near her feet.

We stopped the car and rapidly moved in on the spot where the doe had been. Our flashlights quickly found the fawn. It was crouched quietly on the forest floor. Its neck was stretched out and its head lying on the ground. It made no attempt to run as we walked up and gently put our hands on it. Its soft hooves told us that it had been born within the last few hours; we already knew it was less than three or four days old because it hadn't run when we approached.

The doe stood nervously in the nearby darkness, stamping a foot and snorting loudly while we weighed and measured the fawn. It was a male and weighed seven and a half pounds. As it was too small to wear a collar, we put a metal tag and an orange plastic streamer in its ear.

As we turned to go we discovered its twin, a runt, lying dead under a frond of bracken fern. It weighed less than five pounds and was probably too weak to nurse during the critical few hours after birth. And, so, the crippled doe, just two years old, had already lost two offspring.

The next evening we surprised a fox carrying the front half of a tiny fawn toward its den. She had probably found the dead runt, eaten part, and was carrying the remainder to her pups. The fox dropped the carcass when she saw us. We waited a long time nearby but she never returned. The following day the fragile carcass was swarming with ants and flies, and by a day later it had almost completely disappeared.

We saw the crippled doe often during the summer, sometimes in the late afternoon, grazing in the meadows, sometimes at night, standing nervously in the light of our spotlight. At first her fawn was seldom with her. We knew she had hidden it in a thicket somewhere and would return every few hours to nurse. Gradually, the fawn began to accompany his mother more, and we watched him butting the doe roughly as he attempted to nurse. At the age of three weeks, he was sampling bits of vegetation. His mouth was often alongside the doe's as she grazed, and occasionally he would nibble at bits of herbs projecting from the side of her mouth. In this way he no doubt was inoculated by the bacteria which his four-chambered stomach would need to help digest the woody fibers he ate.

Summer was a good time for the doe and her fawn. Food was plentiful, problems were few. Only the insects seemed to be particularly troublesome and the deer's tails were moving constantly trying to keep them away. The deer ate young sprouts of goldenrod and hawkweed in the meadow and found mushrooms in the cool woods. The fawn grew quickly, still nursing whenever the doe would let him, but was almost independent by later summer.

The crippled doe often passed by our traps, and she sometimes ate bits of corn placed just outside the door. But she never entered a trap again. Nor did her fawn.

And so the year passed. Our work was done and we left the George Reserve. Other people worked there, and occasionally reported seeing the crippled doe.

Her death was not dramatic, at least not to us. She just disappeared. After a few years, no one told us any more of seeing her. She wasn't shot during the annual deer drives. Her life-span had been perhaps five or six years, longer than that of most of her fawns. For a while her home range in the juniper meadow was probably unoccupied. Then as other fawns grew up, one found space there where competition was less, and occupied the area where once the crippled doe had lived.

The body of the doe, however it died, was quickly decomposed by insects and bacteria. Rodents ate the bones for their calcium and phosphorus. And somewhere on or near the George Reserve only a couple of metal tags remain as the legacy of the crippled doe.

153

Merle J. Rognrud entered the Montana Fish and Game Department in 1946, but took leave for two years to earn a master's degree from Utah State University with research on population, range, and productivity of the Nebo elk herd. Returning to Montana, he worked on problems of big game until 1961 when he became a district game manager for two years, then was made assistant to the department's chief of game management.

Mr. Rognrud's career has included research on game birds and the mountain goat, but his primary concern has been elk. Since he made his first pack trip into the Bob Marshall wilderness as a fourteen-year-old boy, he has studied elk on foot, horseback, skiis, and snowshoes, and censused the herds of Montana from planes, helicopters, four-wheel-drive vehicles, and snow machines.

THE ELK
MERLE J. ROGNRUD

The elk calf that we were to know later on as "Crooked Antler" weighed forty pounds when he was born on June 1, in a grass-sage meadow. Although a few newborn calves were seen with the herd of cows while their umbilical cords were still trailing, this one, like most calves, was kept in hiding. He could stagger around quite well in a few hours, but later, when he became too venturesome, his mother pushed him down and forced him to stay quiet. His neck was outstretched, head flat on the ground, and his spotted coat blended into the background. Before going off to eat, she licked and nuzzled him and returned from time to time to nurse him.

Once while she was away, when he was only five days old, he was frightened by a coyote that came too close. Instead of "freezing" as he had always done before when danger threatened, he leaped from his bed and ran, squealing, as far as he could. His mother came hurrying and barking, several "aunts" arrived, and the coyote retreated from their striking hooves. (The calf's cries had brought help that time, but they might have brought another predator.)

155

Three weeks went by and the calf joined the adults and other young. He stayed near his mother whenever he could and sometimes she played with him. Although the cows would not adopt a calf, they did take turns protecting the nurseries from coyotes and other enemies. Sometimes as many as fifty calves were being watched over by three or four cows while the rest of the herd went off to graze.

In August, Crooked Antler lost his birth coat and moulted into a tawny fall-and-winter pelage; he looked much like a small adult except that his neck hair was not as dark or prominent. During the fall migration to the foothills and throughout the winter, he traveled with his mother, although he had been weaned and could have survived by himself.

After unusually heavy snows, the pair returned with the greatly diminished herd to the spring range. It was a severe shock to the young bull when his mother repeatedly drove him away from her and began to look for a secluded place to give birth again. He finally went off dolefully and sought comfort with the other rejected yearlings. Soon after the birth of the new calf, the yearling was seen feeding near his mother with no resentment shown by either one.

Two more years passed and it was late spring again. Crooked Antler spent the quiet months eating, bedding, and ruminating several times a day. Often he was alone, but sometimes he joined his cronies. He selected the choicest green forage and after shedding his winter coat, was sleek and fat. As his antlers grew from the pedicels and then branched, still soft and sheathed in velvet, he had an accident that resulted in a crooked

right beam—and the name Crooked Antler. In spite of the injury, the antler continued to develop, and by August the full set had spread nearly five feet. Then for weeks the bull threshed the saplings and brush with his antlers and at times hooked his brow tines vigorously into the ground. The velvet rubbed off in tatters, leaving blood on the antlers and on the earth, but the friction relieved the "itching," and it felt good. A formidable set of hard antlers emerged.

September brought the rut, the busiest time of the year for all adult bulls. As Crooked Antler's sexual ardor increased, he hardly took time to eat and then not much, nor for very long. His neck was swollen and his eyes dilated. He bugled often—shrilly at first, but as the days passed he grew hoarse with effort. Other bulls answered and the forest resounded with exuberance and rivalry.

The attention of all the adult bulls now focused on the cows. Crooked Antler joined a small band and made it his harem. In the forest he found it difficult to keep the ground intact as the elk mingled with others, and so the harem changed in number and membership. Once an audacious two-year old bull tried to steal a cow when Crooked Antler's attention was diverted. The young upstart was promptly ejected.

Occasionally an older bull appeared and challenged possession but was quickly chased away. The master seldom had to actually fight another bull. His constantly threatening attitude, as he followed and herded his dozen cows, their calves and yearlings, usually kept any rival at a distance.

On one occasion, during a dispute, he stood on his hind legs and sparred with flying hooves. The intruder rose up also and struck back, then suddenly gave in, grunted, stalked off, and found solace in a mud wallow.

The young stayed with their dams in the harem as a matter of course. They seemed to be more interested in the "go-ings-on" than their mothers. Only when there was a particularly spirited encounter between their master and a challenging bull did the cows stop eating long enough to see how the contest came out. Ordinarily they couldn't have cared less.

As each cow became receptive, Crooked Antler followed her about, nuzzled her, or if she did not respond satisfactorily, he sometimes prodded her with his antlers. (Her heat period would last only twenty-four to thirty-six hours.) Since all cows do not come into heat at the same time, the herd bull was constantly checking to determine which cow was in heat or nearing that period.

By the end of October, the breeding urge had diminished until Crooked Antler no longer herded his harem. He had lost considerable weight, and now, as he ate more, he gained some of it back. But he was still tired and thin as the winter began.

This story of Crooked Antler is an introduction to the description, natural history, and management of a hardy breed of mammals, the North American elk. Less frequently but more accurately called wapiti, these animals are divided into three subspecies. The most widely distributed is the Rocky Mountain elk, while the slightly larger Olympic elk is found only in the Pacific Slope forests of Washington, Oregon, and northern California. Once threatened with extinction, the much smaller tule elk, known also as dwarf elk, lives in south-central Califor-

nia. Merriam's elk became extinct in southwestern United States about 1900.

The elk's grayish or tan coat may become somewhat bleached in late spring before it is shed to summer pelage. The head, neck, chest, and legs are a contrasting dark brown, and the buff rump patch is distinctive. Its tail is short and stubby and the neck is thick in proportion to the head. The canine teeth of the bulls are larger, better developed, and more often richly colored than those of the cows; neither sex has incisors in the upper jaw.

Only males possess antlers. Yearling bulls usually have single "spikes," sometimes of considerable length and at times forked near the tips. Two-year-old bulls most often have what are called "rag horns," consisting of three or four points on each side, while older bulls commonly have six and sometimes even seven or eight. Antlers are shed in March; the new growth begins very soon afterward and is completed by mid-August.

Standing four to five feet at the shoulders, the bulls weigh from 500 to 1,000 pounds, depending somewhat on subspecies, age, condition, and time of year. (Animals may lose up to 25 percent of their weight in winter.) The cows vary from 400 to 700 pounds.

During the peak breeding period in September the bull is in a frenzy of activity. Excited and pugnacious, he responds to any challenge, including the hunters' "bugles" and whistles. It is a great thrill to see this powerful creature come stalking through the timber and brush, or across a high mountain meadow.

At this time of year the herding instinct is compulsive among bulls, even in a limited environment. A misplaced bull

157

elk, raised by man, once herded a group of Hereford cows, keeping them away from water until the rancher was able to rescue his domestic stock. Other captive elk have been known to prevent beef bulls from breeding with their natural mates.

In the wild, cow elk seldom fail to mate. Their entire estrous cycle lasts nineteen to twenty-one days, usually measured from one heat period (twenty-four to thirty-six hours) to the next. If not fertilized during the first heat, cows will have recurring heat periods until they are bred or until the end of their estrous. During the following spring some cows either do not produce offspring or do not raise it to weaning age, but the reason for being without a calf is rarely attributed to lack of breeding.

Today, elk occupy only a part of their historic range. The species was much sought after and hunted heavily for its meat, hide, and at times for its teeth alone (formerly used as fraternal emblems), when the west was being settled. The herds were depleted and even locally exterminated.

Now reestablished in many areas, they are found in the mountainous and forested western regions of North America —more commonly in the Rocky Mountains from New Mexico into Washington, Idaho, Montana, and British Columbia and Alberta.

Where there are severe climatic changes, the herds migrate back and forth from the alpine meadows in summer down to the foothills and warmer slopes in winter. Usually there is an abundance of forbs and flowering woody plants on summer range. When autumn comes, the diet changes to shrubs and plants that retain their leaves or remain green.

During the winter where deep snow covers the ground, shrubs are usually the chief food. On open, windswept range, however, cured grasses may be the mainstay. Because of its long, powerful legs, the elk can paw away snow that is not too deep to uncover forage on the ground, and can stand on its hind legs to reach up into high shrub branches and tree limbs. Where the animals are numerous, the trees may become "high-lined," and shrubs severely hedged.

When their migration takes them near ranches, they will feast on haystacks that are not protected by high, elk-proof fences. During extreme winters, great herds have been maintained by the purchase of many tons of hay and pellets. This is an expensive, undesirable management practice which makes elk dependent on artificial forage and results in semi tame, pauperized animals instead of the wild, resourceful species that everyone wants to keep as a part of the native fauna of North America.

Where elk are protected in national parks and refuges, and the predators have been removed from surrounding livestock country, the herds tend to increase to disastrous numbers. They destroy their range by overgrazing and overbrowsing; erosion results until the topsoil may be washed and blown away, and only undesirable weeds replace the former vegetation. Furthermore, the deer, antelope, bighorn, and bison that use the same range are endangered. Weakened by malnutrition, animals become susceptible to infections, and disease increases and spreads.

Overcrowding of hoofed mammals has become a chronic condition in national parks and refuges around the world. One of the most crucial wildlife problems in the United States has been the destruction of winter range in Yellowstone National Park. Toward the end of the last century the northern herd in this park was estimated to number 25,000. Inevitably the increasing overuse of forage led to a catastrophe during the critical winter of 1919–20 when losses amounted to nearly 60 percent of the entire herd. But there were still too many elk for the amount of food available. Even in the 1930's, with an annual increase of 20 percent, the elk were apparently eating themselves and other game into extinction.

Since that time, increased hunting outside the park, live-trapping (to restock other areas), and official kill in Yellowstone have not yet reduced the herd long enough to allow the winter range to recover. Increased efforts are being made to maintain the herd at a level which will allow perpetuation of the range and in turn the elk resource.

Research is essential to manage an elk herd successfully. First, the size of the population in relation to the capacity of its habitat must be determined. Adjustments in numbers, primarily by hunting, are then made according to the amount of forage available. Trends in sex and age ratios of the herd, related to habitat and hunting, will suggest further management that is needed. The elk has a moderate reproductive potential because only singleton calves are born. How well the herd is reproducing, with respect to potential, is a measure of its success under a given set of field conditions.

The objective of scientific management is to maintain herds of maximum size that are in balance with their food supply and provide an annual crop for recreational hunting. In addition to the esthetic value of the elk, the spectacular antlers are most desirable trophies. Sportsmen greatly enjoy and spend considerable time, money, and effort in hunting the bulls.

Every effort should be made to perpetuate this magnificent creature in all suitable habitats of the continent. With knowledge of its life requirements and a will to limit it to huntable populations, the elk should continue to be an important game animal as well as an integral part of our western mountains.

159

The foremost authority on the moose is a native of Texas. A Ph.D. in bionomics from the University of Toronto, Randolph L. Peterson is an associate professor at the university and curator of mammals in the Royal Ontario Museum. His biological specialties range from moose, caribou, and lesser mammals of Arctic Canada to tropical bats of the New World, Africa, and Madagascar. He is the author of nearly forty scientific and popular publications, among them two definitive books, *North American Moose* and the recently published *Mammals of Canada.* Dr. Peterson has been prominent for many years in the American Society of Mammalogists, of which he was president, 1966–68, and he is a councilor of the Society of Systematic Zoology.

MOOSE

RANDOLPH L. PETERSON

The muffled grunts of a rutting bull moose carried clearly in the brisk late autumn air. He was swimming across the still waters of the channel between Simpson and St. Ignace Islands of northern Lake Superior in search of a mate. As he drew nearer, his large ears stood upright between the widespread antlers which reflected the setting sun from its wet, pale-ivory surface. His antlers had reached full development, and the velvet with its rich supply of nourishing blood vessels had recently been disposed of. The freshly exposed bone would soon became stained by contact with vegetation. Only a few days before I had seen this same bull thrashing his bloodstained antlers against a balsam fir sapling, a clear signal that the breeding season was at hand.

The behavior of the bull undergoes a marked change during the rut, from a shy retiring nature to boldness that has been widely interpreted as aggressiveness. Now seemed to be an excellent opportunity to test the reactions of a rutting bull moose toward a human. I hurried to the area where I thought the bull would come ashore. The grunts continued and grew louder as the bull swam closer, and now I could see his muzzle, plowing through the water like a canoe. Only the hump of his back was visible behind his head. As he gained footing, I stepped directly into his path less than ten yards away. He stopped with a snort and became quiet. His ears lowered, the hair on his shoulder bristled, and his nostrils expanded and contracted. We both stood motionless and stared at each other. He took a few steps forward. My heart pounded and I was tempted to beat a hasty retreat to the nearby clump of trees. But this would have been the normal course of action, according to the stories of people who have spent considerable time up in a tree with an angry bull moose pawing the ground below! (I had often wondered what would have happened had these people remained rather than retreated, since there seemed to be no authenticated records of persons having been injured by an unprovoked attack.)

Just as discretion was about to gain the upper hand over valor, the bull slowly turned and climbed onshore a few feet to the side of me. He crashed through thick brush and moved steadily along a trail as he resumed his periodic grunting. I followed . . . After a short distance I let out a grunt like his to see what he would do. Immediately he stopped, turned his head, and stared directly at me. For an instant I felt he might turn and charge. But with a nasal snort he slowly turned his majestic head and resumed a deliberate walk. Not at all belligerent, he appeared merely disgusted with my interruption of his main purpose—to find a suitable, if not a specific, cow in an amorous mood.

The moose is a solitary species, and there is little opportunity for the males to round up a harem. There is evidence that they tend to be polygamous, but the great distance between receptive females imposes limitations. Following the rut. which usually takes place between late September and the end of October, there is a shift from the summer diet of leaves, twigs, and bark of trees and shrubs, augmented with aquatic plants, to the winter diet of the terminal twigs of woody plants such as willow, yellow birch, various species of maples, and other hardwood species supplemented with a high percentage of evergreens, particularly balsam fir. Not long after the rut, the older bulls shed their antlers, whereas the younger males tend to retain them a while longer, occasionally until March.

With the deepening of the snow, the increasingly severe weather, and a reduction in available food, survival becomes more and more difficult, reaching its most critical peak by late winter or early spring. Spring crusting of snow, which can support an attacking pack of timber wolves but cause the moose to flounder, marks the most vulnerable period of the year. (On equal footing a healthy moose is a difficult prey for any carnivore.) I have found a number of winter wolf kills of moose but no evidence of predation at other times. During the summer months when bears are reported to prey on the calves, I have watched wolves approach moose but show no inclination to attack. I have also come across skeletal remains of old moose that had apparently died of natural causes and had not been disturbed by predators.

With the early signs of spring and the rising sap in hardwood trees, moose indulge in a period of heavy feeding on bark and strip it off both standing and freshly fallen trees. Beginning about the

middle of May, the cow attempts to discourage further company with her offspring (if it has been fortunate enough to survive to its first birthday) and selects a sheltered area in which to bring forth her new calf. On one occasion I made motion pictures of a cow striking at her unwelcome yearling as she crossed to a small island where she had a newborn calf. She raised her front foot to head height in a vicious slash which caused the yearling to fall back into the lake and finally to retreat.

Rejection by its mother appears to be a traumatic experience for the yearling moose. Suddenly it must develop the independent behavior of an adult. This adjustment requires a few days, as illustrated by our encounter with a newly rejected yearling that approached us as we were busily constructing an observation tower near a "salt lick" on St. Ignace Island. Despite the noisy activity of three of us—hammering, sawing, and talking

—this young male approached to within fifty yards and stood staring at us with obvious curiosity. We interrupted our work to test his reactions to us, including shouting, waving, and tossing objects in the air in his direction. He nervously stood his ground for a bit, then bolted into the woods only to return a few seconds later to have still another look at us. For over an hour this game continued until finally he failed to return; he obviously had not yet developed the normal fear of humans that is acquired by most adult moose.

The newborn calf is hardly a thing of beauty by ordinary standards. It appears to be all legs and ears joined by a short body covered with reddish-brown hair, a dark stripe extending down the middle of the back, black muzzle, and dusky ring of hair about the eyes. Weighing between twenty-five and forty pounds (usually thirty to thirty-five) at birth, the young calf is usually kept in seclusion for a few

163

days. This protective isolation may be interrupted abruptly, with the calf being enticed into the frigid waters of a lake for a long swim to the opposite shore. On several occasions I have seen young calves struggling to keep pace with their mothers during an extended swim and felt they would surely drown before they reached shore. An occasional one will cling to its mother's rump or rest its chin on her back.

For the most part, the calves not only have the capacity to survive but grow at an extraordinary rate and may weigh as much as 150 to 200 pounds at the end of three months and from 400 to 600 when only a year old. Twin calves are not uncommon, usually occurring in some 10 to 25 percent of births. The multiple births seem to vary from region to region in response to the nutritional level enjoyed by the cows.

While the cows are concerned with giving birth and caring for their young, the bulls concentrate on growing an elaborate set of new antlers which develop at a rather remarkable rate. It has been suggested that the drain on the vitality of the bulls to produce these ornaments may be similar to that of the cow to bring forth a calf. The full-grown antlers are formidable weapons but apparently serve primarily in combat with other bulls for the attentions of an available female. Driving off bears or wolves involves slashing blows with the moose's front feet, which most carnivores have come to regard with a healthy respect.

During our studies on the islands along the north shore of Lake Superior, we constructed a tree-house tower overlooking a series of mineral springs. There we spent many hours, day and night, observing the moose as they formed a procession to the springs to drink from the seeping, sometimes muddy, water. These areas were thought at first to be "salt licks," but a chemical analysis showed very little salt; traces of other elements may have been the attraction. Moose came at any and all hours of the day and night, with perhaps the only noticeable decline in activity being the midafternoon, which appeared to be "siesta" time. From our perch we came to recognize most individuals and catalogued reams of behavioral activities, including the reactions of individuals to a wide variety of both man-made and other stimuli.

We were amazed to find that a moose would make no overt reaction to a strong light when it was suddenly turned toward him in the middle of a dark night! Several times I have also been surprised to see a moose stand and stare at a boat passing less than a hundred yards away while clouds of dark, acrid smoke poured from the funnels and the voices of people on board carried clearly. As the boat passed, the moose would nonchalantly resume drinking from the spring. We were also fascinated by its ability to suddenly appear as if by magic in the middle of the clearing surrounding the springs. Not even a telltale snap of a twig warned us that a moose was coming, but when panic-stricken it would noisily crash headlong through the brush for great distances.

Both sexes are capable of breeding at the end of their second summer, but there is some evidence that the young males may be prevented from doing so by the larger bulls and that only a portion of the yearling females are successfully bred. Antlers tend to increase in size each successive year but with no regular pattern in number of points or tines. Maximum antler size appears to be reached at about seven to ten years, with a gradual decrease thereafter, although the base and burr continue to expand. The longest life-span of moose is not definitely known, but existing evidence suggests that not many live beyond fifteen to twenty years.

The moose is circumpolar in distribution and occurs in the boreal forests of both North America, and the Old World, where it is known as the elk. To meet its habitat requirements it depends upon a continuous succession of new growth in a mixed forest ecosystem supplemented with lake and stream plants for aquatic feeding. Because its ecological requirements are sufficiently distinct from such herbivores as deer, wapiti, or caribou, there is usually no serious competition when they occur in the same area, unless there is a chronic overpopulation of one or more of the species. Every day a moose eats forty to sixty pounds of food which it obtains by foraging over large areas in more or less solitary fashion. In an area of over one hundred square miles the number of moose rarely exceeds one per square mile, although local concentrations may show a much higher population level in favorable feeding areas, such as lakes and streams in summer or protected valleys, used as "yards," in winter.

As a big-game animal, large bull moose offer the hunter between 500 and 750 pounds of highly palatable meat (between 50 and 60 percent of the total live weight). Throughout most of its North American range, the bull moose may reach a maximum weight of about 1,400 pounds and the cows about 900 pounds. In Alaska and adjacent regions where the largest race occurs, the males are reported to reach about 1,800 pounds and the cows near 1,200 pounds. On one occasion I secured a set of scales and off-loaded them on the shore of St. Ignace Island and waited for a bull moose to come to them. At the end of my wait, a fine bull was shot and rolled onto the scale. He tallied in at 1,177 pounds, had a hog-dressed weight (less viscera) of 903 pounds and a dressed weight of 697 pounds (less viscera, head, hide, and feet).

Sound conservation measures provide for cropping of the annual surplus normally provided by most wildlife species, but the management of moose is complicated by the difficulty of distributing the hunting pressure evenly over its range. The result is usually overexploitation in the readily accessible locations and virtually no exploitation in the more remote portions of its range. Since moose are necessarily thinly distributed over large areas as a consequence of their food requirements, and have a relatively low reproduction potential (less than half the cows seem to produce a calf each year), overexploitation must be avoided. It is vital that careful conservation measures be carried out to insure that this survivor of a past epoch can continue to flourish for generations to come as the world's largest living deer.

165

A. W. F. (Frank) Banfield was educated at the universities of Toronto and Michigan. He served with the Canadian Army through the Mediterranean and German campaigns of World War II, retiring with the rank of captain. He was chief mammalogist of the Canadian Wildlife Service, 1946–57, before moving to the National Museums of Canada where he was chief zoologist and later director of the Museum of Natural Sciences.

Pursuing his specialties of mammalian systematics and zoogeography, Dr. Banfield has engaged in field research throughout Canada, as well as Alaska and across northern Eurasia from Japan to Finland. His bibliography of eighty titles includes a book, *The Mammals of Canada,* and papers on systematics, biology, and management of mammals, especially the barren-ground caribou.

CARIBOU

A. W. F. BANFIELD

We were camped on the Canadian "barrens" northeast of Yellowknife, waiting the return of the caribou from their summer pastures closer to the Arctic coast. It was a late August evening. Scanning the hills with binoculars, I spotted a distant herd across the lake. Fortunately, the breeze was favorable and a quick paddle was enough to put me downwind in the path of the approaching caribou.

I sprinted across the tundra and crouched behind a large glacial boulder. The acrid aroma of caribou lichens filled the air as I tried to catch my breath. Above the agitated clicks of a Lapland longspur and softer trills of a flying pipit, I strained to catch the first sound of the approaching herds. Gradually the muffled roll of hoofs swelled and died away.

Over the crest of the hill appeared a row of tall broken velvet antlers as a band of bucks climbed into full view. They broke into a trot down the slope toward me. Soon they were flanked by other bands on the skyline. There were several troops of bucks in their fresh clove-brown summer coats in the van. As they trotted down the hillside they reminded me of squadrons

167

of cavalry. The forest of bobbing antlers resembled lances, and the rhythmic clicking of tendons rolling over sesamoid bones in the feet suggested the clinking of spurs. Next came troops of young bucks and barren does and finally herds of does and fawns.

Soon the leading bands had passed me and the light breeze carried my scent to them. The stags shook their heads and broke into a stiff-legged pacing gait with head and tail held high. However, they ran only about fifty yards and then circled behind my position and stared upwind. (The intermittent rumbling I had heard before was the herd breaking into a short canter, and then slowing to a leisurely walk.) With a toss of the head and an occasional leaping turn they continued their migration.

Now I was surrounded by caribou. The whole hillside seemed to be moving and my position alone remained still. There was an incessant commotion of swine-like belches of the bucks and the bawls of the three-month-old calves. A few of the bands passed within ten yards. When the closest does caught my scent, they quivered and halted stiff-legged. They hunched slightly to urinate, looking in my direction over their shoulders, while others observed the warning sign and trotted on. The air reeked.

The herd took an hour to pass and I estimated ten thousand caribou had come within easy sight of my position. There were perhaps other herds in the migration. Now it was all over. I lay on the tundra and stretched my cramped legs. I had observed one of the greatest North American wildlife spectacles: the caribou migration, a scene that rivaled the bison herds of the mid-nineteenth century on the American plains and the great migrations of East African antelope. I was reminded of the marvelously artistic drawings of reindeer on the cave walls of the Dordogne Valley in southern

France. (Our Magdalenian ancestors depicted the reindeer, along with other postglacial mammals, such as the bison, mammoth, and rhinoceros. Today the reindeer alone survives in numbers comparable to those early scenes in Europe twelve thousand years ago.)

The North American caribou belongs to the same species as the Old World reindeer (*Rangifer tarandus*) that in historical times was distributed in a circumpolar arc from northern Scotland to Scandinavia and Siberia, Alaska to New England, Newfoundland, Greenland, and Iceland. It is a compact, medium-size deer with well-developed lateral "dew claws" located low on the feet to bear some of the body weight. It also has a number of special adaptations to the Arctic environment. The well-furred muzzle is blunt and looks rather bovine. The nostrils are valvular; the ears are short, broad, and heavily furred; the tail is short. The feet are unusually large with big crescentic hooves to facilitate travel over snow-covered or boggy ground. The pelage is dense, composed of long, brittle guard hairs and a close, fine, crinkly underfur. There is a long ventral mane on the throat.

The caribou's crowning glory is its antlers, which are extremely individualistic. Indeed, one is seldom the mirror image of its mate. The bucks carry massive antlers as much as five feet long. Uniquely the does also have antlers, although smaller than those of the males. (In some populations, the Newfoundland caribou for example, as many as 30 percent of the does may be antlerless.)

The basic antler pattern consists of gracefully backward-bowed beams with two palmate tines branching off near the burr. The first swings down over the forehead and acts as an eyeshield. The second swings widely forward. A number of terminal tines branch off the main beams over the shoulder. The annual growth of antlers is approximately six months out of phase between the sexes. Velvet knobs appear on the bucks in March and grow to full height by August. The velvet is rubbed off in September prior to the rut, and the antlers commence to drop in late November. The does' antlers grow during the late summer and are carried until after the fawns are dropped in June.

The color pattern of caribou varies widely with different subspecies and according to season. The basic dorsal color in fresh autumn pelage is clove brown, darker on the face and chest. The cream white of the neck and mane extends in a ribbon across the shoulder and flank. The belly, rump, and undersurface of the tail are also white. The legs are brown except for narrow white socks above the hooves. By late spring this coat becomes dirty grayish-white as a result of bleaching and breakage of the dark tips of the guard hairs.

The sexes differ markedly in size: the males are about 25 percent heavier than the females. There is also a great variation in the size of the subspecies. A large woodland caribou buck may weigh 600 pounds while a small Arctic Peary caribou buck weighs only about 150 pounds.

Caribou are usually observed in bands of a dozen, up to herds of a thousand or more. While there does not seem to be a definite pattern of group leadership, the social order is matriarchal with an experienced doe leading the band. They are gregarious animals, and seen from the air, a migrating herd reminds one of strings of iron fillings being pulled

169

along the well-beaten trails by a magnetic field. Individuals will disperse for feeding but will run together if alarmed to form a compact band. Throughout most of the year, large herds are segregated into bands according to sex and age. The bands consist of bucks, does, and fawns respectively, although occasionally barren does do associate with young or adult bucks. Only during the mating season do all the bands join.

This gregariousness is also associated with nomadism: the herds are almost constantly on the move from one seasonal pasture to another, and their migrations are often very extensive. The tundra subspecies may travel up to eight hundred miles between summer tundra pasture and winter forest ranges. Others inhabiting mountainous regions undertake vertical seasonal migrations from summer alpine pastures to lower forested range in winter. The woodland caribou's movements, however, are more local from open fens to drier forested ridges.

If horses are called hay-burners, caribou should be called lichen-burners because these lowly plants form the mainstay of their diet, especially in winter. Other winter food includes dried sedges, horsetails, and the twigs of birch and willows. The caribou paw through the loose snow to reach their food. The summer diet is more varied and includes mushrooms, lichens, grasses, sedges, forbs, and the twigs and leaves of birch, willows, and certain heaths. Reindeer thrive on ten pounds of lichens per day.

The most important predator of caribou is probably man, and secondly, the wolf. In primitive times, the caribou managed to survive the attacks of both, but the addition of firearms tipped the balance against the prey. There still exists, however, a delicately balanced relationship between wolf and caribou. A healthy calf, a few days after birth, can outrun a wolf. So, quite obviously, the wolf can make a kill only when conditions have been weighed in its favor. Moreover, the caribou herds sense when a wolf pack is hunting and become instantly alert. (When the wolves pass leisurely by, the prey appear little disturbed.) Aside from wolves, the grizzlies, lynx, and wolverines occasionally kill a caribou, and the golden eagles may prey upon fawns.

The rut occurs in October. The bucks are polygamous and spend the period rushing about, threshing bushes with their antlers, sparring with other bucks, panting and bellowing. Rutting occurs promiscuously among the ranks of does. The gestation period is approximately eight months long, and the fawns are dropped between May 15 and July 3. The pregnant does leave the winter range before the bucks and seek rough rocky terrain in which to bear their single young. At birth the fawns are clothed in a crinkly fawn-colored coat and weigh approximately twelve pounds. They are very precocious. Within thirty minutes they can walk with a hopping gait, and following ninety minutes rest, run several miles after their mother. They can outrun a man the second day. The young caribou commence to graze after about two weeks, but depend upon milk for the first month at least. Weaning is often delayed, and in the winter a few fawns are still supplementing their diet by occasional suckling. The juvenile females mature normally at sixteen months.

Caribou constituted an important economic resource for northern Eskimos and Indians before the arrival of Europeans. They provided food, and the pelt was used for light warm Arctic clothing, bedding, and hide tepees. The sinews were used as thread, the bones as utensils, and the fat provided heat and light. Only in recent decades has the caribou been supplanted by other sources of food and manufactured articles. Now the native populations are less dependent upon this natural resource, and with wise management, the caribou herds can continue to inhabit their remote ranges and provide limited resources and pleasure to northern people.

After working as a Forest Service ranger in Colorado, Arthur F. Halloran entered the United States Fish and Wildlife Service. He managed several huge refuges in New Mexico and Arizona, 1941–54, then was transferred to game research. His headquarters, Wichita Mountains National Wildlife Refuge, is the home of a large herd of American bison (buffalo) which he describes in this chapter.

Mr. Halloran is a fellow of the Oklahoma Academy of Science and holds the Silver Beaver Award of the Boy Scouts. He has published more than one hundred technical papers and popular articles on desert bighorn, bison, longhorn cattle, and other mammals, as well as birds. With Mrs. Halloran, he enjoys bird-watching, and they have traveled as far as Tahiti in pursuit of their hobby.

THE AMERICAN BISON, OR BUFFALO

ARTHUR F. HALLORAN

The buffalo cow wheeled and charged. The quick-footed nine-year-old boy turned back, sprinted for the house, jumped the steps, grabbed the door, and slammed it behind him. The cow, inches away, slid to a halt against the bottom step and returned to her calf.

We had just moved to the Wichita Mountains Wildlife Refuge in Oklahoma. Johnnie was playing at a neighbor's when a herd of bison, mostly cows and calves, moved into the intervening park. My wife whistled the boy to supper. Starting home, he inadvertently walked between a cow and her calf. The thousand-pound beast had charged.

The herd grazed on and Johnnie came in. He sat down to his meal, turned to me and said, "Who's afraid of a buffalo? I am!" He was right! Bison are dangerous and can't be trusted. If you are ever afoot and taking pictures of buffalo, be sure you can beat them back to your car or a tree you can climb. These animals carry the genes of ancestors who forced power-packed lobo wolves to prey on only the very young, the sick, and the disabled.

The American bison or buffalo, estimated to number 60 million one hundred years ago, has become one of America's greatest natural memories. The mighty Sioux developed courage and superb horsemanship hunting this powerful monarch. They used the hides for tepees and blankets, meat for food, tails for flyswatters, and horns for ladies. As you can imagine, riding a bronc up to the side of a running buffalo bull and putting an arrow into his vitals was not child's play—especially if one were riding with no saddle, no stirrups, and no hands!

Then came our forefathers. Thousands of California-bound gold seekers were able to cross "The Great American Desert" because buffalo meat could be had for the shooting. This was before the pony express and the days of the hard-bitten hunters who provided buffalo steaks for rough Irish crews who sweated and strained to lay tracks across an untamed continent. We shall return to this story, but first let us peer into the misty wallows of prehistory to learn of the buffaloes' ancestors.

Long ago, there was a land bridge between Siberia and Alaska. The sea receded, and animals, large and small, moved into North America's untouched forests and grasslands. The giant bison nosing into this new range a million or more years ago included bulls whose massive horns spanned better than six feet. (Experts still argue as to how many kinds of these cow-family creatures eventually immigrated or developed in this primeval land.) Today, there are two kinds of bison in the New World: the heavy-coated wood or mountain buffalo of northern Canada and the slightly smaller plains buffalo. Both are smaller than their ancestors. The mountain bison also occurred through the Rockies to Colorado where Mountain Men in the

mid-1800's found them as solitaries or in small bands in high mountain parks. Some scientists believe the wood bison is related to a hairy ancestor of the present-day European bison, or wisent, and that the plains buffalo descended from an earlier migrant. Excellent displays of prehistoric bison can be seen at the University of Kansas Museum of Natural History at Lawrence.

During the eighteenth and nineteenth centuries, pioneers, Indians, and traders all but exterminated the buffalo. Pennsylvania's last herd was slaughtered in deep crusted snow in 1799. The final remnants east of the Mississippi were killed in Wisconsin in 1830.

After the 1850's, Indian trade for buffalo hides grew to enormous proportions. Buffalo overcoats and robes were in high style. As late as the turn of the century, a young blade with a big warm buffalo robe in his buggy provided a snug covering for his girl as they returned from November country socials. Traders along the Missouri could secure a hide worth five or ten dollars for a pound or two of coffee. Many of these sharp dealers made fortunes.

Bison herds even stopped trains, and the railroads ran special buffalo-hunting excursions. Passengers shooting from the coaches often left the meat to rot. Then, professionals entered the picture. Hides dropped to $1.25, and buffalo meat sold for less than a penny a pound—supply quite obviously exceeded demand. Some specialized in shooting bison only for their tongues, which were smoked and sold for two bits apiece. Buffalo meat was even fed to hogs. By 1889, all but a few hundred wild buffalo were gone.

By 1903, less than a thousand bison, fenced or wild, remained in the United States. A few had found refuge in Yellowstone National Park. Some wild wood buffalo were left in Canada. Only the efforts of a handful of dedicated people, including Dr. William T. Hornaday, founder of the American Bison Society, saved the species from extinction. As interest kindled, remnants were assembled in protected herds. A recent census shows that there are about 25,000 buffalo in North America; slightly more than half of these are in Canada. In addition to government herds, there are scores in zoos and on private ranches.

More than thirty years ago my wife and I were spending Christmas with her folks on the wind-driven, deadly cold plains of the Dakotas. After supper, Grandma Cole started looking at early-day photographs. She showed us a 1903 close-up shot of buffalo on the James "Scotty" Philip ranch, west of the Missouri. These animals were descendants of five wild calves caught by the Dupree boys in 1882. Scotty Philip was one of the few who realized the bison was on the brink of extinction and did something about it.

Grandma, too, was very aware of the buffalo in those days. As a "young married" she had pioneered on the prairie in a sod house. Times had been hard. She told of one Christmas when she had picked up "pretty prairie rocks" to put in the Christmas stockings for her two little girls. On that cold December afternoon she had also brought in a load of sun-dried buffalo chips to keep the chill out of her one-room "soddy." She went on to relate of the late seventies and eighties when most of the buffalo were gone; how the settlers had gathered and sold buffalo bones. This was a way to stay on the land. It was said that a ton of bones, bringing eight to twelve dollars, represented one hundred buffalo. The bones were shipped to the East and used

for fertilizer. During the thirteen years from 1868 to 1881, in Kansas alone, two and a half million dollars was paid for bones!

Buffalo size and weight interest many. One record Kansas bull weighed 3,000 pounds. Most bulls weigh less than this. And bulls weighed on the Wichita Refuge averaged about 1,500 pounds on the hoof with large ones weighing close to a ton. Cows are much lighter and smaller. Although few comparative weights are available, it seems that southern plains buffalo are lighter than those raised farther north.

Size records are harder to find than weights. The largest bull I have measured was 10½ feet long and 6¼ feet high at the shoulder. Doubtless there have been and still are larger bulls than this. The horn span of buffalo varies as does weight and size. The largest span in the record books is almost three feet. This fine specimen is found at the Fish-

ing Bridge Museum in Yellowstone National Park.

Bison rub their hides on convenient trees and rocks to ease insect bites and to scrape off their heavy winter coats. Trees that grow at an angle are favorites; both large and small may rub. Rubbing rocks become slick as glass. Buffalo used early-day telegraph poles as rubbing posts. Someone had had an idea to stop this by studding poles with nails. But when the buffalo discovered the nails, he was in his glory. He scratched even harder! This habit still presents a problem. Bulls and cows alike "rub down" stout road signs. One way to reduce this damage is to pile rocks around the base of a signpost so buffalo can't get close enough to reach it. This works, but it is a dirty trick on an old native with an itch.

The buffalo's hide and fur have the peculiar quality of absorbing light, including headlights. So if you drive through a bison refuge at night, be careful. Sometimes the red eyeshine is all you see. Many an indifferent motorist has found himself knee-deep in buffalo with no time to stop.

Buffalo also have a habit of pawing up dirt and then rolling in it. This is called wallowing and is thought to relieve tensions and help soothe an itching hide. I have never seen a buffalo roll over his hump. They will wallow on one side, get up, shake themselves like a dog, and then roll on the other side with their feet in the air. A wallow started by one is sometimes used by many. Old wallows may be from six to thirty or more feet across. Rainwater collects in these depres-pressions, and in contrast to adjacent dry glasslands, moisture-loving plants abound.

When a herd of bison graze unhurriedly across a grassy flat, they are often accompanied by a flock of cowbirds. The movements of the big beasts flush out insects, and the birds walk fearlessly among the hooves to catch and eat disturbed "bugs." This habit was known to early-day plainsmen who called these feathered insect-eaters "buffalo birds."

During the hot summer months, breeding season is in full swing. Bulls herd the cows and there is a good deal of fighting and maneuvering. Calves are born after a gestation period of about nine months. The mother is devoted, always staying between her calf and danger. Bison can have twins, but these are rare. Although buffalo calves may be born in any month of the year, most of them appear in the spring. This is a survival matter; spring-born calves have a long summer and fall to grow before winter comes. In contrast to the brown color of the adults, calves are reddish. As they approach three months of age, the dark color of their parents is first seen along the backbone. By late fall, spring-born calves are the same color as their parents. Calves lack the prominent shoulder hump of mature bison. It is said that one in two million calves is an albino. The white buffalo was sacred to the Indians. It represented something special. We can easily imagine the excitement of such an event. (In Asia the white elephant has brought similar veneration.) During 1933, a white buffalo calf appeared on the National Bison Range in Montana. He was named "Big Medicine." He grew into a magnificent bull with a white coat crowned by a dark-tufted mane between his horns. By the time he died in 1959 at twenty-six, he was probably the most photographed bison in all of history. A life-size mount of this famous animal is housed in Montana's Historical Society Museum at Helena.

There are several accounts of bison crossing with cattle to produce a hybrid, called cattalo. Many of these corral-bred crosses are not fertile. Although some have thought it would be of value to have a breed with the hardiness of a buffalo and the meat and tameness of a cow, no one has been completely successful with such an endeavor. In large fenced pastures where both cattle and buffalo range, the two species do not interbreed and tend to ignore each other.

Through the years a few buffalo have been broken to the yoke and even to ride! Undisturbed herds under fence become docile to a point. However, it is foolhardy to be lulled into a false security; these wildings are always unpredictable. An aroused buffalo will turn and charge a man on horseback. And we say on the Wichita, "You can drive a buffalo bull any place he wants to go."

177

Although Ralph and Florence Welles met in a biology class at San Jose State College, their first career was the stage. For eighteen years, they were respectively director and choreographer of the Palo Alto (California) Community Theater. Always interested in wildlife, they began intensive studies of bighorn in 1954 for the National Park Service. Six years of work resulted in a book, *The Bighorn of Death Valley,* which earned the first award of the Desert Bighorn Council.

The following chapter describes an episode from the Welles' research, which is still continuing at Death Valley and elsewhere in southern California. They also lecture with their orchestrated color films on desert natural history, make shorts for federal and state agencies, and are active in several organizations. In 1969, Mr. and Mrs. Welles were cochairmen of the Desert Bighorn Council.

DEATH VALLEY BIGHORN

RALPH AND FLORENCE WELLES

It was nine hundred feet above the floor of Death Valley and 118° in the shade. A ewe, known to us as Whitehorns, stood alert staring to the north. Her band fed slowly down the ridge toward the spring below. From the south came the great fighting ram Broken Nose. From the north, an equally tough fighter called The Hook.

While we watched, Broken Nose threw up his head. His challenge echoed down the canyon wall. The Hook answered and they both began their breath-taking descent toward the spring. Whitehorns and her band plunged down the ridge, evidently to reach water and get away before the rams could close in. This did not surprise us, for ewes with young often avoid rams until late in the rutting season to prevent being separated from their offspring in the mating chase, which may last for several days.

We began to get our cameras ready. Seven times before during the thirty days we had spent this spring observing bighorns, we had seen and heard head-splitting duels between lesser contestants, but they were always too far away to take pictures, or it was too early or to late for enough light, or it

179

was too hot for cameras to sit in the sun. Today everything looked right.

The echoing, trumpeting sound of a challenge made us look up. The Hook had intercepted the ewe, and now with his hackles rising in rage he stood facing Broken Nose. He rose on his hind legs and sighted down his nose at his enemy. Broken Nose, however, ignored him and rushed headlong at the ewe. The mating chase was on.

This was an ancient game—this procreation of the race. A deliberate, seemingly planned approach to crisis like the rituals of pagan warriors preparing to die for their gods. And the ewe was part of it. The urge to procreation is as strong in her as it is in the rams, but as they approached she turned this way and that. Sliding out from under their lunges at the last split second, she broke away in headlong flight which almost immediately took her from sight beyond the ridge.

Her small band huddled uncertainly in the ravine, waiting, for she was their leader. Then her lamb, bleating anxiously, went bounding over the ridge after her.

We hurriedly gathered up canteens and wet towels to keep our cameras cool enough to handle, and followed the chase.

As we crested the ridge we found the ewe and lamb already reunited. Nearly a quarter of a mile away in the shimmering heat waves, the two rams rose on their hind legs and careened in this erect position toward each other from a distance of about forty feet. Then they lunged head down across the last ten feet between them in a head-on collision that would have killed anything but a bighorn ram.

There is no other sound like it. A two-ton boulder crashing down a cliff fooled us once. When the air is still, either sound can be heard a mile away, echoing through desert mountain canyons.

After the crash the rams recoiled to three or four feet from each other. They

180

stood with their heads up and back, with their eyes nearly closed, as though waiting to regain their equilibrium before another round.

Then they turned and walked away from each other as though that ended the fray. But at some signal only they could know, they turned, rose again on their hind legs, tilted their heads as though "sighting down their noses at each other," and rushed forward.

We counted forty "blasts" with no apparent advantage to either ram. The temperature continued to climb, a hot wind came up from the south, their noses became swollen and puffy, and the "battle bulge" at the back of their heads grew to the size of a bowling ball.

They never saw the ewe leave with another ram, nor did they take notice of us as we finally approached to within a hundred yards of their battleground. After two hours they began to tire and the jousts came farther apart. More time

now was spent by one thrashing his horns in a shrub while the other watched, panting in the heat, or turned away and pretended to browse until another "moment of truth" when the pretenses dropped and they rose with perfect timing and whirled and crashed together again. Once Broken Nose slipped and fell and The Hook stood over him, head up, his swollen muzzle in the air, and waited until Broken Nose had scrambled to his feet.

Shortly after that they stopped and stood, gaunt and bleary-eyed, staring at us for a moment, then turned and walked deliberately away to the deep shade of a cliff where they lay down side by side to rest.

The fact that these encounters are not "battles to the death," may be one of the reasons the bighorn has outlived the camel and others of its hooved contemporaries for over ten thousand years. The margin of survival in the desert is slim

enough without their killing each other.

The matriarchal social pattern is also very important in their survival. The older ewes are the leaders in the mixed band—leaders by example only. The matriarch has no authority, but she knows how to find water, food, and shelter, and she knows where danger lurks in the shadows. Just as she learned from her elders, the new generation learns from her how to reach food, water, and sanctuary in terrain so inaccessible that even the wild burro cannot follow.

When the rams are separated from the herds in off-season they tend to take their cues from the most battered old warrior among them until he voluntarily withdraws from active participation in the rituals of his tribe. We have often seen younger rams abandon the mating chase when an older one entered the arena.

And we have never seen an ill-matched "battle."

On several occasions immature rams were observed trying to "pick a fight" with a mature one, only to be ignored unless the younger one became too much of a nuisance. If this occurred the older one would sometimes turn and without any warning knock the youngster off his feet and walk away. This may end it but it may not. One day we watched a two-year-old ram pester a twelve-year-old veteran for over an hour as he browsed across a mesa. The youngster would rise on his hind legs in the approved manner, tilt his head, blow through his nose, and prance back and forth in front of the old ram, who refused to stop eating even long enough to look up at him. When the young ram finally charged him, he simply turned his massive head enough to catch the blow, then returned to his imperturbable feeding.

This seems to be part of the universal behavior that establishes "pecking order." Six-month-old lambs play king of the mountain at every opportunity; one leaps to the top of a boulder while the others take turns trying to dislodge him. Sometimes when a large enough boulder can be found, several engage in the game at the same time and a general free-for-all ensues. We knew a three-year-old ram who would take up the throne alone while as many as four youngsters would face him at the same time. He simply stood his ground, sparring with them but never returning a charge.

We found the bighorn justly renowned for their ability to traverse seemingly impassable terrain. They train for this from the first day of birth. The previous year, when the ewe Old Mama had returned to the Big Wash with her two-day-old baby, she gently butted him over two or three times a day. And every evening, as the shadows hit the Wash, although the lamb was still wobbly on his legs, she would nudge him with her muzzle, and then with him at her heels, climb for a mile or two up into the safety of the sheer cliffs of Pyramid Peak.

After several months of constant association with us on the mesa and in Big Wash the old ewe had become used to our being around and to the sound of our voices; but one evening we followed her up into her sanctuary and learned that to follow her there was not acceptable behavior to her. In a ravine at the foot of a towering precipice we came upon her suddenly where she lay barely twenty feet away, her eyes half closed, placidly chewing her cud as the last rays of the sun played across her graying face. Her lamb peered at us from where it lay behind her.

When she saw us, a convulsive tensing of muscles shot through her entire body, her head jerked toward us, and one front leg flipped out from under her chest as though she was going to leap to her feet. Instead she froze there, her eyes wide and glowing golden in the sun. For a moment none of us moved or made a sound, then she "blew" at us, the same stentorian snort of warning that bighorns have sounded for the last ten thousand years in this mountain fastness. For a moment we were there in a vast stretch of unmoving time where nothing had changed and where no promise of change was being made. Then the lamb leaped to its feet and the spell was broken.

We suddenly felt apologetic to the old ewe for our intrusion, and we began to talk to her, as we were used to doing when she fed close to us in the Wash at the foot of the mountains. As we talked we began to back away and her tension lessened. She brought up her cud again and folded her front leg back beneath her.

We paused before we dropped from her sight, and as we did, her lamb began to play as bighorn lambs are likely to do in the evening. It ran in circles around its mother and at one point leaped against the cliff above her and bounced off, landing on her ribs with all four feet. From there it leaped up as high as it could and thudded down on her again, before scampering back to the cliff above.

The old ewe accepted this pummeling from her lamb as she accepted the shadow that crept up the canyon to her and over her, draining the golden glow from her eyes as the last fingers of the sun felt their way on up the face of the mountain and out into the night.

After earning degrees in wildlife management, Stewart M. Brandborg studied mountain goats, elk, bighorns, and deer in remote wilderness areas of Idaho for the State Fish and Game Department. In 1954, he came to Washington, D. C., as assistant conservation director of the National Wildlife Federation. Six years later he joined the staff of the Wilderness Society as director of special projects, and in 1964 he was appointed executive director. As a leader on conservation, he played a major role in establishment of the National Wilderness Preservation System. Brandy's long list of published addresses and writings on wilderness and wildlife includes *The Life History of the Mountain Goat in Idaho*, the first detailed account of this little-known mammal.

THE MOUNTAIN GOAT
STEWART M. BRANDBORG

To many who feel at home in the northern Rockies, the mountain goat symbolizes the most rugged of our western wilderness. Sighting these animals—far-off white specks against backdrops of cliffs and broken terrain—is a thrill for the most seasoned mountaineer. It stems in part from our wonder that such large animals can survive the extremes of this harsh, high-country environment.

Despite the name given them by early explorers, trappers, and mountain men, they are not goats. Instead, their nearest relative among North American mammals is the so-called antelope of our prairies, and their white coats, accented by black horns, noses, and hooves, set them apart.

Perhaps the most impressive of their unusual characteristics is the ease with which they move across steep cliffs and down sheer canyon walls. Soft pads, slightly protruding from their concave hooves, give them traction, so that they are more surefooted than any other large North American animal. Even the kids leap and scramble over precipitous heights in mock battles and games of tag.

185

Mountain goats are distinctive in several other ways. Both males and females have beards and sharp, pointed horns that curve backward. Instead of fighting head-on, like mountain sheep and most other hoofed animals, they rush quickly, circling around each other, trying to plunge their horns into chest, belly, flank, or rump. The wounds inflicted are painful and crippling, if not fatal, and neither the victor nor vanquished is likely to go unscathed.

Over thousands of centuries the goats that survived and reproduced were probably the ones that stayed out of combat. As a result, a behavior pattern of caution seems to have evolved; goats do a great deal of threatening and relatively little fighting. Most frequently, instead of rushing at their rivals, the billies stalk around each other, stiff-legged and with heads lowered. While the nannies are also more likely to threaten than to attack, they use their horns viciously when sufficiently annoyed. As a result, even the larger billies weighing 200 to 250 pounds tend to be intimidated by the somewhat smaller nannies.

During most of the mating season in November and December, the males join the groups of females, yearlings, and kids, and it is in this period that larger groups are most common. A habit of the billy during the rut is to paw the ground furiously with a foreleg, throwing snow and earth on his belly, flanks, and hind legs. Competition for females often leads to threats and sometimes to a bloody fight that may eliminate one or both billies from the contest.

About six months after the rut, the female leaves the band briefly to give birth to a kid. Most often she has only one, but twins are not uncommon. It is

likely that multiple births are more frequent on a range where the food is plentiful.

At birth the goat weighs from six to eight pounds, and within a short period it is up and running about. It returns often to suckle, bunting the mother and wiggling its tail excitedly. Kids grow very fast and by August they are so big that they have difficulty reaching under the mother to nurse.

To protect her new offspring, the mother refuses to let her yearling approach or even to tag along behind her. Despite the mother's concern for the kid, it often strays from her side and may become vulnerable to a coyote, bear, bobcat, mountain lion, or eagle. When the kid is frightened, it runs bleating for its mother. Sometimes she tries to cover it with her body, making threatening motions at the enemy with her horns. At least once she has been photographed standing on her hind legs striking at a marauding eagle.

The billy never takes any paternal responsibility, and family life—in the sense of grouping of females and their young with adult males—seldom occurs. Mother goats with kids, other females, and possibly a few yearlings are likely to remain in bands of four to twelve. The yearling, rejected by its mother, may wander alone for a while or join others in a similar predicament. Usually it attaches itself to a group of adults or stays in the same band at a considerable distance from its mother. The adult males keep to themselves most of the year. Only occasionally is an adult billy or two seen with females and young outside the rutting season.

Under normal circumstances, big, healthy mountain goats are unlikely to be attacked by predators as they feed on the steep slopes and mountain ledges. But eagles frequently dive at them as well as at deer and other large animals. Some naturalists believe this is calculated hunting and that the raptors are trying to startle their quarry into falling to their death. Others say that the birds do this as a pastime—"just for fun."

Be that as it may, I once saw a bald eagle attack a young goat. We had been watching two nannies, kids, and a yearling feeding on a cliff late one afternoon. The eagle flew by and circled about twenty-five feet above the goats. One of the nannies saw the bird and moved close to her kid, but, undaunted, it swooped down and landed on a pinnacle of rock only ten feet away. When the mother started toward the eagle the bird jumped from its perch, flew over her, picked up the kid in its talons, and sailed out over the canyon. Only a few days old, the kid (weighing less than seven pounds) dangled helplessly. The eagle glided for a third of a mile, not once moving its wings while carrying its load. Then it began to lose altitude, landed out of sight—and there was no doubt as to what ensued.

The mother goat spent several minutes hunting up and down the slope for her lost kid. The yearling that had been feeding 150 feet away ran to her but she quickly drove it off and continued her search. Fifteen minutes later she resumed her feeding, and as she wandered along, the yearling followed about a hundred feet behind her . . . Life on the cliff went on as usual.

Much more dangerous to the goats than an occasional predator is the advent of winter. Deep snows bury most of the grasses and other low-growing staples

187

of their diet. Their high-country summer ranges, often above ten thousand feet in elevation, may be covered in winter by ten to twenty feet of snow, except where the strong wings blow it away. Even their thick, woolly coats do not always provide adequate protection from winter gales and frigid temperatures at these elevations.

In many areas, the goats migrate distances of several miles to spend winters on sunny exposures in lower canyons and valleys where storms are less severe and preferred shrub and grass forage is more readily available. On coastal ranges, such as in Glacier Bay National Monument, Alaska, these movements may bring them down to ocean level. In Montana, Idaho, and Washington (the only three contiguous states where goats occur naturally) many herds spend the winter and early spring months at elevations of between 3,500 and 5,000 feet. Unfortunately, these favored winter feeding grounds often show severe overuse and depletion of grass and browse.

Winter food shortage is believed to be a principal factor in limiting increases in numbers of goats, for then the animals become emaciated and subject to disease. A high incidence of parasites (ticks, tapeworms, lungworms, and other forms) may also contribute to losses when the animals are weakened by malnutrition.

Although mountain goats are seldom seen to fall, they undoubtedly make fatal mistakes, especially when snow and ice make the cliffs extremely hazardous. Most of the dead animals that we found in late winter and early spring were at the bases of escarpments where falls appeared to be the immediate cause of death. Snow slides may be responsible for more accidental losses than any other natural factor. Rolling rocks and landslides, frequently caused by heavy rains and sometimes by the animals themselves, also result in injuries.

Over the years a good deal of research has been undertaken to provide a basis for protection and management of mountain goats. Some of my most interesting work has been the study of their life history, numbers, distribution, and needs. Because of their remote habitat and the fact that their horns are not spectacular trophies, they have often escaped the heavy hunting pressure of other big game. However, where roads have intruded upon their natural ranges, mountain goats are more easily hunted and have either declined drastically or have been eliminated entirely.

There are still areas in their natural range, which extends northward from the Sawtooth Mountains of Idaho through British Columbia and Alberta into Alaska, where the goats exist in primeval numbers. Some of these animals have been successfully transplanted to several suitable localities, such as the Crazy Mountains of Montana and the Collegiate Mountains of Colorado. Unexpectedly, when less than a dozen exhibit goats escaped from their compound in South Dakota during the 1920's, they founded a population in the Black Hills that may now total over two hundred.

Information on mountain goat numbers is subject to wide error due to the inaccessibility of the animals and the physical hardships faced by the biologists in making field studies on foot and on horseback. Counts from airplanes and helicopters give some measure of population trends, but must be carefully checked against data from ground surveys. In a number of areas, goats have been live-trapped and marked with paint or with metal and plastic clips in their ears so that individuals can be identified during air and ground observations— until the paint wears or sheds off; after that the ear markers continue the record.

Recent estimates for the United States give the following population figures: Idaho, 3,000; Montana, 4,300, and Washington, 5,000. Alaska and the Rocky Mountain provinces of British Columbia and Yukon Territory also support sizable populations.

Nearly 90 percent of the goats that I have seen have been in groups of less than fifty animals. As many as thirty to forty are occasionally seen together in Montana and Idaho in late summer and fall, but most goats spend the summer in smaller groups that range in size from two to a dozen individuals. At other seasons there is considerable variation in the groupings.

The small and scattered bands that I studied in Idaho did not show any marked increase over the years in which continual observations were made— probably because of extremely heavy losses of young goats. There was a consistently high annual loss of between 50 and 70 percent of the kids in their first year. The cause of these deaths was undetermined, and there was little evidence that any of the predators were responsible for significant losses.

Even with our present limited knowledge of the mountain goat, it is clear that the species survives on somewhat marginal terms. If given careful protection, however, it can be preserved and restored to many of its former ranges. Hunting should be limited on the basis of intensive annual inventories, and full protection must be given in years when populations are low. As long as roads and other human developments do not intrude upon its wild mountainous habitat, future generations of people can know and enjoy the mountain goat as one of the most interesting and unusual members of our North American fauna.

A career employee of the Canadian Wildlife
Service, John S. Tener has engaged in field
research on waterfowl in Ontario-Quebec,
1949–50, and on mammals (especially
muskoxen) of the Arctic, 1951–52 and
1955–61. After four years, 1962–66, as
staff mammalogist at the headquarters in
Ottawa (including a year as advisor to the
game department of Uganda), Dr. Tener
became deputy director of the Canadian
Wildlife Service, and was made director in
1969. A fellow of the Arctic Institute of
North America, he has been, or is currently, chairman of several national and
international conferences and committees.
His publications include about twenty scientific papers and the dramatically illustrated and authoritative book, *Muskoxen in
Canada*.

MUSKOXEN

JOHN S. TENER

It was snowing hard; the fine dry crystals whispered raspily along the surface and drifted in sheets across the hills. Our sled squeaked over the snow as the dogs settled down to a steady pull. Attungala and I, although completely clad in caribou skins, were cold in the subzero weather as we continued our search for a herd of muskoxen that lived somewhere in the region. Suddenly the dogs quickened their pace and we knew that something alive was ahead. Attungala stopped the team and anchored the sled firmly; then we climbed a steep slope to peer over the top. Through the occasional lifting of the snow screen, we saw a cluster of dark objects, motionless on top of the next rise. Creeping closer, we found that they were muskoxen. Snow encrusted their long hair as they stood with their backs into the wind, heads down, patiently waiting for the strong wind to drop.

We watched them for several hours—until the cold and approaching night drove us away. Getting back to our sled, we returned to a hot dinner and warm sleeping bags in a comfortable igloo. The muskoxen and other wild animals in that land had to face whatever the elements produced.

How can they do it? How can some of them range even farther north where there is continuous darkness for four months of the year and the temperature goes down to 60° below zero? . . . Just what are muskoxen?

Fossil evidence suggests that the muskox developed in central Asia and spread over northern Asia and Europe. The species reached North America by crossing the Bering Sea land bridge, which intermittently connected the two continents as the sea rose and fell with the coming and going of the ice ages. The species became extinct in the Old World, but survives today in Canada and Greenland.

Introduced populations are also found on Nunivak Island off the coast of Alaska, in Norway, and on Spitsbergen. The thirty-four muskoxen transplanted to Alaska in 1930 had been captured in Greenland, shipped to Norway, then to New York, Seattle, and the Biological Survey's cooperative reindeer experimental station near Fairbanks. Although the 14,000-mile trip had taken more than two months, all animals arrived in good condition. They were kept for six years in a 7,500-acre pasturage for observation and study. During this time, losses by accidental injuries and two killings by bears were offset by the birth of calves. In 1935 and 1936, the survivors and progeny were shipped down the Yukon River to Bering Sea and released on Nunivak Island. Resident Eskimos helped with the landing and over the years have watched the thirty-three muskoxen increase to more than seven hundred animals.

The muskox was given its name by a French officer whose description of the species in 1720 was the first to be published. Since musk was an important in-gredient in the manufacture of perfume at the time, it was hoped that this name for the animal would attract financial backers in Europe for further explorations. The discoverer claimed that the animals smelled so strongly of musk that it was impossible to eat them. Our recent studies revealed no evidence of a musky odor and have confirmed that if a muskox is butchered promptly and properly, the meat has an excellent flavor even during the rut. Attempts to explain the animal's so-called musk included the eye gland as a possible source, but histological examination at the University of British Columbia has disproved this theory.

Superficially, a bull muskox looks something like a long-haired buffalo, but its only living relative is the takin of southeast Asia. An adult bull muskox may weigh seven to nine hundred pounds, stand four and one-half feet at the shoulder, and be about seven feet long. The most striking feature of the animal is its long-skirted coat that hangs raggedly below the knees. This covering is composed of coarse, dark hair which hides the fine, dense, lighter-colored under-hair. The latter has been likened to cashmere and offers what its developers hope will be a new industry in Arctic and sub-Arctic regions—the raising of muskoxen in captivity for their inner wool. Important economic and sociological problems must be solved, however, before a sound industry can be developed. Cost of feeding and care under present procedures would exceed returns from the wool; furthermore, Eskimos are nomadic hunters and temperamentally unsuited to a pastoral life.

The adult bull muskox has a heavy set of horns which nearly unite above the eyes; they sweep down, out, then up, and are used in defense and attack. The horns of females are more slender. In both sexes these weapons appear at about six months of age and take approximately five years to develop fully. Those of old animals are likely to be darker and, in bulls, may have broken tips.

From a distance a muskox appears quite black, although old bulls are apt to be brownish. A closer examination reveals that the basic color of most animals is black-brown to dark brown, and that the animals have creamy white to pale yellow-brown "stockings" and "saddles." The animals on Greenland and on the high Arctic islands of Canada tend to have whiter stockings and saddles than their mainland counterparts. There is some individual variability in color in all populations as well.

The regions inhabited by most Canadian muskoxen (the Arctic mainland and the Arctic islands of the Northwest Territories) are characterized by a glacial climate in which the average temperatures of the warmest months are below 50° F. The climate is one of short, cool summers, long cold winters, and relatively little precipitation. Because snowfall is light, the animals usually do not have to dig through much snow to obtain their food. In fact, the precipitation is so light that were it not for water from summer melting of surface permafrost, large areas in the Arctic islands would be devoid of vascular plants for the animals to eat.

The melt season on the Arctic mainland of Canada begins in the first half of May, and snow is usually gone, except for drifted areas, by the middle of June. On the islands, melting usually starts in early June and is over in about two weeks. Snow may fall at any time in the summer, but normally doesn't remain on the ground in the high Arctic until the

end of August and on the mainland about a month later. The extremely short growing season limits the kinds of plants and new growth, and thus the number of muskoxen that can survive.

Another important environmental factor in the life of muskoxen is the light regime. In the Thelon Game Sanctuary, near the southernmost range of muskoxen, the sun is above the horizon for nearly twenty-two hours on June 21, but only for about three and one-half hours on December 22. The northernmost regions inhabited by muskoxen in Canada and Greenland receive twenty-four hours of sunlight daily from about April 10 to the end of August each year, but none from about October 22 to March 1. During the depth of winter, high Arctic muskoxen must carry on their daily functions in continuous darkness or near-darkness.

Summer ranges of muskoxen on the Arctic mainland are largely centered around water sources, such as rivers, ponds, and lakes. These areas favor vegetation growth, particularly willow, probably the most important summer food of the animals. (Muskoxen will occasionally cross rivers, although they seem to prefer not to.) On the Arctic islands and in Greenland the animals are found less often near water, chiefly because there are fewer ponds and lakes.

In winter, on both the mainland and the islands, muskoxen live on gently rolling hills, slopes, or plateaus, wherever suitable forage exists and snow depth is kept low by prevailing winds. Seasonable movements of the animals between winter and summer ranges vary somewhat in the distances covered, but apparently those areas are generally close to each other.

Apart from willows, which have been

noted as a highly important summer food, muskoxen eat a rather wide variety of other plants in summer, including grasses, sedges, and forbs. In winter the animals on the Arctic mainland use a wide selection of woody plants such as Labrador tea, crowberry, bilberry, birch, and willow. High-Arctic muskoxen have a more restricted winter diet, principally willow, dryas, and dried grasses and sedges. Here, most of the woody food species of the mainland are lacking.

The young calf muskox first sees the light of day in a snow-covered landscape in late April or May. The temperature may be thirty below zero and the newborn is wet and shivering. In an hour or two the brown curly hair dries with the help of the mother, and the little creature is following her about with the herd. The mother's milk has much less fat and protein than that of reindeer and caribou, and within a week the calf is grazing. It continues to suckle when possible, however, sometimes up to eighteen months. The calves remain with the mothers for at least a year and may form part of a family group until adulthood. Cows appear to bear their first calves when four years old, but bulls do not

reach sexual maturity until they are six. Normally a single calf is born every second year but may be produced annually; twins are extremely rare. Preliminary evidence suggests that good nutrition is the key to good annual production.

In poor years very few or no calves are born, but at other times populations may have a relatively high proportion of them. Apart from those years when there are no calves, the proportion of young in herds on the Arctic mainland of Canada has varied between 8.5 and 14.3 percent and on the Arctic islands between 6.6 and 18.1 percent.

The average person may be surprised to learn that in this land of night and extreme cold, the survival of calves to yearling age is about the same as other North American ungulates in much milder climates—about 50 percent. Muskoxen appear to be long-lived animals—twenty years or more. At least one muskox, known to have lived in the wild for twenty-three years, still had fairly good teeth; such an animal would probably attain the age of twenty-five.

Musk oxen are usually found in herds, although many bulls are solitary in summer. Except during the rut, an old cow is apt to be the leader. The size of herds varies to some extent with season and place. Southern herds of muskoxen in summer average about eleven animals each and in winter around twenty. Northern bands consist of approximately eight animals in summer and about fifteen in winter. Much larger groups occur in both seasons, but the average size of winter herds seems to be a behavioral adaptation which results in better survival. In the autumn the solitary bulls join mixed herds or groups composed solely of bulls.

The mating season lasts from late July to early September, but the peak appears to be between the first and third week of August. Almost invariably a mature, battle-experienced bull becomes "boss" of a herd during this period. Occasionally solitary bulls attempt to replace the herd bull by engaging in rather ritualized contests. The two contestants will face each other ten or twenty yards apart, then charge with heads lowered; the point of impact is usually the base of the horns, and the resulting crash can be heard up to a mile away. The animals will continue to charge each other until one acknowledges defeat and leaves. Before giving up, an occasional bull is gored or otherwise severely injured.

Apart from the mating season, muskoxen usually have a quiet disposition and spend their time peacefully grazing or resting and ruminating. Their movements are purposeful and slow unless they are aroused by danger or combat. In spite of short, heavy limbs, the animals can move very quickly across broken ground or up shale slopes and hills, and are able to maintain their speed for several miles.

By no means does a herd always run away at the approach of danger. The scattered, grazing muskoxen may run together to form a closely packed group, with calves and yearlings pressed against the flanks of the adults and with the latter presenting a circle or row of lowered horns to an advancing intruder. If attacked by wolves, an adult muskox, often the herd bull, will run out a short distance in an attempt to gore a wolf, and then quickly back into the herd again.

The effect of wolf predation on muskox populations has yet to be evaluated. It is known that wolves kill bulls, cows, and immature animals, but there is no evidence that wolf predation controls the population increase. There is very clear evidence, however, that in the past man with modern firearms reduced and even extirpated muskoxen. The defense stance of muskoxen, while admirably adapted to wolf attacks, was disastrous when the demand for skin robes attracted hunters in the latter half of the last century.

About 15,000 skins were traded between 1862 and 1916, all from Canada's Arctic mainland. Several thousand other muskoxen were killed on the Arctic islands and in Greenland to meet the needs of explorers and trappers. The decimation of the species prompted the Canadian government to give it complete protection in 1917. As a result, when the last census was taken in 1961, it was estimated that the population had increased to 10,000. Some 1,500 were believed to be on the mainland and 8,500 on the Arctic islands. The Greenland population, also protected, is thought to number about 6,000.

The muskox's rather catholic diet, herd behavior and defense, and superb insulation of hair and other adaptations to Arctic conditions, have enabled this remarkable animal to survive in one of the world's harshest environments.

MAMMALS OF THE SEA

A fighter pilot in the Pacific, 1942–46, Karl W. Kenyon earned the Navy Cross when he survived the loss of a plane to enemy fire. In 1947 he entered the Fish and Wildlife Service and was assigned to research on the fur seal, including pelagic sealing off Japan. Since 1955 he has been in charge of sea otter investigations. (One expedition ended in a plane crash which left Kenyon injured and four men dead.) He has made surveys of walruses, albatrosses at Midway and Hawaii, and international studies in and around Antarctica. Mr. Kenyon is a fellow of the American Association and, among other offices, chairman of the "Seal Group" of the Survival Service Commission, I.U.C.N. He has written chapters in two books and about ninety articles—several of which have been translated and reprinted in European journals.

THE SEA OTTER
KARL W. KENYON

Flying two hundred feet above Bering Sea, Dave Spencer and I counted sea otters and recorded them on a nautical chart. Excellent visibility, a light breeze, and high overcast above the glassy, gray water gave us ideal conditions around Adak Island in the Aleutians. As we flew westward, however, an increasing wind ruffled the ocean. Otters became difficult to detect.

"It looks rougher up ahead," Theron (Smitty) Smith, our pilot, remarked as he looked inquiringly at Dave and me. We both nodded assent; our survey was finished for the day.

"I'll just swing around the northwest flank of Mount Tanaga," Smitty continued, "then head home from there." He added power and banked around the volcanic slopes. The altimeter needle climbed smoothly past five hundred feet.

Suddenly the DC-3 shuddered and lurched wildly. With both hands I clung to the back of Smitty's seat while charts, pencils, and notebooks cascaded aft past my head and dangling legs.

Roaring and vibrating now, as Smitty applied full power, the nose of the plane came up, but we still plunged toward the sea. From the corner of one eye I saw the altimeter needle unwinding down, down, down, past two hundred feet. Through a side window I could see water. Caught in a violent convection wind on the downwind side of the mountain, we continued to lose altitude. Visions of earlier crashes, which I had barely survived, flashed through my mind. Now . . . This was it . . . this was the end . . . this was the end of our surveys.

We had almost reached the waves. Miraculously our plane gained speed and then passed with a thudding jolt from the current of down-flowing wind. We climbed again to altitude and safety. Avoiding the mountains, we returned to our temporary base at the United States Naval Station on Adak Island. Our otter surveys would continue, at least for another day.

Investigations by air are a far cry from the exploratory voyages of Vitus Bering in 1741 and of James Cook in 1778. These sea captains took otter skins to Russian and Chinese ports and precipitated a century and a half of unregulated exploitation. Due to Russian, American, and European hunters, the sea otter became rare by the end of the nineteenth century. Fortunately, some otters still remained in the Rat Islands group of the outer Aleutians in 1911 when laws, primarily for the protection of the northern fur seal, gave protection also to the sea otter.

The first scientific surveys of sea otters began on a small scale during the early 1940's when Frank Beale, Aleutian National Wildlife Refuge Manager, investigated reports of a sea otter population explosion at Amchitka Island. An attempt in 1950 to transplant surplus otters from this increasingly dense population to unoccupied parts of the former range revealed our ignorance of the needs of sea otters. All captured animals died before they could be transported to

new areas. Field experiments on methods of holding the animals in captivity were urgent. Also, there was much that needed to be learned of their habitat requirements, reproduction, and natural history.

In 1959 the United States Fish and Wildlife Service scheduled extensive aerial surveys to determine the abundance and distribution of expanding sea otter populations in several Alaska areas. Dave Spencer, supervisor of National Wildlife Refuges in Alaska, and I made two complete surveys of the Aleutian Islands chain, the Alaska Peninsula, and the Shumagin Islands during our comprehensive surveys up to 1965.

We were fortunate to have one of Alaska's most experienced pilots for the vast wilderness that we covered. Nevertheless our three-to-four-month studies

each year were rugged and frustrating. Rain, fog, chilling winds, isolation, unavoidable delays in transportation and supplies, beset us.

The capture of otters on Amchitka's beaches for tagging and studies always offered excitement. One of these ventures left a vivid impression.

A fierce mid-October storm, building strength through a twenty-four-hour period, reached its climax in winds gusting to eighty knots. It was early afternoon when we drove the jeep pickup to St. Makarius Point. From the low bluff at the edge of the North Pacific we saw five otters resting in sheltered pockets among kelp-covered rocks exposed by low tide.

My Aleut helpers, John Nevzorof and Innokenty Golodoff, each carried a long-

201

handled net, while I had a cage strapped to a packboard on my back, a pocketful of sheep ear tags and pliers. Foam flicked past our ears on the shrieking wind, and strips of Alaria kelp fluttered helplessly in the irregular gusts. Once past the shallow, knee-deep channel between the shore and the reefs, the buffeting wind made walking on the slippery rocks extremely hazardous. But John and Innokenty, born in the islands, were experienced, surefooted stalkers. Soon the first otters—a mother with a small pup—were caught. We quickly removed the pup from the net so that the mother would not hurt it in her frantic struggle to escape. We then clipped a tag in the web of her hind flipper. As we liberated

her, we placed the pup in her path and she grasped it by the loose skin on the back of its neck. Then she plunged into the water and emerged with the now crying pup clasped tightly to her chest with a flipper. She eyed us balefully as she swam rapidly on her back toward a passage between the reefs.

The howl of the wind among rocks drowned the sound of our movements, and other otters only a few yards away remained undisturbed. Within twenty minutes we netted, tagged, and released all but one. This last we reserved to take back to our pool on Adak Island for experimental studies in captivity. It was a fully adult male of just over seventy pounds. Lifting him by his hind flip-

202

pers, we freed him from the net and lowered him into the carrying cage. Then John and Innokenty hoisted him on my back.

By now, the rising tide churned like a river through the channel and nearly topped my hip boots. Suddenly the otter reared up on one side of his cage and threw himself to the other—just as my foot came down on a slippery rock. The result was inevitable: I splashed sideways into the rushing, near-freezing water.

The fall could have been disastrous but for the quick action of John and Innokenty. They immediately grasped the cage and held it upright so that I could gain my footing, pull myself from the swift current, and get back to shore. Soaking wet and shivering, I was glad when the jeep brought us to our plane for Adak Island.

Adak was only 130 miles east, a convenient jumping-off place and supply base. Here our holding pen, a cement pool 15×8×3 feet deep, enclosed by a board fence, allowed free air circulation and was fed by clear water from a tundra stream. This furnished an ideal environment for our captives. We learned that otters, captured in weakened and starving condition, returned to vigorous health on an ample diet of fish that we first froze (to kill parasites) and then thawed.

We had long suspected that the Amchitka sea otter population was overcrowding its habitat and that starvation had caused the death of the many otters that we found on beaches during winter and early spring storms.

We discovered that an adult, captive otter requires 23 percent of its body weight in food each day to remain healthy and vigorous, while growing juveniles consume up to one third of their body weight in food. In the wild, the sea otter feeds primarily on shellfish and other attached invertebrates in coastal waters down to depths of about 150 to 180 feet. It is not surprising that a large population in a limited area can deplete its food resources, and can suffer severe mortality during periods of stress that accompany Aleutian storms.

We also learned from our captives that although a pup only a few days old can eat solid food, it requires milk from its mother's two abdominal nipples for many months.

Smallest of marine mammals, the sea otter reaches a maximum weight of one hundred pounds. It resembles, in some respects, other marine mammals more closely than it does related members of its own family, the Mustelidae. This family includes river otters, skunks, weasels, and badgers. All usually bear more than one young in a litter, but the sea otter, like other marine mammals, normally produces only one. Compared with the river otter, the sea otter pup is relatively large and much more developed at birth. It weighs about four to five pounds, has its eyes open, and arrives with a full coat of warm fur and several erupted teeth. Nearly helpless, however, it is unable to swim or dive until it is several months of age. Much of its early life is spent sleeping, nursing, and being groomed as it rides on its mother's chest and belly. Only while she is diving for food does the mother leave her pup floating on the surface.

Although it is a marine mammal, the sea otter hauls out on the beaches to rest and to bear its young. Mating takes place in the water, and the female deserts the male as soon as she can avoid his attentions which may last up to three days.

Recovery of tagged animals revealed that the otter's home range is probably not more than five to ten miles of coastline, but its sense of territoriality is weakly developed. I have never seen males fight either for females or for territory. Except when interested in mating, males live in great bachelor groups and haul out during all seasons on favorite and limited stretches of beach.

Among marine mammals the sea otter is unique in that it depends entirely for body warmth on an insulating blanket of air trapped in its coat of dense, inch-long fur. I estimate that the number of fur fibers in an adult male pelt is over 800 million, or nearly twice as many as in a fur seal pelt of comparable size. Seals and whales depend for warmth on a subcutaneous layer of fat or blubber, but the sea otter has only limited deposits of body fat—not a distinct blubber layer. For this reason the sea otter is highly vulnerable to death through chilling, if its fur becomes soiled and allows water to reach its skin.

For years, exploiters have wanted to harvest sea otters, knowing that a prime

pelt is worth as much as $2,300. On January 22, 1962, I watched Loren Croxton, wildlife biologist for the Alaska Department of Fish and Game, kill with one well-aimed shot the first of one thousand sea otters whose skins were to be offered for sale at the Seattle Fur Exchange on January 30, 1968. This was the first sale of sea otter pelts in the United States since the species was given protection by the 1911 Fur Seal Treaty.

I participated in the kill with mixed feelings. From an aesthetic point of view I would prefer to enjoy sea otters as living wild animals, but as a biologist I needed to examine the specimens. Our studies had made it obvious that surplus animals could be taken from the thirty thousand wild otters in Alaska without endangering the several populations or the species. In addition, many facts of life history could be gained only through the study of a large collection of anatomical specimens.

For example, our subsequent studies of these animals' stomach contents revealed that soft-bodied invertebrates (clams, rock oysters, mussels, and chitons) and some fish are far more important food items than the sea urchin, often supposed to be a food of primary importance. The latter, although found in more than 90 percent of the samples, may have little food value.

Sea otters feeding near Monterey, California, often hold flat rocks on their chests against which they crack their hard-shelled food. We did not see wild otters do this in Alaska. However, when our captives were given a rock with their clams, they knew just how to use it!

Field observations during all seasons revealed that young may be born in any month of the year. Nevertheless, it was necessary to study a large series of reproductive tracts to discover that most births occur in spring and summer months. Microscopic studies by Drs. A. Sinha and C. H. Conaway revealed that shortly after fertilization the blastocyst enters a resting stage—delayed implantation—indicating that the period between mating and birth may be approximately one year. Since the young otter remains with the mother for about a year, and since pregnancy takes a year, at least two years usually elapse between births. Apparently a mother accompanied by a pup does not come in heat.

Detailed knowledge of the reproductive habits, general behavior, abundance, and distribution are essential to the formulation of a rational management program. With this knowledge at hand it will be possible to maintain healthy sea otter populations and at the same time harvest a useful economic product. Much is still to be learned of the life history, but enough knowledge is now available to assure that the world population of perhaps 35,000 sea otters may, throughout its range along the California coast, in Alaska, and in the Kuril Islands of the Soviet Union, furnish an aesthetic, scientific, and economic return to the various groups of its human admirers.

John J. Burns spent his early life in New York and eastern New England and was a commercial fisherman on Long Island until entering North Carolina State College. After graduation in 1960 he went to Alaska, where he became a marine mammalogist for the State Department of Fish and Game. Graduate work at the University of Alaska resulted in an M.S. degree in zoology and wildlife management in 1964.

Based at Nome, where he lives with his wife and two children, Mr. Burns devotes most of his time to the Pacific walrus. Dwelling as it does in remote Arctic seas, this unique and endangered mammal has had little scientific study in the past. The following account of the writer's observations, therefore, is of particular importance and interest.

THE WALRUS

JOHN J. BURNS

On April 28, I flew in a small plane from Nome, Alaska, to one of America's most northwestern outposts. We landed on the ice field that covers the narrow channel between the American Little Diomede and the Russian Big Diomede islands. Our Soviet neighbors kept us under surveillance from their lookout high up on the side of their rocky island. They would still be watching when Ed and Jim Dunbar, two sport hunters, arrived in the little Eskimo village a week later.

May would be a month of rapid and spectacular change. My studies of walruses and seals had brought me to this and other islands in the Bering Strait during the six previous years. Each visit seemed to be more interesting and informative than the last. Perhaps this was because some of the questions about seal and walrus biology had been at least paritally answered, and in the process new and often more challenging ones had been raised.

By mid-May the tenacious grip of late winter began to loosen. Seals, starting on their northward spring migration from the Bering Sea, appeared in larger numbers. The "landing field" between the two islands was breaking up and drifting away in the strong current. Most spectacular was the arrival of tens of thousands of cliff-nesting seabirds. The Eskimo hunters were concerned because so far only a few walruses had been taken. I was worried, too. The Diomeders needed the food and by-products, and we needed the specimens and data for our research program. But, for days, the only sounds we had heard, other than human voices, were birds and the seemingly endless whistle of the wind.

Very early on the morning of May 28, I was awakened by the shouts of the hunters and the bellowing of walruses which seemed to come from everywhere. Several large herds lying on the moving ice had drifted within sight of the village, and the Eskimos were eager to get at them. I chose to join the crew that was taking Ed and Jim after their trophies. This would give me an opportunity to see more animals, for the brothers would want to cruise from herd to herd before they decided which big bull to shoot. (Unlike the natives, each nonresident is permitted to kill only one bull walrus.)

At 4 A.M. the sun was already high as we left the village in a large walrus-hide boat. Within a few minutes a lone bull was spotted on an ice floe, and we turned toward it to have a look.

Almost a mile separated us. The walrus was only a dark object on the ice. Soon it acquired form, and the big white tusks were visible when it swung its head in our direction. We broke into an open lead and the walrus watched us approach. Our outboard motor was cut and the boat glided to a stop within fifty yards of the great battle-scarred bull. It was an awesome sight for the Dunbars who had never seen a walrus before. Al-though the rest of us had been close to walruses many times, we found their excitement contagious.

Their whispered exclamations prompted a flow of memories. I was only faintly aware of camera shutters clicking on both sides of me and the low murmur of voices. Then, for a few minutes, I drifted back into the past.

. . . my first walrus stares at me with its little eyes in the big, wrinkled, whiskered face . . . now its ungainly body humps over the ice and splashes into the sea . . . a cow demolishes a huge chunk of ice with her tusks and frees her newborn calf from a crevasse into which it has fallen . . . the calf clings to its mother's back with foreflippers as she dives into the icy waters . . . Eskimo hunters are paddling their little skin boats (umiaks) toward a large herd . . . *look out!* . . . an enraged bull almost capsizes one of them . . . the animal is killed and the hunters clamber onto the ice floe, shooting as they advance . . . immediately they begin butchering the meat for the coming winter . . . some of the escaping animals turn and mill around the floe looking for their wounded . . . my seven-year-old son throws snowballs at them less than ten feet away, and is impressed by the fact that he can keep these huge animals from climbing back on the ice with us by hitting them on the very sensitive nose.

"Have a cigarette! Have a cigarette!" someone was repeating. With a start I came back to today, the outboard motor, and the Dunbars. They were still fascinated by the walrus. As with all other adult bulls, the neck, shoulders, and upper chest of this one were covered by a shield of thick, lumpy skin. This secon-

208

dary sex characteristic affords protection when the bulls jab each other with their long tusks.

Our bull had several wounds on his neck, and the left side of his broad, bristly muzzle was partially torn away. It was obvious that he had been fighting with his own kind, although the breeding season was over. When walruses haul out on ice or land, they crowd together, flippers and tusks often touching or on top of each other. A late-comer may have to jab his way through closely packed bodies to find a resting place. Sometimes the sprawling animals make room for a dominant male to pass, but more often there are likely to be arguments. Our bull must have survived a particularly gory dispute and he was now recovering in isolation. Even with the arrival of our boat, he was reluctant to leave his new-found haven.

"He's fat—probably weighs 3,500 pounds!" exclaimed an Eskimo.

"But one tusk is broken," said Jim.

"Oh, let's try for a bigger one!" urged Ed. "Sometimes they weigh close to two tons!" This was certainly the time to hunt walruses. By the end of June the bulls would have lost considerable weight and would not regain it until the fall.

Since it was early in the day, the Dunbars decided to look for a bull that had larger tusks. One of the Eskimos started the motor and we began to pull away. The increased noise and activity were more than the walrus would tolerate. He rolled over, slid into the icy water, and disappeared.

That evening, after a long and successful day, the Dunbars had many questions to ask about walruses and our attempts to manage their populations. Now that they had actually seen the ani-

mals and each had a trophy of his own, the information was more interesting and meaningful for them than it had been during the weeks of waiting.

Walruses are important to the coastal-dwelling Eskimos of Alaska because they supply much of the material needs of these people. The meat is acquired for food; the skins make ropes, coverings for umiaks and kayaks; and the intestines become waterproof parkas. Bone and ivory are used for hunting implements, and the sale of ivory carvings is a vital source of cash income. The importance of walruses in the Eskimo economy requires that their future be insured.

The walrus is a rather long lived animal that matures slowly; its life-span is occasionally as long as thirty-seven years. The age of individual animals can be determined by the number of rings or annual layers observed in thin cross sections of the teeth. During the past several years, Eskimo hunters have been taking one tooth from each walrus they kill and sending it to us for examination. (Our initial attempts at trying to convince these men that we could determine the age of a walrus from a slice of tooth is in itself a comical story!)

Females attain a maximum weight of around 2,200 pounds as opposed to almost two tons in the bulls. The body form is basically seal-like, with smooth contours to reduce water friction. Most of the fore and hind limbs are within the body; only the paddle-like flippers protrude. The hind flippers join the body at what would be a person's ankle. Power for swimming comes mainly from the hind flippers which are moved from side to side. As in fur seals and sea lions, the hind flippers can be rotated forward under the body when a walrus moves across ice or land. Hind flippers of a true seal cannot be rotated forward.

Odobenus, the generic name, refers to their most prominent characteristic—tusks. These modified canine teeth are present in both sexes and frequently grow to more than two feet in length. Cows lack the lumpy skin on the neck and shoulders of the bull; their tusks are more slender, the muzzle is not so broad, and their color is generally darker brown.

Most females do not begin to breed until they are six or seven years old. Mating occurs during February and March, but implantation and subsequent growth of the fetus does not occur until sometime during the first two weeks of June. From conception to birth, the total gestation period is about thirteen months; the time of actual fetal growth is about ten months. Cows in their prime have one calf every other year; older females produce less frequently. A calf weighs about 130 pounds when it is born during late April or early May. The mother takes care of it for eighteen months, and sometimes as long as two and one-half years. If she is killed before the calf is weaned, or at least one and one-half years old, it will die.

At two years of age a walrus weighs about 750 pounds. Although females attain their adult weight by eight or nine years of age, the males continue growing until they are fourteen or fifteen years old. Length of adult females, from nose to tip of the tail is around nine and one-half feet; that of males is almost eleven feet. These average lengths do not include the hind flippers.

Pacific walruses are not restricted to areas along the shore because most of their range (Bering and Chukchi Seas)

is underlain by the uniformly shallow and rich Bering-Chukchi Platform.

Clams provide the bulk of their diet. Only the protruding extremity of the clams is eaten: the "foot" of some types and the siphons of others. As much as 109 pounds of clam feet and siphons have been recorded in the stomach of one bull. These parts are torn away from the rest of the clam by strong suction, a method of feeding for which the mouth of the walrus seems ideally suited. Few if any shell fragments are found in the stomachs. A walrus' mouth is narrow with an unusually high roof, strong, thick lips which are not deeply cleft, and a thick, piston-like tongue. Contrary to popular belief, the tusks are probably not used to dig up the ocean floor. When a walrus is feeding, it glides forward along the bottom using its tusks like sled runners and feels for clams with its broad, bristly muzzle. The importance of the tusks in feeding is that with the neck muscles, they regulate pressure of the walrus' nose against the ocean bottom.

The traditional Diomede Eskimo belief about how a walrus feeds agrees with ours on only one point—the tusks are not used to dig up clams. According to the Diomeders, when a walrus locates a clam, it puts its mouth right next to it and grunts loudly. The frightened clam forgets how to clam up and is promptly relieved of its soft parts.

This hypothesis was put to the crucial test. The Eskimos and I placed thirteen clams in a water-filled pan with sand on the bottom. Several of us took turns grunting at them—with our faces in and out of the water. No success. The clams did what they were supposed to do; they stayed clammed up. We then resorted to a foghorn, banging pots, and a small church bell. One clam expelled water when the church bell was rung. This was, of course, proof of something as far as the local missionary was concerned. However, the question of how a walrus gets a clam out of its shell was not resolved, as it was decided that we could not satisfactorily imitate the sounds of a clam-hunting walrus. We shucked the clams by other methods.

I have frequently joined the Eskimos in taking advantage of the walrus' prowess as a clam catcher by eating clams from the animals' stomachs—either raw or after we cooked them.

Walruses (with the exception of some young bulls) are usually not dangerous to man, but their inquisitiveness, gregariousness, size, and great strength demand caution on the part of those who approach them. The bond between mother and calf is very strong, and neither will abandon the other even when hunters are close at hand. Cows make every effort to rescue their offspring and often carry their dead calves away. Walruses, especially the young males, will frequently push wounded animals off an ice floe and out of the reach of hunters. They commonly return to an ice floe as long as other animals, in pain, fear, or anger continue to bellow, sometimes placing both men and boats in jeopardy. This return is not a reprisal attack, but an attempt to lead the wounded animals and orphaned calves to safety. A man imitating the sounds of a walrus can frequently call them to him.

Tusks seem to be very important during encounters with other walruses; animals with the largest tusks are dominant over the others. When animals hauled out on an ice floe or on land are dis-

turbed, they raise their heads high, prominently displaying their tusks. Animals with smaller tusks usually either move away, lower their heads, or become respectfully quiet. The only serious battles are between animals of about the same body and tusk size.

At one time Pacific walruses were much more numerous than they are today. It has been estimated that prior to 1860 the herds numbered no less than 200,000 animals. After the decline of whales in the Bering and Chukchi Seas, whalers turned their attention to the vast herds of walruses, killing them in large numbers. The number of walruses was at its lowest during the early decades of this century, reduced to perhaps 45,000 animals. Since that time, due to protective legislation, there has been a slow but steady increase in the population and they have apparently reached about half of their former abundance. Unfortunately, hunting loss, even under optimum conditions continues to be high, ranging from 30 to 60 percent of the animals killed. Wounded animals usually escape from the ice floes, and those that die in the water are apt to sink before being harpooned and hauled aboard. Since ivory is a source of income, there is an incentive for hunters to kill walruses solely for their tusks. Recent regulations restricting the purchase and sale of raw ivory and establishing limits on the number of females that can be taken have had a great influence on the size and sex composition of the annual harvests.

The fate of the walrus herds is by no means certain, but if the present concern for them continues, they will be available for future generations of Eskimo hunters to stalk over the frozen northern seas.

Since 1935, Robert T. Orr has been successively assistant curator and curator of birds and mammals in the California Academy of Sciences, and he became associate director in 1964. In addition to these full-time duties he has taught biology at Stanford, California, and San Francisco universities, retiring from the latter as full professor in 1964.

Dr. Orr has been president of the American Society of Mammalogists and the Cooper Ornithological Society. He has published about two hundred articles as well as a number of books as diverse in subject as fungi, mammals, and animal life in general (*Vertebrate Biology* and *The Animal Kingdom,* etc.). His name is synonymous with natural history, especially the marine mammals of the Pacific Coast, from northern California to Peru.

SEA LION
ROBERT T. ORR

It was early in June, just a few weeks after the arrival of the first Steller sea lion bulls on Año Nuevo Island. The most dominant individuals had already established territories and some had harems of cows. A few of the cows had even given birth to pups. However, there were many solitary males near the edges of the harem areas and on smaller reefs and sandy beaches. We conjectured that these young males or bachelors, as they are known, gathered together to console one another.

For several years I had been coming out weekly to this island off the coast of central California, to study the social behavior of sea lions as well as their population dynamics. There were blinds strategically located to permit one to watch without being seen. Most of these were on promontories on the main body of the island, but the one that I planned to use today was on the edge of a reef where a large group of breeding bulls and cows had already formed into harem groups. To get there one had to cross a shallow surge channel on slippery mats of seaweed at low tide. On reaching the edge of the reef it was then necessary to climb ten or twelve feet up a vertical surface

213

of rock and enter the blind from beneath. The latter was built like a room and had one edge overhanging to permit access through a trapdoor in the floor. Once safely inside, the one-way glass windows made it possible to watch the sea lions, which sometimes surrounded the blind on all three sides, without their seeing us.

The tide was low on this day, but a solitary bull was on one edge of the now exposed surge channel. Although he was facing the other way, I could see that he was aggressive and had been in numerous battles, some quite recently, judging from the open wounds on his enormous neck and on the sides of his head. I quietly moved down the edge of the island and was crossing the slippery channel to the base of the reef when suddenly the bull turned, discovered me, and, with a roar, charged. In my struggle to reach safety I slipped and fell on the algal growth. I thought this would be my end, having watched big bulls shake other bulls weighing as much as two thousand pounds. in their massive jaws.

Sometimes a knowledge of animal behavior is of value, and on this occasion I decided to chance all on something I had observed during two previous Steller sea lion breeding seasons. Males in battle face each other, roar, and maintain their heads elevated. The lowering of the head and assumption of a prone position is a submissive gesture and will cause a cessation of aggressive behavior. I decided to be submissive, since there was really little choice. I lay still and prone and the attacking bull stopped about twenty feet away. Finally after a few moments he turned around and faced the other way, toward the sea. This was my cue to rise

quietly to my feet and ascend the rocks into the blind. My thoughts for the next several hours were not on the colonial behavior of sea lions but rather on how I would safely return to the island without any further attack. Before the tide rose too high, however, my problem was solved by the bull leaving the area, probably in search of a more fruitful location.

The Steller or northern sea lion, like certain other members of the order Pinnipedia, has a very definite social structure during the reproductive period. The males come to offshore islands in early May and stake out territories on favored reefs. Fierce battles take place in order that these sites may be maintained, and only the dominant individuals are successful. Once a bull has become established, neighboring bulls become more tolerant, and several such landowners may join forces to prevent any intruders from taking over.

The females or cows come to these areas in late May or early June, at which time a single bull may acquire as many as ten to fifteen females. The females are not kept in the harem areas by the bulls, as is true of the northern fur seal cows, but leave if they wish to go to sea or to another harem. The herd bulls may be as close as ten feet to one another, but generally the space between them is greater. Unlike the females, they remain on guard within their territories day and night for a number of weeks unless displaced by a more dominant individual.

The pups are usually born a few days after the females join the harems, during the month of June or very early July. Unlike their yellow-brown-colored mothers, they have a blackish pelage. Their voice resembles the bleat of a lamb, whereas that of the adults is more like the lowing of cattle. This is in marked contrast to the staccato barking that is so characteristic of the California sea lion, a related species of somewhat more southern distribution. It is often said that young sea lions have to learn to swim, but I have watched newborn pups that have been washed off the natal reefs paddle successfully in high seas for several hours. Their main problem is cold because they lack the thick layer of fat that enables the older animals to survive the chilling waters of the North Pacific.

Young sea lions stay close to their mothers for the first few days of life, nursing when hungry and sleeping much of the rest of the time. As they get older their behavior changes, and by the time they are several weeks of age they gather

into groups and move to the edge of the harem areas or to situations where there is less danger of being crushed by the bulls, who pay no attention to them whatsoever. Here they appear to indulge in play, swim in tidepools and splash ponds, and sleep in groups. By this time the females periodically leave the reefs and go to sea to feed. On returning to the rookery, vocalization seems to be the principal means of communication between a mother and her pup. The female calls as she approaches in the water and is answered by her offspring. Both move toward each other, one on a reef and the other in the water. After the mother comes on land, muzzle contact is finally made and odor recognition seems to confirm the reunion. Any strange pup trying to obtain nourishment is apt to be picked up in the jaws of an irate female and tossed ten or fifteen feet away, sometimes with dire results.

As the summer moves on, the bulls become less aggressive and more tolerant of intruders and the harems start to break up. By the latter part of July the bulls begin to leave the island, accompanied by the young bachelors whose summer has been spent in jousting one another in mock battles that prepare them for more serious contests to come in another year or so. The females and their pups, however, remain on for many months. Young sea lions, unlike young elephant seals or harbor seals, may nurse for more than a year. The latter are weaned in about one month.

By September on Año Nuevo the only Steller sea lions left are females and their young, with a few yearlings still trying to obtain food from their mothers despite the latters' new progeny. The pups have not yet lost their black natal pelage but

are much larger and have left the protected pools to swim in the surge channels and between the reefs. Even here they continue to engage in considerable play and often follow one another or an adult female who serves as a leader.

With the exodus of the Steller bulls from Año Nuevo Island there is an influx of another type of pinniped, the California sea lion, which is the kind most often seen in zoos and circuses. Males of this species come north from their own harem areas, which are on islands much farther south along the coast of southern California and northwestern Mexico. Once here they more or less replace the Steller bulls, which in turn have also moved farther north where they will remain until the migratory urge brings them south again the following April or May. The California bulls are smaller and darker and mingle with the Steller pups and cows with little animosity shown by members of either species. It is not uncommon to see both kinds sleeping side by side or even on top of the very much larger elephant seals, which also inhabit the island but do not breed until midwinter.

By late December a change begins to take place in the Steller sea lion colony. Their numbers, which have been quite high although composed almost solely of females and pups, begin to dwindle. The pups are old enough to go to sea and travel for some distance. Gradually during the next three or four months fewer and fewer individuals are seen, although there is never a time in the year when some are not present. The population reaches its lowest by late April or early May, but this is when the bulls begin to return, and once again this interesting social cycle starts its course.

217

A specialist in marine mammals, Kansas-born Victor B. Scheffer joined the United States Bureau of Biological Survey, now the Fish and Wildlife Service, in 1937 and retired in 1969. For nearly thirty years he studied life in the North Pacific Ocean and Bering Sea—his primary interest being the Pribilof herd of fur seals.

Vic Scheffer was a National Science Grantee to Cambridge University, England, in 1956–57, and an observer for the United States on the first scientific team that visited Antarctica in 1964 under the Antarctic Treaty. Since 1965 he has lectured at his alma mater in Seattle. He is the author of many professional papers and the book *Seals, Sea Lions and Walruses*. His hobby is nature photography.

THE NORTHERN FUR SEAL

VICTOR B. SCHEFFER

A few tens of thousands of years B.P. (before present) the northern fur seals were living in a great arc along the temperate shores of North Pacific. Then came the hunters; nameless men who left no records. They paddled out from shore in skin boats and found the breeding places of the seals, one by one. When the remnant seals were rediscovered, first in 1742 by Georg Steller, they were surviving only on bleak, sub-Arctic islands uninhabited by man.

Now on the fourth of July 1968 I stand on St. Paul Island in the Bering Sea, reading the words of a square bronze plate bolted to a volcanic rock:

FUR SEAL ROOKERIES . . . . ALASKA
REGISTERED NATIONAL HISTORIC LANDMARK

From the north, the sharp sea wind brings the sound of ten thousand seals from the beaches of Lukanin. Far in the distance, across a tundra bright with flowers, I see the low rounded hills where lie the remains of men: the young coast-guardsman drowned in performance of duty; the professor from Stanford who came to this wild island and fell in love with its wildness, and whose ashes were finally returned here; the five seal poachers, surprised on

219

the beach with bloody knives in 1906. One of the hills is named for a theologian and one for a fur trader who took part in a lawless attack on the seals in 1868.

Since their discovery by the Russians in 1786, the Alaska seals have yielded amazing wealth. They now bring about 5 million dollars annually from the sale of pelts and meat, and from the profits of tourism. The harvest of skins fluctuates around 60,000 to 70,000 a year. The output of dark red "sealburger," for animal food, is more than 700 tons and will soon be 1,000.

And where there's money, there's action. As I study the history of the fur seals and man's efforts to manage them wisely, I feel as though I am opening "time capsules" of human and natural history which contain all the important clues to wildlife conservation. I read evidence of greed and plunder, death, cruelty, bureaucracy, native suppression, and national and international bickering. And, at the end of it all, the modern scene.

Four great nations—Canada, Japan, the United States, and the Soviet Union —now cooperate under a convention to keep the seal populations of the north at "the level of maximum sustainable yield." Their scientists meet yearly to swap ideas. Ignoring political and ideological bounds, they work side by side on small vessels and on the respective breeding grounds of the Asian and American seals.

All the northern fur seals breed in summer on islands in, or near, the Bering Sea. On the breeding grounds owned by the United States (the Pribilof Islands of Alaska), their numbers, which had been reduced to about 200,000 in 1910, now reach a summer peak of about 1,400,-000. On the half-dozen or more islands

and offshore breeding rocks owned by the Soviet Union (the Commanders, the central Kurils, and Seal Island) the summer population is about 300,000 and is still growing. The Canadians and the Japanese have no fur seal islands now. However, their nationals abstain from killing seals on the international seas and, in return, share the American and Soviet take of skins each year.

In winter, the seals wander for months on end across the wide, rolling Pacific, feeding and sleeping at sea. Some stray as far south as central Mexico and central Japan. The Asian and American stocks intermingle at sea in winter and on land in summer. They are indistinguishable. Biologists cannot identify the birthplace of a seal unless it happens to be one of tens of thousands now wearing a numbered metal tag that was clinched to its flipper in the first summer of life.

The seals keep warm in the chilly seas of winter, partly because they are enveloped in subcutaneous fat (blubber) and partly because their fur contains about 300,000 water-repellent fibers per square inch.

As I stare across the tundra on this fourth of July I think back to the year 1940, when I was sent as a young biologist to the seal islands by Ira Noel Gabrielson, then director of the Fish and Wildlife Service. He shrewdly suspected that the vital statistics of the seal herd, though printed in neat columns in the government record books, were not the facts. And how could they be? No serious study of seals had been made for twenty years. The pregnancy rate in 1940 was assumed to be 100 percent, though it was actually nearer 60. The mortality rate of pups on land was assumed to be 2 or 3 percent, though it was surely much higher. As recently as 1942, no one could legally kill any seal for study, much less the female sacred cow.

All this is past. Now researchers, including biostatisticians, general biologists, and a veterinarian, work continually to improve the management of the herd and to disclose broad zoological principles. They study a population whose members are remarkable subjects —perhaps the finest subjects in the world—for research on wild animals in their native habitat.

The seals are very predictable. Early in May each year the adult males (bulls), fat and belligerent, land on the Pribilofs. They weigh 420 pounds, on average. In a few weeks they are followed by the adult females (cows), which have an average weight of 100 pounds. Most of the females are pregnant, and in June or July, they give birth to a single black "pup" weighing about eleven pounds. Within a week, the new mother is reimpregnated in the horn of the uterus opposite the one which just delivered. (An official who lectured in the 1920's used to say that "she had a double womb"!)

The period of gestation is about fifty-one weeks. For the first four months, the embryo is quiescent and barely visible to the naked eye. Toward mid-November, however, it suddenly fastens to the pink uterine wall; a placenta spreads and begins to give it nourishment. When it reaches full term in the following summer it is a well-formed little seal, warm-coated in black hair, with open eyes, a strong bleating voice, and about one third of its *permanent* teeth already showing above the gums.

The odds are roughly equal that the pup will be born tail-first or head-first. Twin embryos appear in one or two pregnancies per thousand, though I doubt that a mother could, or would even try to rear twins to healthy independence. Two or three pups in 100,000 are albinos, with white coats, pink eyes, and pinky-white flippers. And some are piebald, mixed black and white. Such freaks are accepted by the other seals and are interesting to naturalists, but they are unimportant in the total picture.

After the mother has given birth and has been reimpregnated, the male loses a certain degree of interest in her. He continues to hold her loosely in a "harem" around which he shuffles many times each day and night. From a low-flying airplane, one can see the well-beaten circles on the rookery that mark the boundaries of each male domain. His attachment to a certain place is stronger than that to a certain seal or group of seals.

From the time the cows arrive he stays on station for an average of fifty days without food or drink, subsisting on his enormous pads of fat. He impregnates about thirty-eight females. This number must be estimated, for not all the females are on the rookery at a given time. Some are out in Bering Sea, feeding on fish and squid to make milk for their pups. After landing in June or July, the average female stays on the rookery for eight days before she leaves. Some females wander 250 miles at sea before they turn toward home.

The distance that the nursing mother must travel to find food is perhaps a limiting factor in population growth. I say "perhaps" because the relationship has not been proved. After the Fur Seal Treaty of 1911 went into effect, the size of the herd grew steadily until the late 1930's or thereabouts, when it leveled off. One explanation goes something like this: more seals—increased competition among nursing mothers for fish near the breeding grounds in summer—greater average distance to be traveled in search of food—longer average time between nursings—less fat deposited on the average pup by the time it faces the hazards of its first winter at sea—thus greater mortality of pups and yearlings —and thus fewer seals in the entire herd. Full circle!

During the four months from birth to weaning, the rhythm of the nursing cycle is quite regular. Dick Peterson verified this by watching seals, day after day, from an observation tower at the edge of Kitovi Rookery. I confirmed it later by examining the ivory layers deposited in the roots of the teeth. (The record stays there in the teeth for life.) On the average, ten or eleven strata, representing cycles of eleven days each, are laid down in the teeth during the nursing period. That is, about once in eleven days the pup gorges on rich milk, 45 percent fat, but no sugar, and then sleeps profoundly while its mother goes off to fill her mammary glands. If she does not return, the pup will die. Among the thousands of crowded odorous seals, each cow mysteriously recognizes her own and will nurse no other.

I would like to tell a story about teeth, only because it illustrates the value of pure research—of research that gives no promise of paying off tomorrow. In the summer of 1949 I undertook to photograph the complete dentition of a seal. I boiled his skull, extracted his teeth, cleaned them in peroxide, and laid them neatly on a glass slab. Then I looked at them sharply. Four puzzling ridges or ripple marks encircled the root of each. Could these be annual marks reflecting

the yearling cycle, first on land and then at sea?

In the routine "kill" of the following morning I looked at the teeth of a dozen males of known ages—three to five years —tagged as pups. Indeed the ridges were annual marks. Here was suddenly a new research tool that could shed light on the age composition of the herd. It could help biologists to express pregnancy rates, mortality, migratory habits, and other phenomena, all with reference to age, and all on the basis of seals that had not been tagged, branded, sheared, or otherwise handled by man.

I will confess that other adventures in seal research did not end so happily. Once I asked the St. Paul Island natives to reenact a scene from 1924, the last year they had counted pups by driving them like sheep along the beach. The enthusiastic staging of the drive got quickly out of control, and before we sensed the danger, forty pups had smothered in a steaming pile among the rocks.

Except the yearlings, many of whom remain at sea for reasons yet unknown, all ages of seals return to the Pribilofs in summer. At age three a few of the females are known to mate for the first time, and at age three a few of the males are presumed capable of breeding. For reasons both anatomical and sociological, however, the female is not sexually prime until age seven, and the male until age ten. Even when the testes of the adolescent male contain viable sperms, he must first win a place on the breeding ground before he can mate. This usually means he must challenge an older and more powerful bull.

Each summer and fall on the Pribilofs, about one pup in twelve dies—generally of starvation, injury, hookworm anemia, or infection. And around the first of November the survivors, 300,000 strong, gradually venture into the stormy Bering Sea and North Pacific. About half of these will die within the next eight months. The ones that do adapt to pelagic life have a good chance of growing up. The average age of breeding males is about eleven years, and of breeding females eleven or twelve. One female in ten thousand born survives to age twenty-five. Survival is even lower in the males, for a man-made reason: more males than females are killed in the annual harvest. Since the fur seals are highly polygamous, 80 to 90 percent of the young males in ages two to five years can be killed without depressing the production rate of the herd.

Young males (bachelors) are easily captured because they rest in groups apart from, but near, the harems. The bachelors approaching six or seven years of age continuously watch for opportunities to raid the rookeries and cut out a few breeding females. The opportunities increase in midsummer when many older bulls, thin and worn from weeks of vigil, depart from the rookeries.

I suggested earlier that the objective of the present fur seal convention is maximum yield. Though this statement is essentially true, the diplomats of certain nations have hinted from time to time that smaller populations would be pref-erable because seals eat commercially valuable fish. The remains of fifty-four species of fish and nine species of squid were found in seal stomachs collected off North America from 1958 to 1966. In 9,580 stomachs containing food, salmon were identified in 239. The important fishes in the diet were anchovy, hake, capelin, herring, sand lance, saury, walleye pollack, and rockfishes. However, the impact of seals upon fisheries has not been measured, and possibly never can be, for the ecology of the situation is complex and ever-changing.

Perhaps I have passed too quickly over the natural history of *Callorhinus ursinus*. There is so much that could be told.

In memory, I climb again through the wet beach-grass. The manager of the Pribilofs has offered to lead me to a vantage point where I can see the famous furbearing seals of Alaska. In single file we follow a fox trail to the top of a cliff. Suddenly we meet a wall of icy wind, rank with the smell of animal bodies, and we hear a great chorus, an unearthly chorus, a sound that will forever echo in my mind. Once again I stare in disbelief at a carpet of moving forms a hundred feet below. Black and brown and gray, they cover the beach and move among the slippery boulders and fade away a mile or more into the everlasting mists from whence they came.

The daughter of writer Philip Wylie, Karen W. Pryor maintained aquaria in her Cornell University dormitory and married a classmate who had a similar enthusiasm for the watery world. Subsequently, the Pryors settled in Hawaii, did graduate work in marine biology at the University of Hawaii, and established the Oceanic Foundation. This organization operates Sea Life Park, the greatest tourist attraction in the Islands, and the Oceanic Institute for research. Mrs. Pryor is curator of the former and director of training of whales and porpoises in the latter. She has published several research papers in scientific journals and (in premarine days) a book entitled *Nursing Your Baby*. Currently she is supervising construction of a new home, which will have a porpoise in the swimming pool.

WILD THINGS IN THE WILD SEA
KAREN W. PRYOR

When we began building Sea Life Park on Oahu and went hunting porpoises, a distinguished scientist discouraged us with the comment that Hawaiian waters are known to have "a very impoverished cetacean fauna." As usual, it was a case of an animal being reported absent in a given area because no one had looked for it there. We now know of at least fifteen species of whales and porpoises (or dolphins) in Hawaiian waters, and most of these have found their way into our tanks.

Of the species we have come to know, each one has its charms, but none is more interesting than the little-known *Steno bredanensis* (rough-toothed porpoise). We saw our first *Steno* in 1964, although we didn't know it. A sign painter decorated our collecting boat, a converted sampan, with a portrait of a porpoise jumping through a life preserver. The man was better at lettering than at artwork. Such a porpoise! It had a long, thin snout like a billfish, no forehead, bulging eyes, and flapping, oversized flippers and flukes. Its color was a mottled, indeterminate brown instead of the elegant steel grays and creams of most cetaceans. There were a good many jokes as the

225

newly painted boat went out—"Don't catch one of *those*"—but of course we did. The sign painter had made quite a good representation of *Steno bredanensis,* the rough-toothed porpoise!

Steno is an ugly animal, as porpoises go. We know little about its life at sea so far, but its bulky, bulging rib cage, its large mobile flippers which act as diving planes, its wide, powerful tail, suggest an animal which dives deep and stays down a long time. Equally unorthodox is its habit of swimming. Most porpoises, creatures of the interface between air and water, cruise at or just under the surface, rolling to the air and even leaping out quite often. *Stenos* cruise fifteen feet or more below the surface, coming up only to breathe. Perhaps this is why they are seldom reported as seen at sea.

Stenos are covered with scars, many of them circular. As one reporter wrote, "A *Steno* looks as if it spent its finest hours fighting with a switch-blade." Most porpoises are extremely careful to protect their delicate skin; rough-tooths simply don't care. In captivity, they bang themselves up and get cut and scraped, play with sharp objects and stick their noses into abrasive drains with tiresome frequency. Gentle with each other, they are real roughnecks with people and porpoises of other species, and have to be trained to pull their punches. A wild-caught *Steno,* learning to feed, does not simply swallow his fish. He destroys it. Given whole fish, even tiny six-inch smelt, he will gut them, dehead them, fling them around the tank, bang them on the walls, and then eat them.

Why? We don't know. We can surmise that *Steno,* instead of feeding on surface life such as flying fish, as a proper porpoise does, dives to four or five hundred feet and hunts large squid which have to be attacked and subdued; hence the circular scars and the bold and brassy approach to life. But we have seen them feeding on flying fish, too.

We know, now, where to find our rough-toothed porpoises: there seems to be a resident school that can almost always be located in one coastal area near Honolulu. We have released tagged animals into the school and observed them at sea from underwater chambers. Scientists at Sea Life Park's neighbor, the Oceanic Institute, have a continuing program of studying the wild *Steno* on his own home grounds.

Meanwhile, since the day when the first Steno was brought ashore, individuals of this species have been working for us—and teaching us more about themselves—in our research and exhibit tanks.

The first captive was a female. Most porpoises suffer on being captured, not from the handling or the strange confinement of tank walls, but from being alone for the first time, away from the constant voices and presence of their species mates. The new *Steno* was no exception. Shocked and terrified, she would not eat or swim. It was imperative to try to catch another immediately. Small craft warnings were up, unfortunately, and the collecting boat's long pulpit was rigged for whales, which, like the porpoises, are snagged in a lasso as they pass across the bows of the ship. The collectors found *Stenos* again, but, in fifteen-foot seas and a thirty-knot wind, could not reach them because of the over-sized whale-hunting pulpit. Over the radio came reports of the worsening condition of our female *Steno*. Lashing the wheel, the two men let the ship drift and smashed the whale pulpit. Amidst its drifting wreckage they started the boat up and noosed a *Steno* from the bow itself.

All our veterinary skill could not save the first porpoise, which weakened and contracted pneumonia. But she lived long enough to help acclimatize the second, a male named Kai (ocean) by our Hawaiian collector, to commemorate the rough sea he was caught in. By the time the third *Steno* came in (a female named Pono) Kai was feeding well and had learned to press a lever, ringing a bell, in return for a food reward.

It often takes a new porpoise, even with a tame species-mate to imitate, several days to learn to eat in captivity and two or three weeks to begin to catch on to the idea of working for food. Pono was dropped into the tank in the evening. The next morning, before attempts began to lure her to eat, Kai was given a short session with his bell. He rang the bell and was fed, four or five times. Pono watched. Then Pono swam up, slammed the bell nearly off the wall, took a fish reward, and swallowed it.

Learning by observation is commonplace in porpoises, but the fearless participation in work shown by Pono less than twenty-four hours after capture, was our first lesson in *Steno* precocity.

We have come to discover that almost nothing fazes a *Steno*. Most other porpoises, before being trained, are as shy of strange objects as an unbroken colt. But if you show a newly caught *Steno* a harness, such as scientists use to attach instruments to porpoises, he will quickly grab it from you and wrap himself up in it. On the other hand, ask a high-strung *Stenella* (a surface dolphin) to swim through a hoop, and it may take

three or four days before he comes down to your end of the tank, near the strange equipment. Put a hoop in a *Steno*'s tank and before you can get your hand in the fish bucket he may swim through it, jump over it, swim under it, grab it, and take it away with him.

We soon began using *Stenos* for our most demanding work. In discrimination experiments, we found that they have a remarkably long attention span. Learning to select a black-marked card placed at random among white cards, a female *Steno* named Malia would work steadily for two hours or more, long past the time when the human experimenter was willing to give up. Furthermore, puzzles interest the rough-tooth. Give him a promising problem, and he will work long past the point of expected interest —without apparent concern for rewards. Malia often accepted a fish politely when her response was correct, dropped it casually to the tank floor, and returned for another chance to work.

In 1964, our Oceanic Institute and Sea Life Park trainers took a trained porpoise to sea; it was the first of many such projects and led to extensive use by the United States Navy of trained porpoises working at liberty in the open sea, performing such tasks as carrying messages and locating lost equipment. The animal preferred for this work has been *Tursiops truncatus,* the Atlantic bottlenose, or his cousin, the Pacific bottlenose. Tractable, intelligent, and friendly as a poodle, *Tursiops* seems to thrive on open ocean work. Occasionally a Navy porpoise goes AWOL for a few hours, but it always comes home to boat, trainer, and floating kennel, in due course.

Why not try *Steno* at sea? We wanted to study the physiology of the animal during deep dives; the species seemed so highly trainable that we thought it would work for us in a disciplined way even when free to go wild again.

We were both right and wrong. We chose Pono first, and trained her to press a lever on a target which we proposed to lower to progressively greater depths. We then took her to sea by the rather crude method of moving her, on a stretcher, to a dock-side tank, and then dropping her in the harbor and asking her to follow our boat. So she did, with every appearance of joy, and worked hard at her lever-pressing for an hour or two. Then she became very frightened, and we soon saw why; half a dozen small sharks were circling the lever. Pono panicked and vanished.

For three days we circled the area, broadcasting the sound Pono had been trained to answer, but saw no sign of her. However, later in the summer, while the collecting boat was in a school of *Stenos,* both the collector and the senior scientist aboard observed an animal scarred like Pono. The loudspeaker was lowered, the recall sound turned on. The suspected Pono peeled out of formation, came to the boat, and tapped the loudspeaker as Pono had been trained to do. Of course, we shall never know absolutely if it was Pono.

We decided to try our experiment again; this time with precautions. We reasoned that Pono might not have panicked if she had been given a floating cage to retreat to, and that stricter training might have also been valuable. So when we set to sea with Kai, we had a cage and a much more elaborate regimen. Kai was required to wait in his cage for his orders; to press a button at the surface giving him his command to dive; to dive through a target hoop, car-

rying a recording instrument in a collar; and to return to his cage for his fish reward. By the very fact of its complexity, we hoped that such a routine would give us more control over the animal.

For five days Kai worked like a champion, three sessions a day, ten or twelve dives a session, his behavior flawless. He ignored the flying fish around him, the passing ships, the underwater photographers. On the evening of the fifth day, he suddenly departed from his routine, circled the ship twice, gave us a long look, and then left in the direction of the sunset, chasing flying fish and leaping in the red evening light.

Perhaps he had become bored, or perhaps five days in the open sea was too great a temptation to have expected him to ignore, or perhaps he felt he had done his work and deserved a real reward. In any case, Kai is welcome to his freedom.

If we ever see him again we shall recognize him by his collar.

As we continue to work with *Steno* in captivity—with Hou, who astounded science by learning to invent her own tasks; with Malia, who pats your hand with her fin when she thinks you are doing a good job; with *Stenos* trained to work blindfolded, using sonar; with *Stenos* being trained to carry tiny transmitters so we can turn them loose to track the wild schools; with *Stenos* who jump through hoops, slither out on dry land, decorate underwater Christmas trees, and execute all manner of frivolities for the amusement of Sea Life Park visitors—as we work with all these attentive and obviously happy animals, we can no longer forget that *Steno* is not a member of the family, a kind of domesticated seagoing dog, but will always be a little wild at heart.

Carl L. Hubbs began a busy career at Field Museum, then went to the University of Michigan where he rose from instructor to professor in zoology, curator of fishes, and first director of the Institute for Fisheries Research. Moving to Scripps Institution of Oceanography in 1944, he became resident biologist and, in 1956, emeritus professor. He has collected fishes in all fifty states, Latin America, eastern Asia, and elsewhere.

Dr. Hubbs has been president or vice-president of many learned groups, and is a fellow of numerous science academies (two of which have conferred medals on him). A former editor of *Copeia* and currently review editor of *American Naturalist,* he is author of over five hundred articles, papers, and books, mostly on fishes, but also on marine birds and mammals, oceanography, ecology, archeology, evolution, and general systematics.

THE GRAY WHALE

CARL L. HUBBS

One day in January 1968, Rick Grigg, one of the many scuba divers at Scripps Institution of Oceanography, a SeaLab II aquanaut, broke all records for intimate contact with a gray whale. While conducting research in seventy feet of water, he was startled by a whale leisurely moving by. After taking remarkably fine photographs of the beast's head (he was too near for a full-length picture), he reached out to learn what a live whale feels like and to push himself clear of the beating, barnacle-roughened flukes. The whale responded by a tail stroke that knocked off Grigg's mouthpiece and face mask. He made a safe though bleeding ascent to the surface, and later insisted that the whale didn't really attack.

I have had encounters almost as close, but never so exciting. In 1947, when I was initiating, with Errol Flynn, the first movie of this remarkable cetacean, three gray whales swam side-by-side directly under and barely below our small craft. Nothing happened, but the anticipation of danger was almost overwhelming.

Another time, an assistant and I had hove to in a small boat on the whales' migration path, with engine silenced, to learn whether gray whales continue migrating under bright moonlight. Increasingly loud spouting—with a clearly audible "whoosh!" on the dead-calm sea—indicated a whale approaching on a course that should have brought it a hundred feet or so away from us. When nearly abeam, the big fellow, now clearly visible at the surface, abruptly turned to swim directly at our drifting launch. We grabbed the gunwale in anticipation of an inevitable crash, but the whale submerged just enough to avoid scraping the boat.

Later, in a lagoon where many gray whales calve, while we were immobile because we were retrieving a trawl, a crash again seemed inescapable. A large gray whale suddenly surfaced, belly up, and then bore down directly on us; but it also just avoided a collision. On many occasions I have been close enough to touch gray whales (but have refrained)! I have been deluged by showers from watery spouts—incidentally learning that at least in the lagoons, the gray whale is not affected with halitosis often attributed to large whales.

In all my studies on gray whales only one attack occurred. After the whales in a Baja California lagoon had been pestered almost continously by a hovering helicopter during the first use of such aircraft in the study of whales, one of the beasts repeatedly rammed the skiff of turtle fishermen so hard that the craft would have been destroyed had it not been flat-bottomed and light. But other scientists in recent years trying to capture or to implant instruments in gray whales have had their small craft stove in, suffering the fate that befell many whalers in the mid-1800's. These earlier sailors characterized the gray whale as the most dangerous of all whales and called it "devilfish," as did the Japanese, using an equivalent name.

The fifty-foot-long "devilfish" is able to smash a small ship, but it does not attack unless wounded or repeatedly provoked. Its straight mouth bisects the narrow, compressed head that is sprinkled with a few sparse hairs. About three hundred yellowish baleen plates in its mouth strain vast quantities of food from water and mud. Although the diameter of its throat is only a few inches, it swallows many tons of tiny ocean animals during the feeding months. Barnacles and whale lice infest this whale more than any other cetacean, and algae and even kelp may grow on its skin. Like all whales, the grays propel themselves through the ocean by their flukes and steer with their flippers.

The gray whale has two habits that are unique among cetaceans. If temporarily stranded on a sandbar, its chest does not collapse and cause it to suffocate like other whales; instead, it floats off easily when the tide comes in again. Secondly, the gray whale gives birth to young, not in the ocean, but in shallow, muddy lagoons.

Its life history is astonishing. For about four ice-free months the eastern Pacific herds of gray whales feed heavily in the frigid waters of Bering Sea and even in Chukchi Sea beyond Bering Strait. They grow sleek and fat on the abundant scuds, krill, small fish, and other food in the fantastically productive water. Thus they ready themselves for the twelve-to-fourteen-thousand-mile, roughly three-month journey to Baja California, Mexico.

On this long trek southward, as well as during the several weeks spent in and near the Mexican lagoons, and for at least much of the return journey, the whales (with empty stomachs) rely for their vast energy needs almost entirely on the blubber and fat that they have stored in the summer. At the end of this annual roundtrip of 24,000 to 28,000 miles, they have lost nearly half of their weight. (This may be one of the reasons they have been called scrag whales.)

Gray whales now exist only in the Pacific. Under scientific observation during the last twenty-two years, their coming and going has been remarkably regular, as though the animals were equipped with built-in calendars. Leaving the Arctic in autumn, they generally travel close to shore, even swimming through beds of kelp.

Soon after they arrive in Mexican waters, they make an abrupt turn to the southeast, following a depth contour rather than a compass direction. Do they sense the depth by echolocation? Porpoises locate objects by timing the return

of sound signals, and perhaps whales share this faculty. Incidentally, for years the gray whales defied efforts to discover if they make definite sounds, but recently their vocalization has been recorded and measured.

Passing by southern California on their way to the Mexican lagoons early in December, the run gradually increases until Christmas and then continues strong through the first week or two in February. During their late winter and early spring stay in Mexican waters, great numbers of these whales can be seen lolling or frolicking in and near the surf close to the mouths of the lagoons. Sometimes they roll about in small groups, or breach into the air and fall back with a mighty splash. Most of the whales outside the lagoons are males, waiting for the cows to emerge.

Inside the lagoons, in the tortuous tidal channels where strong currents often flow, the cows give birth to single

calves. Larger than the bull, the cow is up to fifty-five feet long, weighs possibly thirty-five tons and is well able to produce her fourteen-to-seventeen-foot-long offspring. Lying on top of the water, she nurses the monstrous babe beneath her by almost explosively expelling cheese-like milk from the nipples in the rear part of her abdomen. Being underwater, the calf does not breathe while nursing.

When the cows, with their calves, come out of the lagoons to head north, they are met by males and bred. Copulation is a short process and in horizontal position. The males are polygamous and the females that are not served here may mate in the ocean on the return trip.

A major hazard during the migrations are the thirty-foot-long black-and-white killer whales with conical teeth, powerful jaws, and voracious appetites. Although the gray is much larger, it cannot go as fast, and it has no teeth or other means of retaliation. The killers attack in schools, biting at the gray's lips, tongue, flippers, and belly—occasionally until their prey bleeds to death or drowns. Some grays escape with deep gashes and missing or mutilated flippers; others are luckier.

When the cow hears or sees the killers coming, she tries to hurry her calf toward shore and shallow water where the predators often dare not follow. If there isn't time to get away, the mother may come between the enemy and her calf, or even lift it up on one of her flippers. The cows are so solicitous of their calves that whalers of long ago often killed a calf first to ensure the continued presence of the cow. Without the incentive of maternal defense, a gray whale in

immediate danger is said to sometimes lie on the water, belly up, apparently paralyzed with fright.

While traveling, gray whales cruise from two to twelve miles an hour—usually three to six. In a crisis, however, a calf has been able to keep up with adults for three miles when they were chased at fifteen to twenty miles an hour. On the average, the grays come up for air every four or five minutes, but if they are alarmed and racing, they are likely to surface every minute or two. Yet, on deep dives, they may stay underwater as long as twelve minutes. (Calves usually come up to breathe twice as often as the adults.)

When whales surface, they expel their breath several times from the blowhole (the nostrils) on top of their heads; this warm air condenses upon contact with the colder atmosphere, and forms vapor ten to twelve feet high. People who have thought that the whales were spouting water are surprised to learn that ordinarily the animals are merely breathing normally. Gray whales in a pod tend to surface simultaneously, and the numerous spouts at one time are a thrilling sight.

At night, during their migrations, the grays continue on their way if there is moonlight; otherwise they usually stop and rest. Probably because the cows must nurse their offspring for six to eight months, they do some feeding on the long journey back to the Arctic.

As can be seen, whales are remarkable animals, and we should take a look at their extraordinary history. Of ancient lineage, they have vestigial hind limbs buried in flesh that prove they were at one time land mammals. Teeth still ap-

pear in the fetus, but are replaced by baleen as the animal develops. The gray whale in particular is called a "living fossil"; its position on the evolutionary tree might be likened to the green tip of an old basal branch, otherwise dead.

The only gray whales left in the world are now found in the Pacific Ocean, and at least twice they have been brought to the brink of extinction. During 1851, after depleting whales elsewhere, enterprising Yankee whalers discovered and promptly began exploiting the gray whale whose shore-bound habits rendered it easy prey.

Captain Charles M. Scammon, one of the most enterprising among them, and surely the most learned, contributed in 1871 (in his *The Marine Mammals of the North-western Coast of North America*) most of what until very recently was known of the species. When he discovered that this whale entered lagoons to calve, he made tremendous profits—until other whalers learned his secret. Thereupon, slaughter in the lagoons as well as near coastal whaling stations rapidly brought the species close to extinction. Only one whale was reported taken in 1880. Presumably as a result of the virtual cessation of commercial

take, a slight recovery was noted by 1886.

Around the turn of the century the species was thought to have become extinct until Roy Chapman Andrews, studying whales in 1910 along the Korean coast, found indications of its continued existence. Upon later confirmation, he and others designated these grays as a separate Asiatic herd, wintering and calving in Korea and summering and fattening in Okhotsk Sea. Persecution by Koreans, Japanese, and Russians through the 1930's may have depleted this herd, but its present status is uncertain.

Meanwhile, on the American side of the Pacific, the gray whales slowly recuperated. But again, in the 1920's and 1930's they were subjected to commercial assault until finally they came under international protection by treaty in 1938. By then, the population had once more been so depleted that many authorities believed that the species was exterminated.

However, in 1946 a considerable number of gray whales were seen going south as though heading toward the traditional calving lagoons of Baja California. This finding led me to undertake a census of the southward migration. Beginning in the winter of 1946–47, with the aid of colleagues, I carried on this work for several years at Scripps Institution in La Jolla. From here we could clearly see the migrating whales by the use of mammoth binoculars captured from the Japanese on a Pacific island.

By courtesy of the Coast Guard I also made two trips by plane over the Mexican calving lagoons and roughly charted the renewed whale concentrations. Longing for a closer look, I induced Errol Flynn to sponsor an expedition by helicopter, planes, and boats to San Ignacio Lagoon. Otherwise, for some years I, with associates, ran the long and tedious census of whales, in lagoons and along the coast, from shore.

Beginning in 1952, our California-based census was taken over by the Fish and Wildlife Service. This set us free to concentrate on the lagoons, and through the patronage and skillful piloting of Dr. Gifford C. Ewing, we undertook an annual census by airplane, in which we placed greater faith. Judging from our last serial count in 1964, at least 3,000 and possibly as many as 6,000 gray whales winter in Mexico. (I regard as unwarranted and unbelievable the newspaper and other estimates that approximate 10,000 and up to 15,000 or more. Did the "census takers" sometimes count spouts instead of whales?)

During the years of the return of the gray whale, a new whaling industry developed—whale-watching. From the decks of well-patronized whale-excursion boats that operate out of San Diego and other coastal ports, and also from the superb and much promoted vantage point of Carrillo National Monument, atop Point Loma, and from other pro-

montories along the coast as far north as Oregon, thousands of people enjoy watching the gray whales each winter as they file by along their traditional and unique migratory path, close to the rocky shore.

Although park rangers and knowledgeable guides regale the whale watchers with natural-history facts, the excitement of watching the grays swim by does not equal the thrill of seeing them gathered by the hundreds in the Baja California lagoons. Many persons come by plane, helicopter, and boat to marvel at the congregations.

By mid-February the first whales returning northward pass the last stragglers heading south (neither group accompanied by calves). The northward journey past San Diego and La Jolla extends through March and April, rarely into May. This return run is much less spectacular because the whales are now more scattered, farther offshore, and more wary than when they were traveling south for the serious business of procreation.

Recently, the protective measures which permitted the eastern Pacific herd to recover from apparent extinction have been relaxed to the extent that one hundred migrants are killed annually. The information thus gained is needed for science and for the regulation of any further harvest. This innovation has disturbed some biologists who fear that it is only the opening wedge to a larger commercial killing. Their alarm is echoed by people who believe that the continuing esthetic pleasure and economic gain from the annual whale-watch outweighs the temporary revenue gained by rendering a unique marine creature into oil, meal, and cat food.

INDEX

Turtles, sea
  green, 23–25, 27
  hawksbill, 24, 26
  leatherback, 23, 24–25
  loggerhead, 24–25
  ridley, 24, 25
Tusks, 208–11

Van Gelder, Richard G., "Skunks," 116–21
Viviparity, 46
Viviparous Quadrupeds of North America, The
    (Audubon and Bachman), 88
Vultures, 56

Wallowing, 177
"Walrus" (Burns), 207–11
Walrus, 207–11
Wapiti, 155–59
Weaning
  of caribou, 171
  of mule deer, 144
  of polar bear, 79
  of raccoon, 96
  of sea lion, 217
  of walrus, 210
Weasels, 87–91
Weight
  of black bear, 66
  of bobcat, 130
  of buffalo, 176

Weight *(Cont.)*
  of caribou, 169, 171
  of great-horned owl, 10, 12
  of grizzly bear, 71, 73
  of moose, 163–64, 165
  of mountain goat, 186
  of mountain lion, 124
  of North American elk, 157
  of polar bear, 77, 79
  of raccoon, 94
  of sea turtles, 25
  of seals, 221
  of timber wolf, 112
  of walrus, 209–10
Welles, Ralph and Florence, "Death Valley
    Bighorn," 178–83
Whales, 204, 211, 225, 226, 232
  gray, 231–36
  killer, 234
White-tailed deer, 147
"Wild Things in the Wild Sea" (Pryor), 225–29
Wildcat, 129–33
"Wolverine" (Pruitt), 99–103
Wolverine, 99–103, 171
Wolf, 162, 171, 195
  timber, 111–15
Wood buffalo, 174
Wylie, Philip, 224

Yellowstone National Park, 159, 174–76
Yeti, 103